W9-BER-840

Every Child, Every Day

A Digital Conversion Model for Student Achievement

MARK A. EDWARDS

Superintendent,
Mooresville Graded School District,
North Carolina

PEARSON

Boston • Columbus • Indianapolis • New York • San Francisco • Upper Saddle River
Amsterdam • CapeTown • Dubai • London • Madrid • Milan • Munich • Paris • Montreal • Toronto
Delhi • Mexico City • São Paulo • Sydney • Hong Kong • Seoul • Singapore • Taipei • Tokyo

Vice-President, Editor-in-Chief: Aurora Martínez Ramos
Executive Editor: Linda Bishop
Developmental Editor: Diane Rapley
Senior Marketing Manager: Christine Gatchell
Editorial Assistant: Michelle Hochberg
Executive Marketing Manager: Krista Clark
Production Editor: Karen Mason
Production Coordination and Electronic Composition: Element LLC
Text Design and Illustrations: Element LLC
Cover Coordinator: Laura Gardner and Jenny Hart
Cover and Interior Photos: Tanae McLean

Copyright © 2014 by Pearson Education, Inc. All rights reserved. Manufactured in the United States of America. This publication is protected by copyright, and permission should be obtained from the publisher prior to any prohibited reproduction, storage in a retrieval system, or transmission in any form or by any means, electronic, mechanical, photocopying, recording, or likewise. To obtain permission(s) to use material from this work, please submit a written request to Pearson Education, Inc., Permissions Department, One Lake Street, Upper Saddle River, New Jersey 07458, or you may fax your request to 201-236-3290.

Many of the designations by manufacturers and sellers to distinguish their products are claimed as trademarks. Where those designations appear in this book, and the publisher was aware of a trademark claim, the designations have been printed in initial caps or all caps.

Between the time web site information is gathered and then published, it is not unusual for some sites to have closed. Also, the transcription of URLs can result in typographical errors. The publisher would appreciate notification where these errors occur so that they may be corrected in subsequent editions.

Library of Congress Cataloging-in-Publication Data

Edwards, Mark (School superintendent), author.
 Every child, every day : a digital conversion model for student achievement / Mark Edwards, Superintendent, Mooresville Graded School District, North Carolina.
    pages cm
Includes bibliographical references.
ISBN 0-13-292709-8
1. Educational technology. 2. Electronic information resources. 3. School improvement programs. I. Title.
LB1028.3.E4237 2014
371.33--dc23
                    2012051023

10 9 8 7 6 5 4

ISBN-10: 0-13-292709-8
ISBN-13: 978-0-13-292709-3

About the Author

Dr. Mark Edwards currently serves as superintendent of the Mooresville Graded School District (MGSD) in Mooresville, North Carolina, where he has led an innovative digital conversion initiative.

Following graduation from the University of Tennessee, Dr. Edwards began his career in education as a science teacher in Brooksville, Florida. He then obtained a master of arts degree in school administration from Tennessee Technological University and a doctorate in educational leadership from Vanderbilt University. Over the past 30 years, he has served students in Tennessee, Virginia, Florida, Alabama, and North Carolina, first as a teacher and then as an assistant principal, principal, dean, and superintendent. He has also served as vice president for Business Development at Harcourt Assessment.

Dr. Edwards has led two Virginia school districts, Danville and Henrico County, in the role of superintendent. In Henrico County, he directed one of the first major one-to-one computing initiatives in the United States, in which 26,000 laptops were deployed to students in grades 6–12. This initiative was recognized as a benchmark for one-to-one computing and honored with numerous awards. Dr. Edwards was named Virginia Superintendent of the Year in 2001 and North Carolina Superintendent of the Year in 2012. He received the Harold W. McGraw Prize in Education in 2003.

Dr. Edwards is considered a pioneer of one-to-one computing in public schools. He was recognized as a ComputerWorld Laureate in June 2012 and received the Sylvia Charp Award at the 2012 ISTE Conference. Dr. Edwards, a father of three, lives in Mooresville, North Carolina.

Acknowledgments

First and foremost, I would like to thank my wife, Marcia, and our children, Adrian, Autumn, and Luke, for their love, support, and blessings throughout my career and throughout the writing of this book. My thanks also go to my mom and dad, Bill and Ernestine Edwards, for being the best teachers in my life.

Thank you to Pleasant Ridge Elementary and West High School in Knoxville, Tennessee, to Cookeville High School and Tennessee Tech University in Cookeville, Tennessee, and to the University of Tennessee and Vanderbilt University for many learning experiences that have guided my direction in life.

I would also like to thank the colleagues and students who taught me so much at D.S. Parrott Middle School, Baldwin Elementary, Erin Elementary, Bay Haven Basics Plus Elementary, Northfield Elementary, Wake County Public Schools, Danville Public Schools, Henrico County Public Schools, and the University of North Alabama.

My appreciation goes to the Pearson team of Diane Rapley, Aurora Martinez, Scott Drossos, and Linda Bishop for their support and guidance in the development of this book. I am grateful to the colleagues who reviewed drafts and shared their insights, including John Bailey, Executive Director, Digital Learning Now!; Adam P. Frankel, Executive Director, Digital Promise; Thomas W. Greaves, Chairman, The Greaves Group; Terry B. Grier, Superintendent of Schools, Houston Independent School District; Jeanne Hayes, President, the Hayes Connection; Keith Krueger, CEO, Consortium for School Networking (CoSN); Leslie A. Wilson, President, The One-to-One Institute; Dr. Vicki B. Wilson, Former Assistant Superintendent, Henrico County, Virginia; and Randy Wilhelm, CEO and Co-Founder, Knovation.

A special thank you to MGSD Public Information Officer Tanae McLean for her tireless assistance with many details in the preparation of this book.

And finally, I wish to convey my deep gratitude to all members of the Mooresville Graded School District family who made this story possible—teachers, principals, support staff, central office administrators and staff, school board, parents, community, and, most of all, students.

Contents

Foreword

Digital learning can serve as the catalyst for transformational change in education. For the first time in history, we can truly help every child reach his or her full potential by customizing instruction so that students can learn at their own pace, anywhere and at any time.

As governors, we learned that a comprehensive roadmap to reform helps rally support, focuses attention, and drives results. We released the "10 Elements of High Quality Digital Learning" to serve as a guide for policymakers to provide the flexibility needed to explore new innovations and models of learning.

North Carolina's Mooresville Graded School District represents what is possible when a school system embraces these principles. Students are using laptops to access digital content, online assessment data is providing real-time feedback to teachers, and new learning platforms are supporting differentiated instruction for students. As a result, graduation rates and assessment scores are up, dropout rates are down, and more students are going on to college.

In *Every Child, Every Day*, Dr. Mark Edwards provides a candid description of the challenges and celebrations associated with radically reorienting a school culture to focus on the needs of students. The inspiring account describes how Dr. Edwards empowered a team of caring and committed educators to rethink old approaches and reinvent learning for their students. A brilliant teacher and leader, Dr. Edwards brings clarity to what is often a challenging process of leading change in today's education system.

Such transformations are easy to dismiss as too difficult to replicate in today's challenging budget climates. But Dr. Edwards proves that it is possible as long as leaders establish priorities, align resources to clear goals, and thoughtfully reallocate resources. He notes throughout the book that Mooresville is a school district with only modest per-pupil funding, but by leading a continuous process of strategic planning, he was able to create an educational model for the rest of the nation. *Every Child, Every Day* offers pragmatic, helpful advice to other school leaders for how they, too, can replicate Mooresville's success.

—Jeb Bush

Former governor of Florida, co-chair of the Digital Learning Council

—Bob Wise

Former governor of West Virginia, co-chair of the Digital Learning Council,
president of the Alliance for Excellent Education

Prologue

Our Path to Digital Conversion

"Despite the challenges, there was a sense that we could improve. I knew that indeed we could and would do better."

In March 2009, our second year of digital conversion, I visited Connie Austin's fourth-grade class at Mooresville Intermediate School, along with the principal, Mrs. Morrow. Connie, then in her 32nd year of teaching, was working with a group of students around a table and was so focused that half the class noticed our arrival before she did. Once she spotted us, Connie showed us around the room, beaming with pride. At one table, several students were advising another student who was working on a presentation. Students at two other tables were working independently, reading from their laptops and making notes. Other students were taking an online math quiz that provided immediate feedback.

"I truly thought I would retire when we started this whole digital conversion thing," Connie whispered to me. "I thought I was too old to learn this techie stuff. But I'm starting to get the hang of it. I never thought I'd be teaching like this, but I'm loving it, and my students are really taking off."

Student performance was indeed on the rise in Connie's class, as it has been throughout the Mooresville Graded School District (MGSD) since we embarked on what we call our "digital conversion" initiative. Like the more common term *one-to-one computing*, *digital conversion* means that students and teachers each receive a laptop computer for 24/7 use. But we have coined the term *digital conversion* to encompass far more than hardware and software. Our students' success is the result of one-to-one computing combined with many other factors, described throughout this book, including a culture of caring and a relentless focus on data to improve student achievement.

Connie's classroom illustrated how far we had progressed after 18 months of learning and changing. Teachers were hitting their stride, growing more confident about their technical skills, changing their teaching style, and increasingly incorporating online content, assessments, and other resources into instruction. Students were engaged in their work, collaborating on projects, and helping each other.

There was a sense in every MGSD school that improved achievement was within our grasp. To reach this point, both the district and the community had gone through many steps on the path to digital conversion.

Our Community

Mooresville, North Carolina, is similar to many other small cities across America. It has evolved from a mill town into a more diverse, middle-class economic and cultural community and is now home to several NASCAR race teams and the Lowe's Home Improvement corporate offices. Many residents commute to Charlotte, the largest city in the state, about 30 minutes away.

Mooresville has grown rapidly over the past few years, with an influx of families from New York, New Jersey, Ohio, and Pennsylvania. The population is now around 27,000. Downtown Mooresville may give the impression that Andy Griffith's fictional Mayberry of the 1960s is alive and well. But in reality, like its many counterparts across the nation, the city is evolving both positively—with greater diversity, new businesses, and housing market increases—and negatively—with increased poverty and signs of gang activity. The recent decline in the national economy created a rising sense of apprehension about the future as well as an increase in the unemployment rate in Mooresville.

Mooresville Graded School District

MGSD is a city school district serving approximately 5,600 students in seven schools and a technical education center affiliated with the high school. The free and reduced lunch population has increased from 30 percent to over 40 percent in five years, as more families have struggled with the impact of the economic downturn.

> **MGSD Demographics**
>
> - 5,600 students
> - Title I district
> - 72% Caucasian
> - 18% African American
> - 8% Hispanic
> - 2% other
> - 12% special education
> - 7% English learners
> - 40% free and reduced lunch

In the early 1990s, MGSD was recognized for implementing a year-round design, with a four-track system and eight weeks on/two weeks off, but the program faded away after a few years because of budget issues and declining interest. Although MGSD was viewed as a good school system overall, the 2006 graduation rate was only 64 percent, and the 2007 academic composite at Mooresville High School was 68 percent. These data points, along with significant performance gaps for several student subgroups, gave the MGSD board of education a mandate for improvement as board members were in the process of hiring a new superintendent.

First Steps

When I interviewed for the position of superintendent of MGSD in 2007, I outlined to the board my experience as a school principal; superintendent of Henrico County, Virginia; dean of the College of Education at the University of North Alabama; and vice president for Business Development at Harcourt Assessment. I described how, during my tenure in Henrico County from 1994 to 2004, we had deployed 26,000 laptops to students in grades 6–12 as part of our Teaching and Learning Initiative, which had received national attention as a benchmark for one-to-one computing and was recognized with numerous awards.

When the board expressed interest in a similar initiative, I was very positive, but I stressed that substantial analysis and groundwork would be required.

FIGURE P.1

Mooresville Schools

Grade	PVES	RRES	SES	MIS	EMIS	MMS	MHS	Totals by Grade
K	164	140	144	—	—	—	—	448
1	157	137	137	—	—	—	—	431
2	140	147	146	—	—	—	—	433
3	170	145	123	—	—	—	—	438
4	—	—	—	238	203	—	—	441
5	—	—	—	279	212	—	—	491
6	—	—	—	233	209	—	—	442
7	—	—	—	—	—	472	—	472
8	—	—	—	—	—	439	—	439
9	—	—	—	—	—	—	454	454
10	—	—	—	—	—	—	395	395
11	—	—	—	—	—	—	342	342
12	—	—	—	—	—	—	364	364
Totals by School	**631**	**569**	**550**	**750**	**624**	**911**	**1,555**	**5,590**

PVES: Park View Elementary School (K–3); RRES: Rocky River Elementary School (K–3); SES: South Elementary School (K–3); EMIS: East Mooresville Intermediate School (4–6); MIS: Mooresville Intermediate School (4–6); MMS: Mooresville Middle School (7–8); and MHS: Mooresville High School (9–12).

Numerous discussions with school board members helped to develop a clear understanding of the road ahead. I was very excited to be offered the position of superintendent, and I had high expectations for success, but I had no idea at the time that we would see today's rates of student improvement.

Although we had seen great results in Henrico County, it was not possible in that initiative to truly evaluate the impact of properly implemented technology, since we were one-to-one computing pioneers and the level of implementation varied widely across schools. MGSD offered a new opportunity to implement a consistent one-to-one initiative and the other important factors that are key to success, such as a culture of caring and data-driven decision making.

In my first days and weeks on the job, I discussed digital conversion with all stakeholders—teachers, administrators, students, and community members. There was keen interest, and there was also a lot of concern. Many people commented on both the growing digital and opportunity divide among students in the district. Another worry was that performance data were declining in many areas. Despite the challenges, there was a sense that we could improve. I knew that indeed we could and would do better.

Several community events helped galvanize public buy-in and support. Lowe's Home Improvement was an early supporter, with a check for $250,000 for infrastructure costs. Meetings with school, business, and community leaders—including members of the Chamber of Commerce and Economic Development Commission representatives—built awareness of the educational, moral, and practical need for digital conversion.

A meeting attended by more than 1,000 parents and community members in January 2008 that featured several nationally recognized speakers was a benchmark in the development of community support for digital conversion. One of the most important lessons I had learned in Henrico County was that internal and external support is essential to success and always a work in progress.

Ongoing Call to Excellence

MGSD embarked on an in-depth digital conversion initiative, implementing the new strategies and tactics outlined in this book. As a result of our work, at MGSD today the daily work of teaching and learning relies on 21st-century tools such as computers, online resources, wireless networks, and interactive whiteboards.

As they will need to do in today's workplace, students use technology to accomplish basic and complex tasks, solve problems, do creative work, and collaborate in teams. Teachers guide students individually and in groups, within a working culture of teacher efficacy and student engagement that courses throughout the system and brings learning to life.

By living our motto of *Every Child, Every Day*, incorporating data into instructional planning, increasing student engagement, and building a strong sense of family, we believe we have turbo-charged student achievement. A "power surge" of relevance is connecting students' work today to their dreams for tomorrow. Despite a very modest resource base—we rank 100th out of 115 North Carolina districts in funding—in 2011, our graduation rate jumped to 91percent (second in the state) and our composite academic performance to 89 percent (third in the state).

VISITOR FEEDBACK   *"What we see in Mooresville is the whole package—using the budget, innovating, using data, involvement with the community, and leadership."*

—Karen Cator
Director of Educational Technology, U.S. Department of Education

Our path to digital conversion has been informed by much reading and discussion. A couple of years ago, our administrative team got together to read Malcolm Gladwell's *Outliers* and discuss the 10,000-hour rule he identifies as a marker on the road to excellence. We were fascinated to learn that the Beatles were not just hugely talented but had practiced more than any other band and that the young Bill Gates was able to put in many hours working on a mainframe computer, unlike most other young people at the time.

FIGURE P.2

Community Meeting Flyer

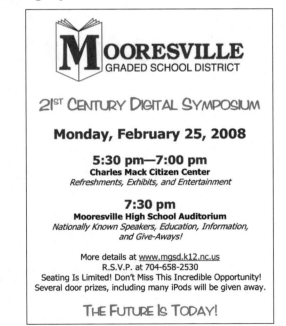

"I believe our district is an outlier," said Crystal Hill, principal of Park View Elementary. "We have the profile." She suggested that digital conversion was allowing our district to become excellent because we put in countless hours of practice—focusing on every child every day and practicing all the key factors that have made our implementation successful, as described in this book. I believe that Crystal was reflecting our cultural call to excellence, the end result of all our work. You can see, feel, and hear the ongoing call to excellence in our schools.

"If we really buckle down and stay focused we could hit 92 percent," said Scott Bruton, Mooresville High School Science Department chair, in response to my question about how he thought we would do on the 2011 biology end-of-quarter (EOC) exams. "You're way too modest. I bet you'll hit 95 percent," I replied, with the intent of pushing the expectation. In 2007, the pass rate on the biology exam was 68 percent, but Mr. Bruton had embraced the role of department leader and was enthusiastically using data to map out instruction. Each year, we had seen significant improvement, and in 2012, 95 percent of students passed the biology EOC exam—a prime example of excellence.

Chapter One

Digital Conversion and Academic Achievement

"The DNA of our student improvement has been the intertwining of digital resources, academic focus, a culture of caring, and a commitment to second-order change."

I don't know exactly how to explain the feeling Julie Morrow, Mooresville Intermediate principal, and I had one November day in 2010 after walking through the school and visiting every class. We didn't see anything extraordinary, and yet we were profoundly excited and exhilarated. Class after class of students was fully engaged. Students were using their laptops for a huge range of activities, gathering in small groups in most classes and working together. Often the teacher was working with a small group on reading or math. Many students were using online content or software for their own personalized work. Some students were moving around the room, with purpose.

We passed students working on projects in the hallways and others on their way to the media center for research assistance. Many students were either creating or sharing something. Teachers were highly engaged. There was a hum of activity in the air, a discernible energy and synergy that anyone could feel, a "learning pulse." I believe that this is the pulse of successful digital conversion.

Since the time the first laptop was handed out in the Mooresville Graded School District (MGSD), we have linked our digital conversion initiative directly to student achievement. The DNA of our student improvement has been the intertwining of academic focus, digital resources, a culture of caring, and a commitment to second-order change—all discussed in detail later in this book.

> **VISITOR FEEDBACK**   *"MGSD has adopted a laser focus on data that drives its ability to improve student outcomes. But at the same time the district has supported deep cultural change, acknowledging the importance of caring relationships between adults and children in building success."*
>
> —Randy Wilhelm
> Chief Executive Officer, Knovation

What Is Digital Conversion?

A mother who serves on our parent advisory committee told us she was very impressed with the video math problems her daughter watches at home on her laptop. "I couldn't possibly help her with her algebra," she said. "But she can watch this expert teacher teach a problem as many times as she needs until she understands it. It's like bringing her teacher home."

Digital conversion refers to the transformation of instruction from a paper-based world to a primarily digital world, in which every student and teacher has access to a personal computing device and the Internet anytime/anywhere. Digital conversion profoundly changes the nature of teaching and learning.

We use the term *digital conversion* to go beyond the more common term *one-to-one computing*, to indicate far more than hardware and software. Our students' success is the result of one-to-one computing combined with many other factors. The combination of factors has put us on the path toward second-order change.

Moving to Second-Order Change

Larry Cuban, in *The Managerial Imperative and the Practice of Leadership in Schools*, says that first-order changes in education aim only to improve efficiency, assuming that the status quo is basically adequate and that only certain policies and practices need to be improved. He writes:

> "For schools, such planned changes would include recruiting better teachers and administrators; raising salaries; distributing resources equitably; selecting better texts, materials, and supplies; and adding new or deleting old content and courses to and from the curriculum.
>
>   When such improvements occur, the results frequently appear to be fundamental changes or even appear to be changes in core activities, but actually these changes do little to alter basic school structures of how time and space are used or how students and teachers are organized and assigned."

Most school reform efforts over the years have focused on first-order change, with little impact on the basic structures of schooling established over 100 years ago. Second-order change, on the other hand, aims for a deep level of transformation, according to Cuban:

> "Second-order change aims at altering the fundamental ways of achieving organizational goals because of major dissatisfaction with current arrangements. Second-order changes introduce new goals and interventions that transform the familiar way of doing things into novel solutions to persistent problems."

At MGSD, we have adopted second-order change principles as a core tenet of our digital conversion. We are not trying to add on to old ways of teaching and learning. Rather, we are trying to "rethink school" from the ground up, enabled by today's technologies and guided by the demands of the 21st-century workplace.

As we strive to move toward second-order change, some things stay the same. Our classrooms still feature colorful maps and posters, books, globes, and other traditional learning aids. The essential role of hands-on learning in subjects such as science, music, and art has not changed, although it is now enhanced with interactive software and dynamic online content. In the Career and Technical Education (CTE) program at our N.F. Woods Advanced Technology & Arts Center—in classes such as health occupations and technology and industrial skills—both hands-on and online learning play a part.

Eighth-grade students at Mooresville Middle School

PD [] TOOLKIT™

Listen to the author describe some of the key characteristics of digital conversion.

But digital conversion goes far beyond traditional learning modalities. It supports second-order change by enabling a fundamental shift across all aspects of daily life in our schools. It affects instruction, pedagogy, professional development, student and teacher motivation, student–teacher roles, learning experiences, and relationships. It creates a new vibrancy and energy that come from the currency and connectivity among students and teachers.

STUDENT FEEDBACK *"I never will be able to knit or play my trombone via computer screen. However, computer resources can help me to practice and to find criticism for my work. We still do many hands-on projects, but projects on the computer allow us to explore the digital world in which we will live."*

—Mooresville High School student

As we move along this path, we sense that the constant coursing of rich online resources throughout our learning activities is making learning more authentic and accessible to every student in every class every day. Teamwork and real-world phenomena are producing a new level of collaborative and connected learning—experienced as an audible "productive hum" in our classrooms—that is defining new learning trajectories for our students.

Addressing the Needs of Today

In the past, of course, the digital workplace did not exist and was not a factor in preparing students for life after school. And many young people were successful in school without the benefit of technology, often because they were lucky enough to have dedicated teachers and a family that could provide books and enrichment. But many less fortunate students did not fall into this category and were not successful. Even today, many children in our country have never owned a book, let alone a computer, and many attend underperforming schools that offer them limited hope for the future.

Digital conversion allows educators to level the playing field and provide every student, including at-risk learners, with anytime/anywhere access to resources and the opportunity to develop the skills they need for today's workplace. And the time has come. In the words of Adam Frankel, executive director of Digital Promise:

accessibility

"While technological innovation has transformed other sectors of our society and economy in recent decades, our education system has been largely resistant to change. There are a range of challenges that stifle innovation in education, from policy and political hurdles to school culture and market failures to outdated infrastructure in our nation's classrooms. But these are challenges that can and must be overcome if we are going to offer all our students the world-class education that's an essential ingredient in their—and America's—success."

At MGSD, we believe that school must address the challenges of today and align with what students need to know today. Today's workplace demands not only digital skills but also the ability to work collaboratively and creatively and engage in independent research—all skills that are enabled and enhanced by technology.

STUDENT FEEDBACK   *"I constantly hear how today's students need a 21st-century education. My thoughts? We are 12 years into the 21st century. Perhaps it's time to stop talking about it and do what's right. I am glad our district had the courage and insight to understand that while it wouldn't be easy to implement such change, it was the right thing to do for us."*

—Mooresville High School student

Critical Success Factors

In 2010, a team of researchers who studied one-to-one computing implementations in almost 1,000 schools across the country found that fewer than one percent were practicing all nine "key implementation factors" identified by the study. The findings were published in *Project RED, The Technology Factor: Nine Keys to Student Achievement and Cost-Effectiveness.*

The *Project RED* study found that one-to-one computing was most effective in schools that understood second-order change and the importance of the key implementation factors. In those schools, one-to-one computing significantly improved student achievement, and MGSD was cited as an example of that type

A milestone achieved at Park View Elementary School

of successful implementation. *Project RED* shows that one-to-one computing is complex and involves many factors in addition to hardware and software—a finding that is borne out by our experience at MGSD.

We have coined the term *digital conversion* to encompass the interplay of the factors that are critical to our success, starting with a laptop for every student and going far beyond. We believe that our digital conversion initiative is positively impacting student improvement because of our dedicated attention to many success factors:

Digital Conversion Critical Success Factors

- A commitment to every child
- A shared vision
- A culture of caring and collaboration
- Embrace of the moral imperative
- Relentless focus on achievement
- Personalized, relevant, connected learning
- Deep transformation of instruction
- High expectations
- Digital resources and infrastructure
- Ongoing professional growth
- Ubiquitous leadership
- In-depth planning
- Data-driven decision making
- Creative resource alignment
- All hands on deck
- Joy, laughter, recognition, and celebration
- Understanding of second-order change

Digital Conversion Is for Everyone

More and more districts are embarking on the path of digital conversion and starting to see success. Schools have come a long way since the early days of one-to-one computing, and now educators can take advantage of a new body of experience. Success is within the reach of all, provided that schools have the commitment and the passion to reexamine old ways, take on new challenges, plan carefully, and be willing to learn and change as they go.

Budget limitations, for example, are often seen as one of the major barriers to digital conversion. But they are generally less of an obstacle than schools fear. MGSD is not an affluent district, but we have addressed the budget challenge by carefully repurposing resources—a strategy that all schools can follow.

VISITOR FEEDBACK *"The experience and proven results evident in the MGSD digital conversion bolstered our collective confidence in our ability to tackle such a potentially overwhelming project. Furthermore, the expertise provided by the MGSD administration saved us valuable time and dollars in the implementation during a mid-year rollout to over 5,850 students, teachers, and administrators."*

—Bennie Hendrix
Chief Technology Officer, Rutherford County Schools,
Forest City, North Carolina

There are 14,000 school districts in the United States, and 75 percent of them are the size of Mooresville or smaller. In fact, 70 percent of districts have demographics and budgets similar to those of Mooresville. Every school and district can make a start, as we did, and work toward a deep level of transformation and improved student achievement.

You Can Do It Too: Getting Started

- Bring stakeholders together and start the conversation.
- Learn from other districts.
- Build relationships.
- Study second-order change and integrate this thinking.
- Start small, with one or two schools.
- Expand gradually and learn as you go.
- Review all the critical success factors, beyond technology.
- Examine your school culture.
- Look for outside support from initiatives such as Digital Promise, the League of Innovative Schools, and *Project RED*.

Academic Achievement

In 2012, one of our high school graduates was particularly excited about his future. Despite having been in trouble on a regular basis earlier in his school career, this student had been offered academic and athletic scholarships to attend Gardner-Webb University outside Charlotte. He explained the change as follows:

> "The main reason I made a change in my life was because of the way the MHS teachers treat you like family. It's just unreal how the teachers all care about you personally. I didn't want to let down so many people who had helped me and lifted me up. They helped me change and prepared me, and now it's up to me."

The *Every Child, Every Day* focus of faculty, coaches, counselors, and administrators helped this student turn around his attitude and his academic performance, positioning him for a promising future.

PD **[d]** TOOLKIT™

Listen to the author describe the Mooresville community and the impact of digital conversion on families and community spirit.

Our student performance data is a source of pride for our students, teachers, and entire community. Although we rank 100th in the state of North Carolina out of 115 school districts in per-pupil funding ($7,463 per student per year), in 2012, we ranked third in the state on our district graduation rate (90 percent, up from 64 percent in 2006) and second in test scores (89 percent composite), ahead of districts that spend at least $1,500 more per student.

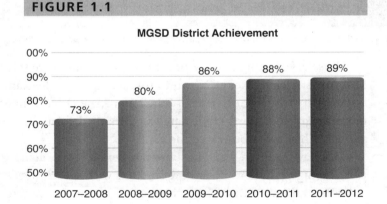

FIGURE 1.1

MGSD District Achievement

- 2007–2008: 73%
- 2008–2009: 80%
- 2009–2010: 86%
- 2010–2011: 88%
- 2011–2012: 89%

We have been very watchful of our overall MGSD trajectory, and we like what we see—steady-as-she-goes academic achievement improvement in all content areas and at all levels for all students. Although the path to excellence gets steeper at the top—and we have seen an increase in the poverty rate of 25 percent over the past four years and an increase in class size in grades 4–12—the trend lines are still looking good. What is most exciting is that we feel the momentum of energy and the pulse of collective learning in our schools every day.

Our digital conversion, our focus on student achievement, and our pervasive cultural dynamic of *Every Child, Every Day* are seriously lifting student performance across the curriculum. When we see all subgroups performing above 90 percent on a math test, we feel the wave of momentum and the surge of excellence coming up through the ranks of our students.

FIGURE 1.2

Third Grade Math Data by Subgroup									
	All Students	Asian	Black	Hispanic	Two or More Races	White	Economically Disadvantaged	LEP	Students with Disabilities
Proficient 2010–11	>95.0%	>95.0%	93.2%	94.7%	92.9%	>95.0%	94.1%	93.3%	92.3%
Proficient 2009–10	94.3%	>95.0%	82.1%	90.0%	83.3%	>95.0%	88.5%	90.9%	77.3%
Proficient 2008–09	90.2%	>95.0%	79.4%	81.0%	77.8%	93.0%	80.5%	60.0%	60.0%
Proficient 2007–08	80.0%	71.4%	50.7%	70.6%	60.0%	87.7%	61.3%	50.0%	58.1%
4-Year Growth	15.0%	23.6%	42.5%	24.1%	32.9%	7.3%	32.8%	43.3%	34.2%

Scores above 95% are reported by the North Carolina Department of Public Instruction as >95%.

It is very exciting to track our third-grade data, since third grade is the first year students take the North Carolina end-of-grade exams. When I had an opportunity to brief Secretary of Education Arne Duncan in March 2012, he saw our disaggregated third-grade data and remarked, "You did more than close the gap with this level. You erased the gap!"

We have reduced—and in some cases erased—the achievement gap for our disadvantaged students, including students with special needs, English language learners, and minorities, despite an increase in our free and reduced lunch population from 30 percent to over 40 percent in four years due to the economic decline and increase in unemployment.

The personalization offered by digital conversion has helped our special needs students work at their own pace and level, and the organization of student work on the Angel learning management system (LMS) has helped them improve

FIGURE 1.3

Third Grade LEP Students & Students with Disabilities			
	All Students	LEP (Limited English Proficient)	Students with Disabilities
Proficient 2010–11	>95.0%	93.3%	92.3%
Proficient 2009–10	94.3%	90.9%	77.3%
Proficient 2008–09	90.2%	60.0%	60.0%
Proficient 2007–08	80.0%	50.0%	58.1%
4-Year Growth	15.0%	43.3%	34.2%

Scores above 95% are reported by the North Carolina Department of Public Instruction as >95%.

their organizational and time management skills. And our special education teachers are utilizing the functionality of the hardware and digital content to incorporate multiple learning modalities into most lessons, with audio, text, movies, and photos to appeal to different learning styles.

At the high school level, the number of dropouts and suspensions has decreased, and attendance and college rates have gone up, as students have become more engaged in school and more confident about their future, thanks to personalized learning and our relentless belief in them.

FIGURE 1.4

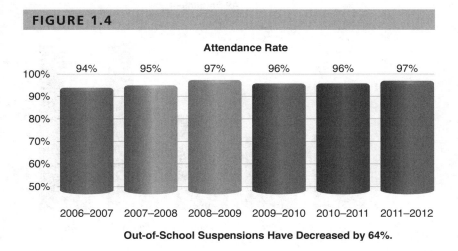

Attendance Rate

94%	95%	97%	96%	96%	97%
2006–2007	2007–2008	2008–2009	2009–2010	2010–2011	2011–2012

Out-of-School Suspensions Have Decreased by 64%.

FIGURE 1.5

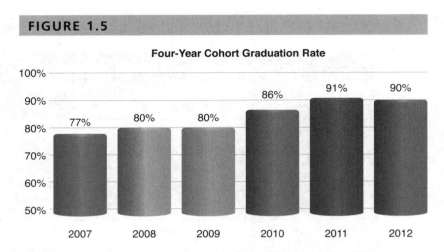

FIGURE 1.5

Four-Year Cohort Graduation Rate

In 2012, our graduation rate topped 90 percent for the second consecutive year, along with only one other North Carolina district, although our graduating class was smaller by 50 students.

In addition, almost 14 percent of our juniors and seniors are now enrolled in community college classes through the North Carolina Huskins Program, which allows them to earn concurrent college credit while in high school.

Especially exciting is that we have seen Advanced Placement (AP) course enrollment more than double, with some students taking multiple AP courses. We offer 16 AP courses, including several online options in subjects not taught in school, and we are adding more.

FIGURE 1.6

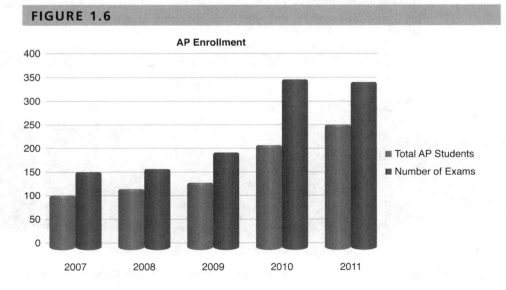

AP Enrollment

FIGURE 1.7

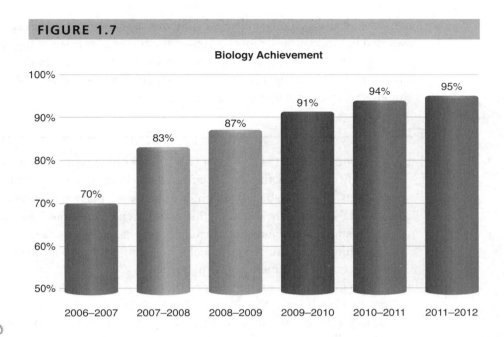

Biology Achievement

Mooresville High School's performance in biology moved from 68 percent in 2005 to 95 percent in 2012. Every North Carolina high school student takes this end-of-course exam, so our teachers are excited and proud of the progress we have seen. The key to success has been the continuous attention to individual student data that drives our instructional planning every day.

Digital conversion has had a direct impact on the number of students who are able to attend college, regardless of their socio-economic background. For six

[handwritten margin note: Continuous attention to individual student data]

FIGURE 1.8

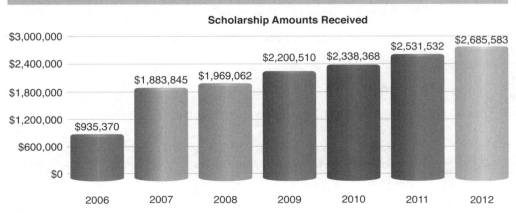

Scholarship Amounts Received

consecutive years, Mooresville High School has set new records in scholarships awarded to graduating seniors and eased the financial burden of higher education for struggling families, with an increase in scholarship dollars of over 300 percent. The hope divide and the opportunity divide are diminishing at MGSD as more students receive scholarships and continue their education after high school.

At the end of the 2011–12 school year, another high school graduate spoke movingly about how the MGSD culture had changed her life and future prospects. "I used to be into all kinds of bad stuff, partying, drugs and alcohol," she said. "I didn't care about anything, and then I found out I was pregnant. I was fifteen. I was absent a lot during my pregnancy. It was hard, but Mr. Shinn kept telling me he saw the potential in me, and Mr. Karriker made me try to keep up and helped me open up to get help.

"So many great teachers helped me—Mrs. Graham, Mrs. Kalio, Coach Watson, Coach Stith, Mrs. Verley, Mrs. Jiminiz, Mrs. Mcgee, Mr. Haglan, Mrs. Huntley, Mrs. Rollins, and Mr. Wirt. They all showed a special support for me, and now I'm going to college to be a nurse. I'm so happy for my baby and me, and I'm so thankful."

REFLECTIVE QUESTIONS

1. What first steps can you take to get started on digital conversion?
2. How can you connect your technology initiative to student achievement?
3. How will you measure your progress toward second-order change?
4. Which critical success factors will support your technology initiative?
5. What impact do you expect to see on day-to-day school life?

REFERENCES

Cuban, Larry (1988). *The Managerial Imperative and the Practice of Leadership in Schools.* New York, NY: SUNY.

Greaves, T., Hayes, J., Wilson, L., Gielniak, M., & Peterson, R. (2010). Project RED, *The Technology Factor: Nine Keys to Student Achievement and Cost-Effectiveness.* Sheldon, CT: MDR.

Chapter Two

The Moral Imperative

"The moral obligation to bridge the digital divide is the driving force behind our digital conversion initiative."

It was late August 2008, and even though it was not quite 9:00 AM, it was already hot and sticky outside. A line of parents, students, and family members stretched all the way down the sidewalk and into the parking lot. There was excitement in the air, as students from Mooresville Intermediate School were about to receive their laptops. Families and students were lining up to go through our registration and orientation process, in which they pay a $50 maintenance fee and receive training and instructions about their responsibilities.

As I scanned the line, full of anticipation and excitement myself, I saw an elderly woman in a wheelchair with three young boys, all tall and lanky, standing around her. She had on a print dress with a faded floral design like my grandmother used to wear. As I greeted her, she said, "These boys are so excited—we've never had a computer in the house before."

As we made our way to the registration table, she motioned me closer and whispered, "I know I'm supposed to have $50 for each boy, but I only have $37 and wanted to know if I could make payments. I'm raising these boys. I'm their grandmother." I said, "Ma'am, that's not a problem. The Mooresville Education Foundation can cover the full cost of the fees," and I showed her where to register for financial assistance.

Later, when I saw the family again, each boy was proudly wearing his new backpack with a MacBook inside, and the grandmother said to me, "Everything went just fine. Now, boys, what do you have to say?" A loud "thank you!" came from the three boys in unison. "You sure are welcome, and I know you'll take good care of those laptops," I said to the boys. "Yes, they will," she replied firmly, looking at each boy. She grabbed my hand and said, "Thank you, sir, this is a dream come true for us." I noticed a tear in her eye, and I felt a tear in my own eye also.

Laptop deployment days are some of the most fun and exciting days of the year in our district. I love hearing students say, "I've been waiting all summer for this," or a parent say, "This is all she's been talking about for the last two weeks!" Even though, as of this writing, we're preparing for our fifth year of digital conversion, the thrill hasn't diminished one bit.

For the many families who had never dreamt they could be part of the information age, laptop deployment days are especially happy occasions. Not only do they receive a computer for the first time, but the $50 maintenance fee is also covered by the Mooresville Education Foundation, and families without broadband Internet access can buy it for $16.99 a month, thanks to an arrangement with our local ISP, MI-Connection. Interestingly, although over 40 percent of families are eligible for help with the maintenance fee, only 24 percent have requested this assistance.

Digital conversion allows us to address the moral imperative of education— to equalize the conditions of students and serve each one of them, regardless of socio-economic status or special needs. Digital conversion is today's great equalizer because it includes every student, enables individualized learning, and makes extended learning outside school hours possible for all students, not just those fortunate enough to have a computer at home.

STUDENT FEEDBACK   *"To me it was more than just a laptop, it was an opportunity. Coming from a home where I did not have access to a personal computer made this opportunity a life-changing one. As a college student now, I value those laptops more than ever. The skills I have gained* *from having such a technology-driven school are priceless. Formatting papers, making iMovies and PowerPoints, and using online college programs such as Blackboard Learn are a breeze, and I would not have the abilities and advantages I have today without the help of MGSD and their laptop initiative."*

—MGSD graduate

The moral obligation to bridge the digital divide is the driving force behind our digital conversion initiative. We believe that, provided with the right tools and support, all students can be successful academically, regardless of socio-economic status, first language spoken, or special needs.

Bridging the Digital Divide

About 12 years ago, when I was working in Henrico County, Virginia, the office receptionist at an alternative high school told me one day how motivated the students were to get their laptops. She mentioned that one student had brought in a jar of coins, over $50 worth, to cover the laptop maintenance fee. He wanted her to keep the jar safe because he was afraid his stepfather would take it if he left it at home.

In the past 15 years, we have seen the emergence of a digital divide in this country. Students who have access to technology—computers, software, digital media, online resources, and the Internet—can access a wealth of information, broaden their knowledge in amazing ways, and be hopeful about their prospects in higher education and the 21st-century workplace. Those without access fall farther behind educationally each day and are growing up with limited hope for the future.

PARENT FEEDBACK   *"The most important aspect is how the laptops have leveled the playing field for low-income students. The laptops have helped to hold the interest of these students as well as given them an opportunity to compete despite whatever may be going on in their households."*

—MGSD parent

PD **td** TOOLKIT™

Listen to parent Leon Pridgen speak about "changed destinies" for MGSD students.

Before we embarked on our digital conversion initiative, many students in our district had no access to technology at home. Computer access in public libraries was limited, and many students lacked transportation to get to a library. Nor did they enjoy most of the other educational and enrichment opportunities available to students in more affluent communities. Many were destined for lower earning power and limited upward mobility.

However, the three boys mentioned at the beginning of this chapter and the many others like them are entitled to the same opportunities as their peers from more affluent families. Our digital conversion effort aims to give all students, regardless of their socio-economic background or special needs, a chance to succeed in today's digital world. According to an article by Eric A. Hanushek in *Education Week*, "Education and the Economy: Our School Performance Matters":

> "Achievement in schools matters, and it matters for a lifetime. Somebody who graduates at the 85th percentile on the achievement distribution can be expected to earn 13 to 20 percent more than the average student."

STUDENT FEEDBACK   *"This initiative provides an opportunity to face the largest problem in our history—the savage inequalities amongst poor and rich schools and poor and rich students. When I attended Mooresville, I always had access to a computer at home. But the fact is, many of my friends did not. This lack of access puts these students at an immediate disadvantage, and in a country founded upon ideals of equal opportunity, such a lack of access is atrocious. So, when I see a laptop in the hands of every student, I see access to information and equal opportunity in the hands of every student."*

—MGSD graduate

Whether students are preparing for college, the workplace, the military, or just to function in 21st-century society, they need to know how to use digital tools and online content, sort and manage information, and work in the technology-based world. The digital revolution has changed the composition of work and posed a challenge for education no less profound than the challenge posed to society by the change from horses to automobiles over 100 years ago.

High Expectations for Every Student

Melody Morrison, who recently retired as special education case manager at Mooresville High School, has seen the impact on her students of high expectations on the part of everyone in the school community. "I have students who might not have graduated five years ago who have graduated. In our school culture, they're not just my kids anymore, they're everybody's kids—all teachers throughout the school are doing their best for them and expecting them to do their best," she says.

Michael Fullan has emphasized the power of the moral imperative in his work on school reform and stressed that system-wide adherence to the moral imperative must always underlie high expectations for students. Fullan advises that when we care for and believe in students, including at-risk learners, high expectations follow as a natural consequence.

Our administrators have read and discussed two of Michael Fullan's books, *All Systems Go* and *The Six Secrets of Change*, in our leadership team meetings. The ideas in these books have brought clarity to our purpose as school leaders, galvanized our team beliefs, and helped us collectively embrace the moral imperative as we strive to live up to our motto, *Every Child, Every Day*.

Our students are constantly encouraged and acknowledged—the essential foundation for high expectations. Just as parents encourage, coach, nurture, and love their children, at MGSD we embrace a caring and loving disposition toward students. Our expectations are part of that caring, and our students know it.

We make both the expectations and the caring clear to students every day. When I visited her class, Susie Hudson, English department co-chair at Mooresville Middle School, said privately to me but out loud for all her students to hear, "We have great students, and we have very high expectations for them, Dr. Edwards, and I know they will rise to the challenge. In fact, when you and I are old, we'll be fortunate to have these students in charge."

As I walked the campus of N.F. Woods Advanced Technology & Arts Center, sister school of Mooresville High School, with Principal Dee Gibbs, he stopped several students to ask how they were doing or if they had followed up on an assignment. He generally finished up a conversation by saying, "You know we care about you," or "Dr. Edwards, you can be proud of this young man." Our students receive a constant flow of support from teachers, administrators, and staff. Every time I visit classes at N.F. Woods, teachers always acknowledge their students for working hard and for just being great kids.

Eighth-grade students at Mooresville Middle School

Special Education Students

PD **TOOLKIT™**

Listen to biology teacher Samone Graham describe how she helps special needs students succeed.

High expectations—along with digital tools, data-driven decision making, and our culture of caring—have allowed us to make substantial progress in closing achievement gaps, including for special education students. The organizational functions and personalization offered by digital tools have had a very beneficial impact on this group of students, who often suffer from poor organizational skills and need to work at their own pace and skill level.

STUDENT FEEDBACK   *"I think that since we have had the laptops, my productivity has gone up ten-fold regarding school work. While there are some distracting features to access on the laptop, I think most would agree with me that the laptops are beneficial to our learning. I have a lot more organization, and it is harder to make excuses to procrastinate, as I have all of what I need right in front of me most of the time."*

—Mooresville High School student

One data point we are particularly proud of is that in 2011, 92 percent of third graders who received special education services scored proficient on the state end-of-grade math exam—a very rigorous application-based test—only three percentage points below the score for all students.

English Language Learners

Digital conversion is helping English learners meet expectations and thrive along with their peers. Lenoa Smith, curriculum resource teacher at Park View Elementary School, has been very excited by the opportunity digital conversion provides to her students. "So many students go home and the only language spoken is Spanish, and the parents struggle with learning English as well," she said. "But with the laptops and our software, students can listen to the text in English and Spanish, and so can the parents. This is really helping them reinforce language acquisition skills at home as well as at school."

Minority Students

During an administrative meeting a couple of years ago, one of our high school department chairs commented that Mooresville High School had always had high expectations for students. But Vanessa Peoples, the second-grade chair from Rocky River Elementary, spoke emotionally about her experience as an African American student growing up in Mooresville at a time when high expectations were not the norm for her and her friends. We acknowledged the truth of her experience, and Vanessa said, "But it's a new day now—new hope—with high expectations for everyone."

> **PARENT FEEDBACK** *"Our students are very proud of the laptops. I saw some students at a bus stop, and I think they're standing a little taller—they know someone cares about them."*
>
> —MGSD parent and former school board member

Culture of Student Collaboration

One year, at the senior class project presentations, a young man walked up to give his presentation, accompanied by another student, who kept his hand on the boy's shoulder during the presentation. The young man stumbled over his words a few times and looked over his shoulder once at his friend, who smiled encouragingly, as did everyone in the audience, but he completed the presentation successfully.

This young man has a severe speech impediment and is very shy. One day in class, his friend had put his hand on the boy's shoulder as he was trying to practice his presentation with the teacher. Everyone involved was thrilled to see what a difference it made. The young man was able to make it through the presentation as long as his friend's hand was on his shoulder—a powerful form of collaboration.

Digital conversion has created a vibrant new student collaboration culture at MGSD, one in which students support each other and help to address the moral imperative. They mentor and tutor each other, work on projects together, and participate in online discussion boards. Students with special needs are

Seventh-grade students at Mooresville Middle School

learning from their peers, and other students are learning from them. As Thomas and Brown write in *A New Culture of Learning*:

> "Students are both willing and capable of learning from one another in deep and profound ways. They turn diversity into strength and build their own networked communities based on interest and shared passion and perspective."

We set out to develop a framework within which students can build their capacity to work together to the benefit of all, no matter the skill level. Today, our visitors often comment on the "productive hum" as students collaborate in our classrooms. Our teachers have moved the instructional focus from teacher direction to student collaboration, where students work in small groups and in pairs for discussion and research projects.

It takes planning and commitment, but, as we have increasingly viewed student collaboration as a standard instructional practice, students have increasingly embraced the opportunity to work together and help each other, playing their part in addressing the moral imperative to help every student thrive.

At a recent annual meeting of the Mooresville NAACP, Vice President Rev. William Conrad spoke about the impact of the digital conversion initiative on families in Mooresville. "Now that all our students have 21st-century laptops, they all have the same opportunities. The district has leveled the playing field, and the students know it," he said.

REFLECTIVE QUESTIONS

1. What is the moral imperative in your district?
2. Is your moral imperative integrated into daily practice?
3. Do your current practices bridge or perpetuate the digital divide?
4. How can you help low-income families with the costs of digital conversion?
5. How are high expectations for every student reflected in your school culture?

REFERENCES

Fullan, Michael. (2010). *All Systems Go: The Change Imperative for Whole System (Reform.* Thousand Oaks, CA: Corwin.

Fullan, Michael. (1993). *Change Forces: Probing the Depth of Educational Reform.* Bristol, PA: Falmer Press.

Fullan, Michael. (2008). *The Six Secrets of Change: What the Best Leaders Do to Help Their Organizations Survive and Thrive.* San Francisco, CA: Jossey-Bass.

Hanushek, Eric A. (April 2011). "Education and the Economy: Our School Performance Matters." *Education Week* 30(27), April 6, 2011, pp. 34–35.

Thomas, D., & Brown, J. S. (2011). *A New Culture of Learning: Cultivating the Imagination for a World of Constant Change.* Lexington, KY: CreateSpace.

Chapter Three

A Culture of Caring

"I strongly believe that digital conversion cannot succeed without a pervasive culture of caring."

Several years ago, when I was superintendent in Henrico County, Virginia, I tried to visit every class and thank every teacher every year—a challenging task with 70 schools in the district. In my ninth year on the job, when I was visiting one of the elementary schools, a teacher came up to me at the end of class, took my hand, and said that she knew that I was going to say thank you but that she loved hearing it. Gratitude and caring had become the norm in the district.

Today in the Mooresville Graded School District, our principals, assistant principals, and central office staff acknowledge the great work of teachers, staff, and students every day, just as teachers acknowledge the great efforts of students. A high level of appreciation and caring continually fuels a "can do" attitude that drives successful teaching and learning. I strongly believe that digital conversion cannot succeed without a pervasive culture of caring.

School Mission: The Foundation of Culture

On a visit to Matt Harriger's fifth-grade class at Mooresville Intermediate School, I saw students at one table creating an iMovie about a research project, students at another table reading a novel, and students at a third table practicing math with an online game that provided immediate feedback. Students were moving around the room, with several quiet conversations going on at once. Mr. Harriger walked from table to table, providing encouragement and assistance, orchestrating student work while helping individuals or small groups, as needed. No longer standing at the front of the class surrounded by books, he was teaching "from the inside out," as we like to say, focusing on each student's work, purpose, and progress.

PD **CO** TOOLKIT™

Listen to MGSD staff speak about the district mission and student-centered learning.

Our district motto is *Every Child, Every Day*, and we love it. I say it every day just to hear it. Everyone at MGSD knows it, unlike the mottoes in other districts where I've worked, and most people believe in it. It's concise but says it all. It expresses our mission—a commitment to caring, student-centered learning.

The culture of a class, school, school system, business, or any other organization—"how we do things around here" or "how we treat each other"—affects everything that happens every day. I believe that a school's culture provides the guiding principles, values, and operational framework for every interaction between students and adults and among all the adults in the system. To develop a strong school culture, employees and students must believe in the mission and be aware that the little things we do every day add up to create the whole.

> **STUDENT FEEDBACK**   *"As a student attending Mooresville High School, I can strongly support our motto. Every Child, Every Day is what defines our system. Our motto motivates our students, teachers, and advisers to make a difference in everyone's education."*
> —Mooresville High School student

A Commitment to Every Child

The foundation of our mission and culture is an absolute belief that every student can learn and succeed, along with a relentless commitment to attaining those goals for all students and caring for each one of them. Every time I visit one of our schools when classes are changing and students are coming and going, I see teachers call students by name, look them in the eye, greet them as they come into class, and shake their hands or pat them on the shoulder as they leave. As

Ron Edmonds's research on effective schools makes clear, a caring environment is a vital ingredient in academic success, especially in the case of students with learning or social difficulties.

One day, as I was entering Mrs. Suther's kindergarten class at Park View Elementary, the principal, Mr. Cottone, offered a cautionary note: "Mrs. Suther has a very challenging class this year, including three new students who have major social and academic issues. But she's working on it." Once inside the room, we saw an alphabet activity on the interactive whiteboard and the students singing along and dancing to the alphabet song, with Mrs. Suther leading the way—in her 28th year of teaching. Soon Mr. Cottone and I were joining in.

One of the little girls asked me if she and her classmates looked like first graders. "Yes, you do," I replied. She explained that they were acting like first graders even though they were really kindergartners because Mrs. Suther had said people would notice, and Mrs. Suther commented for all to hear, "This is the best class at Park View and one of the best I've ever had, Dr. Edwards." As Mr. Cottone and I walked down the hall, he said, "Even through all the struggles, she believes in every child."

First-grade students at Park View Elementary School

Like any other school district, we have difficult student disciplinary issues, but our environment, with its daily focus on building caring, positive relationships, has paid huge dividends. Student suspensions have dropped by 64 percent, and we have seen a positive impact on student attitudes, as well as on grades. Just as teachers respect and care for students, students know that we expect them to respect and care for each other, help each other when needed, and contribute to the wider community. When visitors comment, "You have such great kids," we believe they are observing the impact of our school culture.

Influential Texts

In our leadership meetings, we have read and studied together many books that have influenced our thinking about our mission and about culture and caring. We have taken to heart the findings of Ron Edmonds, from the 1960s, that emphasized high expectations for all students, a caring environment, collaboration, and a focus on achievement, as well as humor, recognition, and celebration.

We have also learned about the importance of organizational culture from writers such as Margaret Wheatley, Michael Fullan, Daniel Pink, Roland S. Barth, Linda Lambert, and Malcolm Gladwell. Lee Bolman and Terry Deal, well-known experts on school culture, have provided valuable insights on how organizational improvements can help school leaders focus on building a strong school culture.

Cultural "Force Field"

Margaret Wheatley, in *Leadership and the New Science*, describes *culture* as "force fields that influence behavior." We at MGSD are consciously developing a cultural force field that undergirds our mission of *Every Child, Every Day*. You can feel the force field when you walk down the halls of our schools. It's forged by a sense of caring and connectedness. It reminds us that we are all working together for a common purpose, and it impacts the work of students and staff and the pursuit of excellence by all.

Although Margaret Wheatley's field is quantum physics, her work has had a profound impact on my understanding of organizational theory as it relates to school systems. She writes about how nature is a prime example of systemic influence, and in one riveting section, she states that love is one of the most powerful forces in the universe. Coming from a scientist, this made a great impression on me.

When a school faculty develops a critical mass that embraces love and caring as the natural order of things—and fully accepts responsibility for the success of every student—something almost magical, and certainly something very tangible for students, evolves. A cultural force field of positive vibes lifts and influences all.

Establishing a Caring Community

Listen to Sharon Markowski and science department chair Scott Bruton talk about extra help for students and their changing attitudes to their profession.

In the spring of 2011, I was walking down a hallway at Mooresville High School when I saw Sharon Markowski, our math department chair, sitting with two students, working on math problems as they were eating sandwiches. "We just need a final tune-up before the algebra end-of-course exam," she explained. "And these fine fellows are working through their lunch, since they couldn't make the tutorial session yesterday afternoon." Sharon was also working through her lunch. And she was leading several after-school tutorial sessions for students who needed further review.

Most of our teachers provide additional help to students outside the classroom through tutorial sessions at school, online discussion boards for use from home, and other avenues. When employees know that their work is valued and that the school and district care about them, they will almost always go the extra mile for their students. Our teacher leaders influence their colleagues with a pervasive can-do spirit, which creates an environment that is more fun to work in, more likely to lead to student success, and more motivating. As discussed by Daniel Pink in *Drive: The Surprising Truth about What Motivates Us*, one of the books we have studied in our leadership meetings, motivation comes from within—not just from within the individual but also from within the culture.

PARENT FEEDBACK　*"They don't make them any better than Mrs. Conley. She stays after school two or three days a week and tutors my son. He doesn't want to let her down because he knows how much she cares because of all the extra help she's giving him."*

—MGSD parent

The Cultural Conditions for Caring

Several factors have come together to permeate our culture with caring for every child and every adult:

- A commitment to every individual
- Committed leadership at all levels
- Communication of caring expectations in meetings and professional goals

- Ongoing appreciation of individuals and teams
- Professional development on how to care for students
- Involvement of every employee in the mission of learning
- Management of negative elements
- Participatory decision making at all levels to ensure buy-in
- Laughter and fun as cultural norms

Transitioning to a New Culture

We have worked through many ups and downs during our transition to a caring, student-centered culture. Looking in the rearview mirror, I offer the following guidelines:

- Understand that bias and reluctance to change are tough to weed out.
- Be patient and persistent.
- Celebrate veteran teachers who have embraced change.
- Recruit new teachers who are excited by the mission.
- Look to principals to lead cultural and instructional change with vigor, daily modeling, and monitoring.
- Develop teacher leaders to influence others.
- Learn from outside your district and from outside education—from books, online communities and blogs, conferences, and other educators.

Honoring Teachers

Honoring teachers and their work is a major part of our culture. We acknowledge the daily work, spirit, energy, and focus teachers provide. I love visiting classrooms and shaking teachers' hands and thanking them, or conveying to students how lucky they are to have such great teachers. Teachers, principals, and teams celebrate together on occasions such as birthdays, weddings, and new babies, to demonstrate for employees that, as they strive to do their best, administrators care about their personal well-being and are thoughtful about their family and personal challenges.

Teachers leaving the MGSD Convocation, August 2011

We have learned much from Michael Fullan's *The Six Secrets of Change*, in which he talks about the impact of a loving community on staff commitment to the common good, and we have found that, when high expectations are communicated in a caring, supportive, and respectful fashion, most teachers will rise to the occasion. A culture of appreciation, responsibility, and teamwork is a powerful motivator and can greatly enhance individual and team success.

"Pervasive Efficacy"

At MGSD, we work on building a sense of what we call "pervasive efficacy," whereby a daily pulse of efficacy and expectation, based on caring for each individual, lifts and propels students to do their best work. I believe the best test of pervasive efficacy is asking a student, "Does Mr. or Mrs. Teacher care about you?" I am confident that a tremendous number of our students believe that their teachers love them and work hard to ensure their success.

We have seen so many students, including at-risk learners, demonstrate significant improvement as a result of teachers relentlessly believing in them and staying committed to the goal of *Every Child, Every Day*. Pervasive efficacy is our daily cultural vitamin. It's not easy, but the energy that comes from success keeps our spirits up!

Caring for Everyone

Of course, we have many trying days when we have to dig deep on the caring and pervasive efficacy to help some of our students. One afternoon, I saw a young boy walking away from school, with Mrs. Shauna, our after-school coordinator, running after him. She told me he had thrown a ball in her face and cursed her and the other students. I caught up with him, called him by name, and asked him to talk through with me what had happened and help figure things out. But he started cursing and running toward the woods. One of our parent leaders saw what was happening and joined me in pursuit of the student.

We jogged after him until the police and his mom arrived, but when the young man spit on both of them, the officer put cuffs on him and took him to the station. The next day, the principal helped the mother line up services and support, and the MGSD staff who were involved with the boy focused on getting him the help he needed.

We approach our daily student and community challenges from a foundation of caring and a sense of responsibility. It's not always easy to see the potential in students who are acting out, but they are usually the ones who need our help the most.

STUDENT FEEDBACK   *"My class was special as I can remember the high school both with and without the laptops, and the school was so much better off with them. The overall quality and morale at the school was better. The teachers were more into their work, the students seemed more willing to work. There was a decrease in fights as well as better respect among peers and teachers."*

—MGSD graduate

Support, Laughter, and Joy

I believe it is logical to make work a positive place since we spend such a large part of our lives there. Most of us have gone to work on occasion feeling stressed or tired but felt better after our coworkers offered support. I think this is an attribute of strong and healthy work cultures, and I believe it happens every day in our schools. Each school has developed a sense of collegiality, shared responsibility, and mutual caring that serves as an energy boost, expressed as a "we are with you" smile or hug and a very real sense of family—a culture that many of the researchers and journalists who have visited our schools have remarked on.

PARENT FEEDBACK   *"My children are surrounded by caring, compassionate, and concerned teachers, counselors, and adults. They are not only learning, laughing, and living but being loved!"*

—MGSD parent

This cultural phenomenon is exemplified by our annual convocation, an assembly of all 800 employees, complete with our Blue Devil Pep Band marching into the auditorium and everyone standing and clapping to the Mooresville High School fight song. As individuals are recognized with awards or profiled

Students at Park View Elementary School launching balloons with the school address attached to see how far they travel, as part of a science/geography project

in iMovies about each school, teachers and staff members cheer loudly for their colleagues. It is inspiring to see the affection that faculty and other employees demonstrate for each other. The support and "spirit synergy" experienced at this event also translate into their day-to-day work.

When I was moving from my position as principal at Northfield Elementary in Tennessee to my first central office job in Wake County, North Carolina, I had an experience that brought home to me the importance of fun and laughter in education. Some of the teachers had asked their students to create mementos for me, and one little boy, who struggled as a student and had a tough home life, wrote a message I have never forgotten: "I will always remember hearing Mr. Edwards laughing out loud in our classroom and in the hall. I will miss hearing him laugh." I imagine this boy did not hear a lot of laughter at home.

Schools are full of humor. Kids are naturally funny, quirky, and goofy and provide countless opportunities for a good laugh. In our schools, we laugh a lot. Teachers smile at students, and students smile back. From the smiles and laughter and caring, and from the shared success of students learning and teachers teaching comes a wonderful thing—joy!

The Impact of Negativity

Unfortunately, caring, student-focused school cultures are not as common as we might wish. Cynics, pessimists, and "negaholics" can suck the joy out of a school and create a stifling hold on the positive spirit schools must have in order to be successful. Many educators and students have had the misfortune of trying to work and learn in a culture made toxic by negaholics who lack the heart or the capacity to see beyond how students are today to how they could be in the future.

I recall a principal in another district telling me several years ago that his students didn't care about anything. I knew better, even though I did not know a single student at the school. I did know that the school had huge challenges and a poor academic record. A few years later, a new principal made several staff changes, pulling out the negative disbelievers and replacing them with relentless believers. The students responded with compelling improvements in performance, increasing their pass rate on the state English exam from 68 percent to over 90 percent. Very few students can flourish academically in a negative and toxic school atmosphere.

In our district, Todd Wirt, principal of Mooresville High School and North Carolina 2010 High School Principal of the Year, implemented a positive behavior support program called Capturing Kids' Hearts. One of his first sessions focused on acknowledging students and greeting them with a pat or a handshake. The objective of the program was to build relationships with students through caring and respect.

One of the participants walked out of that first Capturing Kids' Hearts session. However, during the next two to four years, over 95 percent of the teachers at Mooresville High School came to fully embrace the culture of caring. The teacher who walked out is gone, along with others like him. The teachers who remained have embraced the major changes needed to inspire their work with children and colleagues. If we allow anyone to diminish our work through negativity, cynicism, or pessimism, we are aiding and abetting the destruction of hope, and we need all the hope we can get in our schools.

What to Do About Negaholics?

Many staff members who start out with a negative attitude toward digital conversion can change over time with the appropriate support. I offer the following guidelines:

- Treat negaholics with respect and affirm their good qualities.
- Affirm small steps and be kind at all times.
- Provide examples of positive teacher work and its impact on student performance.
- Use data. Show negaholics that teachers who embrace cultural and instructional transformation get better results.
- Get a witness. Use testimonials from formerly reluctant teachers to demonstrate that all teachers can embrace change.
- Evaluate negaholics with a focus on attitude, willingness to grow, teamwork, and student performance.
- Stand firm and expect negaholics to "get well."

"All In"—School Culture Is for Everyone

The commitment to caring and appreciation extends beyond students and teachers at MGSD. It involves everyone from the principal to the custodians, from the bus drivers to the food service workers, from the office staff to the technology team. All employees need to know they are valued and making a significant contribution to the progress of our students. And they must truly believe in the mission of student-centered learning—*Every Child, Every Day.*

Schools need all hands on deck. Every adult in the district must understand and embrace the physical, emotional, and intellectual effort required to get the job done. We call this "all in"—which is a two-way street. "All in" means that every adult and every student counts in a major way—and we want them to know it— and every adult and every student is counted on in a major way—and we want them to know it.

Collective Leadership

On a visit to Mooresville Intermediate School, I asked a new teacher what she thought about her job. "The support here is phenomenal," she replied. "I didn't have to ask for help. Everyone on the fourth-grade team has come to me and offered me help, advice, and encouragement." The fourth-grade team in this school did not have to be asked to show the leadership required to help a new colleague. They see it as part of the culture.

I believe a huge component of our success has been a commitment to collective, ubiquitous leadership that supports our culture of caring for each other. Central office leaders are highly engaged with principals and teachers on a daily basis. Principals and assistant principals are leaders in classrooms, hallways, and the cafeteria, interacting with students, teachers, and other staff. Teacher leaders model effective instruction, lead collaborative efforts by department and grade level, and offer help. Student leaders work hard in class and show respect for other students.

VISITOR FEEDBACK *"You have so many leaders, and they all seem to be on the same page."*

—John Tate
North Carolina State Board of Education

Collective leadership serves as a daily catalyst for reaching a little higher and helps maintain the focus on every student. Our experience supports this finding of the 2010 *Project RED* research study: "Good principals contribute to distributive leadership, in which team members surrounding the principal play an important role."

Commitment from the Heart

Successful leadership involves a commitment from the heart. Getting our schools pumping with positive vitality starts with leaders of all kinds putting their hearts into their work. I hear our principals say over and over, "We have great kids," and teachers exclaim with visible enthusiasm, "I'm so lucky to have such great students!" They mean it, and our students know they mean it. Leadership researchers Bolman and Deal echo our sentiment when they write:

> "Perhaps we lost our way when we forgot that the heart of leadership lies in the hearts of leaders. We fooled ourselves thinking that sophisticated technique could respond to our deepest concerns."

Our leadership model is all about serving, supporting, and caring for each other. Central office administrators work every day with principals, teachers, and staff to provide professional development activities and collaborate on improvement planning or implementation. The leadership team also provides enthusiastic and caring feedback, direction, and analysis that support the culture.

Principals and assistant principals are the service providers for teachers and students and are highly visible throughout our schools—in classroom hallways and meetings—talking to staff and students, smiling, connecting, encouraging, caring, and building the culture.

Participatory Decision Making

Max De Pree, in *Leadership Is an Art*, suggests that participatory decision making is needed to ensure strong organizations. We have embraced participatory decision making throughout our district as part of our concept of caring, ubiquitous leadership and to help us build a culture where individuals respect each other even when opinions differ.

When we are hiring new employees, we assemble teams, which include parents, to interview candidates and participate in the decision-making process. Our teachers help select principals and other teachers. And when we need new online content or products, we put together a team to review the options and make recommendations.

MGSD teachers, principals, and central office administrators plan together, design staff development together, and use a participatory process to accomplish most tasks. Teacher and parent advisory committees meet throughout the year and provide input on important matters, such as policies and calendar recommendations, influencing the district and the culture as a whole.

When employees feel that they have a voice and that others care about their point of view, they are more likely to embrace challenges with a can-do attitude. This doesn't mean we take a vote on everything we do, but there's no doubt that we see our best results when we use a team approach. However, it takes practice to become a team, and working on teamwork must be ongoing.

Impact on Student Success

Dee Gibbs, the principal at N.F. Woods Advanced Technology & Arts Center, which also houses our alternative program, has helped many students make it through to graduation with special help, second chances, and allowances for difficult circumstances. A couple of years ago, the mother of a student who would not graduate until August and would therefore miss the graduation ceremony was terminally ill. Dee asked that we make an exception and let the student's mom see him "walk." He was allowed to walk with his class at the graduation ceremony. His mother died a few weeks later, and he finished his requirements in summer school, with support from his teachers. I believe our culture of caring supported him that day and will be with him for the rest of his life.

We have seen time and again that good relationships based on mutual respect, caring, trust, and high expectations have a huge impact on everyone in the school community and ultimately on student achievement. As noted by John Medina in *Brain Rules*, students need teachers who are committed to understanding them as individuals and caring about their personal circumstances in order to improve academically, and teachers need to feel cared for, supported, and safe in order to perform well and be effective.

We have worked hard to create these feelings of caring because we believe they are the foundation of student success, and the caring extends to all members of the community. Parents feel welcomed and are treated with huge respect in our schools. Custodians feel proud of their contribution, and their pride is obvious in the cleanliness of our buildings. On my school visits, I routinely check in with the food service workers, bus drivers, and office staff and chat with them about their lives and our students.

I visit every classroom in MGSD two or three times a year, with a focus on thanking teachers and all other employees, and I encourage our principals to visit classrooms every day to send a daily message that school is all about the relationships between students and adults and the work they are doing together. The words *team* and *family* are used all the time in our district, and we have several teams outside the instructional realm. A team of MGSD teachers, administrators, and staff has formed a choir and performs at our convocations, and faculty teams are prominent in local philanthropic efforts such as cancer awareness.

A positive, caring culture based on a team spirit is particularly important in a digital conversion initiative because teachers must learn and change a great deal as they explore how the digital world can improve student learning. Learning how to navigate and thrive in this new world can be especially challenging for non-digital natives. Individuals and teams who have a positive attitude, contribute to the culture of caring, and support each other in the learning process help to build student success in the digital world.

I always look forward to the end-of-year digital presentations our high school occupational studies students give about their internships. One year, a young man with a slight palsy on his left side, his leg bent inward, and his hand curled up as he held the mike, read his first slide in a soft, deep voice: "Custodian."

He described his work as a custodian intern at Mooresville High School and Davidson University. We saw photos of him sweeping, mopping, and emptying trash, with some of his mentors and by himself. He showed a chart detailing how many hours he'd worked and some of the skills he'd learned. Photos of his classes showed him and two other boys with their arms around each other's shoulders, smiling for the camera like any great team would.

His speech impediment was pretty significant, but the audience was able to understand most of his descriptions. His mom's pride in him was obvious, with her big smile, focused attention, and "mother" eyes (pure love). The last slide summed up what he had learned: "1. You have to work hard. 2. You have to be on time. 3. You need a sense of humor." He looked over at his mentors, three Mooresville High School custodians, and smiled and waved to them. I could see that Mr. Johnson, the head custodian, had tears in his eyes. The young man said he wanted to thank his teachers, teacher assistants, his mentors, and most of all, his mom.

REFLECTIVE QUESTIONS

1. How does every adult in your school contribute to student success?
2. What impact do you think caring has on student performance?
3. How often do your teachers "go the extra mile"?
4. Do you have a way to recognize every student's achievement?
5. How do you manage negativity?

REFERENCES

Barth, Roland S. (2001). *Learning by Heart.* San Francisco, CA: Jossey-Bass.

Bolman, Lee G., & Deal, Terrence E. (2011). *Leading with Soul: An Uncommon Journey of Spirit.* San Francisco, CA: Jossey-Bass.

De Pree, Max. (1990). *Leadership Is an Art.* New York, NY: Dell.

Edmonds, Ronald. (1982). "Effective School Research." *Educational Leadership.* 40, 4–11.

Fullan, Michael. (1993). *Change Forces: Probing the Depth of Educational Reform.* Bristol, PA: Falmer Press.

Fullan, Michael. (2008). *The Six Secrets of Change: What the Best Leaders Do to Help Their Organizations Survive and Thrive.* San Francisco, CA: Jossey-Bass.

Gladwell, Malcolm. (2008). *Outliers: The Story of Success.* New York, NY: Little Brown.

Greaves, T., Hayes, J., Wilson, L., Gielniak, M., & Peterson, R. (2010). *Project RED, The Technology Factor: Nine Keys to Student Achievement and Cost-Effectiveness.* Sheldon, CT: MDR.

Lambert, L. (1998). *Building Leadership Capacity in Schools.* Alexandria, VA: Association for Supervision and Curriculum Development.

Medina, John. (2008). *Brain Rules: 12 Principles for Surviving and Thriving at Work, Home, and School.* Seattle, WA: Pear Press.

Pink, Daniel H. (2009). *Drive: The Surprising Truth about What Motivates Us.* New York, NY: Riverhead Books.

Wheatley, Margaret. (2006). *Leadership and the New Science: Discovering Order in a Chaotic World.* San Francisco, CA: Berrett-Koehler.

Chapter Four

Digital Resources and Infrastructure

"Digital resources not only transform teaching and learning, they are essential preparation for today's workplace."

On a recent visit to Jemma Conley's third-grade class at Rocky River Elementary, I saw a student leading a group lesson about Venn diagrams on an interactive whiteboard, other students engrossed in online interactive social studies content, several pairs of students developing digital presentations, and Mrs. Conley working with a group of students who were discussing a reading activity. I observed lots of talking, lots of learning, lots of interest—and lots of digital learning resources.

One little boy showed me what he was doing. "See, I click on this button, and a page comes up with all these famous Americans. Then I click here, and it goes to Thomas Edison. That's who I'm researching. Then I can look at this little movie or choose another one of these things here," he told me.

PD **TOOLKIT**™

Listen to the author describe the importance of planning and communication.

Needless to say, extensive research and planning took place before Mrs. Conley was able to provide her third graders with engaging digital learning opportunities such as these. We began the planning effort in 2007, when we put together a team to lead decision making and develop a detailed timeline. The team was charged with guiding the transition to digital resources as the foundation of our instructional program.

Digital resources are one of the essential DNA strands of our digital conversion initiative, along with a culture of caring and a relentless focus on achievement. Digital resources not only transform teaching and learning, they are essential preparation for today's workplace.

STUDENT FEEDBACK   *"Technology at our school, such as the MacBooks, makes things get done quicker, and learning is a lot more fun. This helps ensure that we have a bright future."*

—East Mooresville Intermediate School student

Collaborative Planning

"Do you really think we we'll have visitors even in the first year?" Principal Julie Morrow asked no one in particular after a long, frustrating meeting in our first year of planning. At that time, we were all feeling the effects of meeting overload, and accommodating visitors felt like one item too many on a long agenda. "I believe if we do a really great job that we will have visitors—and early in the process," I responded, but without enthusiasm.

Everything seemed distant and abstract at that time. Nevertheless, an underlying sense of excitement and the power of teamwork kept us going. We believed that together we could make digital conversion come to life and change the lives of our students and teachers.

Our digital conversion planning team met every week for several hours during the first two years of the initiative and then every month, until we finally rolled the planning process into our regular principal meetings in 2012. From the beginning, our collaborative approach to planning created a strong sense of partnership and helped us develop our problem-solving, decision-making, and teamwork skills.

The planning team has always included a broad array of MGSD leaders—directors of instruction, principals, technology staff, the chief technology officer

(CTO), the chief financial officer (CFO), and myself. Other staff members attend when appropriate to the topic under discussion, and we regularly invite service providers to present information on hardware, software, and infrastructure options.

Planning Objectives

We began by defining our planning objectives, which functioned as an important yardstick against which we evaluated the options under discussion at every meeting. The following objectives kept us focused on our priorities throughout the process:

- Start small and learn from experience.
- Focus on student achievement as the goal.
- Bridge the digital divide.
- Personalize instruction.
- Integrate engaging and current content into instruction.
- Extend learning outside school hours.
- Evaluate student and teacher performance in real time.
- Support collaborative learning.
- Plan ongoing professional development.
- Communicate with all stakeholders.
- Develop leaders at all levels.

Evolving Agenda

We started with broad topics—goals, planning team members, technology, and stakeholders—and each of these topics soon expanded to include multiple items. As the meetings progressed, each team member reported on the items in his or her area of responsibility, including:

- Instruction
- Content
- Students
- Discipline

- Staff development
- Research
- Laptops
- Infrastructure
- Wireless capacity
- Warranties
- Repairs
- Servers
- Service and support
- Help desks
- Acceptable use policy
- Staffing
- Security
- Parent communication
- Community involvement
- Finance
- Facilities
- Visitors

We constantly fine-tuned the agenda, recognizing that the best-laid plans might need to change the next week, as our understanding of digital conversion evolved. It helped to underscore every meeting with a healthy dose of "Let's hold hands and stick together." We also enjoyed a shared sense of excitement about the very special opportunity ahead for Mooresville students and staff and the community as a whole.

Preliminary Planning Documents

Two key preliminary planning documents guided us through the first phases: a new vision of teaching and a communication plan.

A New Vision of Teaching   This far-reaching document, which became part of our master plan, included a digital conversion work statement that provided a framework for our planning team, spelled out the rationale underlying the transformation of our instructional program, and incorporated specific objectives aligned with North Carolina State Board of Education expectations. It informed much of our work and focused on five major goals:

- Shape a new vision of teaching with embedded digital resources coupled with an evolving role of the teacher as the facilitator of differentiated learning.
- Engage students using personalized and relevant real-time content.
- Use project-based, inquiry-based, and collaborative learning as primary instructional strategies.
- Integrate global awareness and digital citizenship into daily activities.
- Foster reflective practice using data and self-analysis.

STUDENT FEEDBACK   *"Before we had the laptops, we'd have an EOQ [end–of-quarter benchmark test] and we wouldn't do well, but the teachers would talk as a whole class. Now since we have the laptops, every student has a teacher helping him out with what they have been struggling with. The laptop is kind of a teacher that is always willing to help you."*
—Mooresville Middle School student

Communication Plan   Recognizing that communication would be critical to the success of our initiative, we developed a comprehensive communication plan that both defined communication strategies at the school and district level and differentiated according to separate audiences—students, district employees, and parents and the community. We also identified channels of communication appropriate to each group, such as workshops, newsletters, community events, and the district web site.

Focus on Employee Growth

In the beginning, new expectations and impending changes created mixed emotions and made many teachers uneasy. But one of the books we read together in our early planning sessions, Linda Lambert's *Building Leadership Capacity in Schools*, helped infuse our dialogue and subsequent implementation with the foundational belief that we had to invest in the growth of all employees in order to bring everyone on board and make digital conversion work.

We used several principles from Lambert's work as early strategies to help diminish fears and kindle enthusiasm. We focused on building collaboration across the organization and involving leaders at all levels in the decision making process. We transitioned to a policy of data-driven decision making, guided by the inquiry process and ongoing personal reflection. And we kept the goal of student achievement front and center at all times.

Learning and Planning Together

A major building block of our evolving culture was a commitment to expanding our knowledge and skills as individuals and teams. As we learned and planned together, we were often inspired by leading thinkers and researchers, believing that we needed to look outside our own small world for ideas on how to successfully tackle our challenges. One influential book we read together was Michael Fullan's *The Six Secrets of Change*, which we discussed at an administrative leadership retreat.

Gina Flannigan, assistant principal at Mooresville High School and now a principal in Boston, expressed very well what we learned from this book. "The two ideas that really left an impression on me were transparency rules and love," she said. "I really believe that when we create a loving environment for employees and students, it just makes things better. And then, when we are open and honest with everyone about how we're doing, the community will know it and appreciate it."

We went on to implement these principles throughout our plans at MGSD, but it was exploring and learning about them together that really allowed them to take hold.

Initial Staff Development Planning

We invested a great deal of time in planning the first phases of professional development, including the initial training on the system, basic software, change management, and the first steps in classroom reorganization. We stressed the long view and the need to take baby steps together, knowing that some of us would run and others would walk or even crawl.

In the second year of implementation at Mooresville Middle School, the science department chair, Mr. Dunagan, echoed the sentiment of many when he predicted that the switch would take time. He could not have been more right. In fact, his school did not really start to take off with digital conversion until 2011, when another science teacher at the school, Mrs. Burklow, told me, "I know it took me a couple of years, but we're flat out on it now!" We believe that everyone, including teachers, learns at his or her own pace, and we took this into account throughout the staff development planning process.

Communication Planning

A detailed communication strategy, directed at both internal and external audiences, was a vital part of the planning process from the beginning. In retrospect, it is clear what an important role this effort played in building support for our digital conversion initiative.

We held a couple of initial meetings that were very important in developing a public dialogue to create awareness of the needs and obligations and to build synergy around the concept. In our first meeting, MGSD administrators, teacher leaders, Chamber of Commerce representatives, elected officials, economic development leaders, and other community leaders discussed the concepts of one-to-one computing and digital conversion, and I shared my experiences in the Henrico County one-to-one computing initiative. Many different viewpoints were aired, but an evolving synergy was in the air.

At a second meeting, in January 2008, attended by more than 1,000 parents and community members, several nationally recognized speakers described the skills students need to compete in today's job market and the role of technology in helping improve academic performance for all learners. A reception followed the presentations and allowed us to get together and discuss our responses. This event proved to be a benchmark in the development of community support for digital conversion in the district.

To build and sustain support, we developed plans for parent technology nights, which we held a couple of times a year, and various other community forums, including civic organizations, Chamber of Commerce events, and NAACP meetings. We posted digital conversion FAQs on our web site and reported on progress at each school board meeting. We also scheduled parent advisory, teacher advisory, and student meetings to offer information and opportunities for discussion.

Building the Digital Foundation

PD [] TOOLKIT™

Listen to Dr. Smith
speak about
the process of
changing teaching
and learning with
technology.

In an early planning meeting, when the team was evaluating projected bandwidth needs, our CTO Dr. Scott Smith said, "It's like the movie *Field of Dreams*—build it, and they will come." We decided to pump up bandwidth capacity since we anticipated heavy use of online multimedia content, an approach that has since been validated by enthusiastic student and teacher use of online resources. It is clear now that stepping up to the plate on the bandwidth issue was a critical factor in our success.

We decided to begin the change process during the 2008 fall semester, with a pilot program at Mooresville High School that allowed us to work out the kinks and develop a planning reference for the rest of the district. In April 2012, Nancy Gardner, Mooresville High School English department chair, described the pilot program to a group of visitors as follows: "We knew we would hit some bumps, and we did, but we kept working, learning the software, changing how we teach, and learning how to collaborate, and here we are."

Pilot Program

In our pilot program, laptop carts were deployed in every high school English classroom. Each cart contained approximately 25 MacBooks and had an Apple AirPort Wi-Fi access point, and the laptops did not go home with students at the end of the day.

We selected the English department as the place to launch the pilot program because all high school students take English each year, and we wanted every high school student to get some baseline experience with digital conversion. We also had a very strong and committed English department chairperson, Debbie Page, and several other English teachers who were willing and able to take on the challenge. In fact, these teachers later went on to develop our first digital conversion professional development programs based on their experience in the pilot program. We planned the pilot program carefully and established the following goals:

- Build teacher confidence.
- Allay fears about change.
- Lay the foundation for instructional planning.
- Refine classroom implementation.

- Initiate student use guidelines.

- Begin professional development planning.

- Troubleshoot infrastructure issues.

- Begin communication planning.

- Develop a planning reference.

Teacher Laptops

Our teacher laptops were selected and rolled out first, in December 2007, right before winter break and before the first community meeting. We put a red bow on each laptop box. School board members attended the event, and we thanked each teacher personally for his or her work as we handed out the laptops, urging the teachers to jump in and have fun. Initially, teachers and all instructional staff received MacBooks, but we have since moved to the 13-inch MacBook Air, based on teacher preference.

Some teachers were very excited and made comments like, "One of the best Christmas presents ever," while others accepted their laptops with little enthusiasm. We immediately embarked on a professional development program focused on the Apple operating system and related software.

Giving teachers their laptops well in advance of students was an important change management buffer for our staff. Teachers will be the first to tell you that students are way out front in understanding and using technology—further evidence of the urgent need to get technology going in our schools—and many teachers find the adjustment to the digital world scary and challenging.

We elected to give teachers a period of time during which they could familiarize themselves with the technology and begin to catch up with students. And in each of our schools, we saw early adopters step up as role models and provide robust leadership that helped others become more comfortable.

Student Laptop Selection

Educators know that durability is a huge factor in selecting student computers that travel between school and home every day, and we expected it to be especially challenging in our schools because we anticipated very high laptop usage, constant movement, and multiple work locations. Since we were planning that homework, assignments, assessments, grading, and many class projects would all be done online, reliability was also a major concern. We based our decision on the following selection criteria:

- Durability
- Reliability
- Built-in software
- Virus management
- Support for creativity
- Support for instructional goals

Built-in software functionality, particularly in regard to creative multimedia applications, was a very important consideration. Expecting that students would be enthusiastic about the availability of online digital tools—music, movies, photos, graphics, and so on—and intending to use these assets for instructional purposes, we wanted to ensure that they were an integral part of the hardware package.

We selected the MacBook based on the iLife toolset for creative presentations and instructional activity, the lack of viruses, and the recommendation of another North Carolina school district, Greene County, which had been using this student device and was pleased with the durability and virus-free learning environment.

In the summer of 2011, we upgraded the student hardware to the newer 11-inch MacBook Airs. The resale value of MacBooks was strong at that time, and we were able to use the proceeds from the sale of the MacBooks to help fund the upgrade.

STUDENT FEEDBACK   *"Before we got the laptops, a typical project would have been some pictures glued on to a poster board or a report. Now we can create a Keynote, iMovie, Comic Life, Virtual Graph and timeline, and a song, all on our laptops. Our teachers have taught us to think outside of the box. They never give us exact outlines for a project; they allow us to use the technology however we want."*

—Mooresville High School student

Staged Laptop Rollout

In the fall of 2008, we began to roll out the student laptops. Every student at Mooresville High School and Mooresville Intermediate School received a MacBook for 24/7 use. In January 2009, MacBook carts were placed in every class at Mooresville Middle School and East Mooresville Intermediate School. By the fall of 2009, every student in grades 4–12 was equipped with his or her own laptop, and MacBook carts were deployed at the third-grade level.

In the fall of 2011, every third grader received a laptop for school use. Students in grades 4–12 have possession of their laptops 24/7 and use them for most, if not all, homework assignments. Third graders do not take their laptops home, although we are considering this option. All K–3 classrooms now have interactive whiteboards, and laptop carts are shared among K–2 classes.

We now refresh the student hardware on a regular basis, preferably over the summer, to address wear and tear and replace laptops as needed. We collect the laptops at the end of each school year, service and update them over the summer, and deploy them again in the fall, with some laptops reserved for summer school students, as needed.

Laptop Deployment Days   We make sure that laptop deployment days are full of excitement and energy. We set up different tables for each step of the deployment and staff them with enthusiastic MGSD employees—tech staff and each school's faculty and principal. We always coordinate laptop deployment days as a team. We create a special sense of occasion and celebration for all involved, and we offer the following tips to other districts:

- Meet and greet students and families to promote the culture of caring.
- Include school and district leaders and school board members to add weight to the occasion.
- Assist qualifying families with maintenance program costs.
- Negotiate with an ISP for reduced home Internet cost for qualifying families.
- Plan parent and student training for safety and responsibility.

Laptop deployment day for intermediate schools, August 2011

Laptop Deployment Process   We planned the deployment process carefully in the beginning and have improved it ever since. Each student receives his or her laptop individually, in a process that takes less than an hour and involves the following:

- Distribution of laptop, backpack, and charger
- Login and password setup
- Attendance by students and parents

- Required use policy review and signature
- Short training session on appropriate use, online safety, and parent monitoring
- Payment of $50 maintenance fee
- Financial assistance application, as needed

FIGURE 4.1

Laptop Rollout Timeline

Date	Distribution
August 2007	400 MacBooks on carts rolled out to MHS English department
December 2007	MacBooks distributed to all teachers
August 2008	1,650 MacBooks distributed to MHS students
	750 MacBooks distributed to MIS students
	80 interactive whiteboards installed in K–2 classrooms at PVES and SES
November 2008	200 MacBooks on carts rolled out to MMS language arts classes
	100 MacBooks on carts rolled out to EMIS 6th grade
January 2009	100 MacBooks on carts rolled out to EMIS 5th grade
March 2009	100 MacBooks on carts rolled out to EMIS 4th grade
June 2009	Laptop collection at MHS and MIS
August 2009	MacBooks rolled out to every student in grades 4–12
	Interactive whiteboards installed in every K–3 classroom
April 2010	Staff, EMIS, MIS, and MMS laptop refresh started
August 2010	MHS and MIS laptop refresh completed
September 2010	Laptop carts distributed to PVES, RRES, and SES
August 2011	Laptop upgrade to 11-inch MacBook Airs for all students in grades 4–12
September 2011	Laptop carts distributed to 3rd-grade classes at PVES, RRES, and SES and two laptop carts distributed to K–2 classrooms

Key to the abbreviations: PVES: Park View Elementary School (K–3); RRES: Rocky River Elementary School (K–3); SES: South Elementary School (K–3); EMIS: East Mooresville Intermediate School (4–6); MIS: Mooresville Intermediate School (4–6); MMS: Mooresville Middle School (7–8); and MHS: Mooresville High School (9–12).

Laptop Maintenance Fees   We decided on a maintenance fee of $50 per computer per year, payable by families, to cover the costs of repairs. The Mooresville Education Foundation covers this cost for qualifying families, and we provide assistance to any other family that requests it. Some families with three or four students ask if they can pay over a few months, and we have accommodated such requests. Each year, we estimate how many families we think will need assistance and ask the foundation to provide the funding.

Wireless Network

Based on our experience in the high school English classes and my experience in Henrico County, we recognized from the start that a robust network with more-than-sufficient bandwidth would be essential to our instructional goals. Planning and implementing the wireless infrastructure was a huge "all in" effort for our tech team, and several service partners helped us plan for short- and long-term needs.

We made the decision to move forward with Cisco 802.11n technology, an upgrade that was slightly more expensive but significantly increased the quality and capacity of our network. At that time, Duke University was the only other educational organization in the country using this cutting-edge infrastructure.

Anytime, Anywhere Access   We wanted to make sure that students could access the Internet anytime, anywhere—from the school lawn, in the park, and from home. To accommodate students who did not have Internet access at home, we extended the hours in our school media centers, which we staffed with existing resources, until 5 PM, and we worked with the public library to provide wireless access. Our small but vibrant Mooresville downtown has Wi-Fi, and many local restaurants provide free Internet access.

Discounted Internet Service   We made an arrangement with our local ISP whereby families without broadband Internet access could buy it for $16.99 a month. This is a vitally important part of the planning equation and one that I believe can be replicated in other communities, since ISPs are motivated to create economical packages in today's competitive marketplace.

Wide Area Network   Since our instructional program relies largely on digital resources, we needed to ensure a high level of functionality, speed, filtering, and compatibility, as well as 99 percent, if not 100 percent, uptime, to support our instructional goals. We have implemented a robust wide area network (WAN) throughout the district.

WAN connections between schools and the technology department are 1-gigabit fiber connections. In addition, we now maintain a 250-megabyte (MB) pipe to the Internet, an increase from 100 MB due to the fact that we added over 2,000 laptops to the network in the 2007–2008 school year. Currently, MGSD supports nearly 5,000 laptops and 1,000 desktops on this infrastructure. We also believe in supplying as much wireless connectivity as possible to devices, which in our case means providing secure 802.11n technology through a managed network infrastructure across nine physical locations in the district.

Moving to the Cloud   We are working with the North Carolina Department of Public Instruction (DPI) on a cloud pilot project that is using Race to the Top funding to build and support comprehensive cloud services to all school districts in the state. We have already transferred our network filtering to the North Carolina DPI cloud, for a savings of $40,000 a year, and we anticipate additional savings to come.

Online Content and Tools

We use a variety of math, science, social studies, and other content area programs that provide individual practice, often in an engaging game format, differentiated according to student needs. These programs align with specific objectives and include progress reports that teachers and students can view. We selected netTrekker Search from Knovation as our district search engine because of the high level of security it provides for students doing online research.

Most of the online content available today includes links to other resources. The content and the links work together to create an enormous reference library for school and home use that has super-charged our learning environment. As we continue on the path of digital conversion, we are excited about the development of new and improved digital content.

Software Evaluation Criteria   We use a large array of online instructional content, and we constantly review new products and services. In the beginning, we focused our instructional software choices on a few key evaluation criteria:

- Aligns with state accountability assessments
- Includes built-in assessments with adaptive functioning
- Flows well and is easy to use for teachers and students

- Is compatible with our hardware and learning management system (LMS)
- Supports creativity and inquiry-based learning
- At the high school level, matches courses such as algebra and biology

The Discovery Education science content, which includes video vignettes and mini-assessments, was an early model of the type of functionality we have since looked for in all content. As teachers review new content and tools and work as a team to make decisions, we try to balance the value of familiarity with the need for innovation. Our service providers are constantly improving the functionality and quality of their products, and we have discovered that they are keenly interested in our feedback and questions.

STUDENT FEEDBACK   *"In band we use a great program called Smart Music. It allows us access to thousands upon thousands of musical works that we can sight-read. Tests are given on Smart Music. It tells us the percentage of notes we played correctly."*

—Mooresville High School student

Alignment to Standards   As part of the online content selection and staging processes, we aligned our online content with the North Carolina Course of Study and national standards for literacy, mathematics, science, and social studies. We enlisted teams of teachers from all levels to work through the alignment process over the summer months to ensure tight alignment between the standards and the digital content.

During this time, we also built and updated our end-of-quarter benchmark tests (EOQs) to ensure standards alignment. Several service providers assisted us in the process, and we benefited from their professional expertise.

Assessment Considerations   One of the huge value-adds of digital conversion is the availability of built-in online formative assessments that give students and teachers valuable information every day to drive student improvement. Since we planned to implement a learning management system at the heart of our software program, we had to make sure that any software under consideration was compatible with our LMS and included embedded assessment functions with broad disaggregation capability.

Real-time data about progress and needs have since become a daily influence on teaching and learning in our district, with an assessment framework that aligns with our learning management system to create an integrated instructional environment.

Learning Management System

Learning management system (LMS) functionality was one of our most important planning considerations since we intended the LMS to be the "clearinghouse," or hub, of much of our instructional program. We were looking for an online grade book and a learning repository for student work.

We wanted our LMS to be the means by which students submit homework and other assignments, and we needed alignment with multiple assessment packages, so that formative assessments could be administered online by grade level and content area, for maximum efficiency and fast teacher response.

Students, parents, administrators, and staff now all depend on the LMS for a variety of functions. Our LMS drop boxes for student work and teacher collaboration have become part of daily life. The LMS also serves as a parent portal where parents can check grades, assignments, and the calendar and communicate with teachers. Collaboration tools in our LMS and the collaboration functionality embedded in many online resources fuel the interactions between stakeholders every day.

PARENT FEEDBACK *"We can engage in email correspondence with teachers, often after hours. In addition, the student's progress is posted in real time on a site personal to each student, and the parents have access to this at any time. Our experience is that the laptops have resulted in more parent engagement in what is actually going on in the classroom because we are able to see it for ourselves."*

—MGSD parent

Media Center Tools

Scanners, digital cameras, digital voice recorders, and digital video cameras are available for checkout from our media centers and by department and grade level. In addition, our laptops are equipped with cameras and video and audio recording software so that students have robust multimedia toolsets available to them at all times. However, the demand for media center tools has increased because students always want the best audio and video quality available.

Social Networking

We made the choice not to enable commercial social media for students, primarily based on concerns about student safety and community acceptance. We had seen many examples of bad social media behavior, from both students and adults, and the benefits did not appear to outweigh the problems.

We use blogs and discussion boards that permit social interaction in a learning environment. We clearly see the promise of collective learning in a digital world and are investigating new social media providers that offer fine-grained control features and a secure environment.

STUDENT FEEDBACK   *"The chat rooms Mrs. Higgins gives us are one of the best parts of class. Of course, there is a strict rule of no text speak. We write our opinions out as befits us as AP students. I know how to speak to people both aloud and in text, and knowing how to write an intelligent, expressive email will benefit me in the world I'm maturing in."*

—Mooresville High School student

Required Use Policy

Listen to teacher Chris Gammon describe required use training for students and parents.

Two years ago, at parent and teacher advisory meetings, we studied the need to change our laptop acceptable use policy to a required use policy, to strengthen the message and the rules. In 2012, we revised this policy again as of a review of all MGSD school board policies. It has become a required use policy in accordance with North Carolina School Board Association recommendations. This policy provides specific guidelines for students, staff, and parents about what is and is not permissible regarding laptop and Internet use. It is essential to make clear that discipline violations using digital resources are included in the code of conduct and will be handled just like any other violations.

Parents were very supportive and even adamant in their support for the stronger language, and they have consistently supported the required use policy. We have since taken extra steps to increase awareness among parents and students of cyber-bullying and online predation. An evolving curriculum of digital citizenship and continuous monitoring of student online activity are part of our daily activity.

Monitoring of Online Activity

A remote desktop security feature allows our administrators and technology staff to monitor student laptops and view their screens while they are on our network. Principals and assistant principals use this tool, and students and parents understand that we monitor Internet use daily and will address any inappropriate use.

Staffing

We are frequently asked if we had to add staff to support digital conversion, and the answer is no. We repurposed our lab coordinators to become tech facilitators, with a combined technical/instructional focus, and this change has worked extremely well. We also redefined some teacher assistant positions as help desk coordinator positions. And a help desk in each school is staffed in part by high school students who are enrolled in a credit course on help desk operation.

Initially, we had to recruit students to take this course, but now we have strong enrollment, and some students are even choosing tech support as a possible career path. The help desks have become a vibrant model of self-sufficiency and an object of fascination for visitors. One of our high school students explained recently to a room full of visitors, "If you can stay for 17 minutes, I can repair the broken screen on this laptop from start to finish. I work better under the clock, kinda like NASCAR, and I can take the broken screen off and install a new one in less than 20 minutes, but my best time is 17 minutes," she said.

Each school has a full-time help desk manager, a media coordinator—a librarian with extensive knowledge of online resources—and a technology facilitator, teacher-support, and trouble-shooting position. One member of the district tech team has primary responsibility for each school, which creates a strong bond between the district and the school. Our tech team, which includes the chief technology officer and one clerical staff person, is made up of eight people, all highly respected for their service, hard work, and dedication.

Initial Training

After the pilot program in our high school English classes, our English department teachers and chairperson Debbie Page stepped up in a major way to become lead scout on our learning expedition. Several of them led professional development sessions over the summer, based on their experience in the pilot program.

Having peers show the way with a big "yes, we can" attitude proved to be very important, because in our first year we had plenty of doubters and a healthy dose of fear. We settled on a one-step-at-a-time strategy as we were growing our capacity in the early days.

We were quick to identify veteran teachers, some with 30 or 40 years of teaching experience, who jumped in early and served as models of change leadership. These veterans embraced the use of digital resources and were not afraid to say that they were better teachers as a result of the learning process. We lost a few teachers along the way, but very few. Over 90 percent have grown and thrived, although in some cases it took two years or more.

We began a voluntary annual Summer Institute in July 2008, and we have since added many other opportunities for professional learning, including early release days, graduate programs in partnership with local universities, tuition reimbursement, teacher leader workshops, content- and grade-level workshops, leadership retreats, and service provider training sessions.

Second-Order Change Management

As we have reviewed our progress, we have regularly addressed the concepts of change management and second-order change—concepts that we believe teachers, principals, and staff must understand and buy into—while recognizing that frustration and resistance are normal byproducts of cultural change. To help our teachers through the second-order change process, we consciously adopted a program of support that includes:

- Emotional intelligence
- Sensitivity to the impact of change
- A combination of nurture and direction
- Acceptance of different rates of progress
- A one-step-at-a-time strategy
- Calm, forward-focused leadership

Service and Support

We expect all our service providers—of hardware, software, content, and infrastructure solutions—to work in partnership with us and be there when needed to troubleshoot crises and manage ongoing issues. We also expect them to team with us to ensure effective training, implementation, and fidelity to the plan. Vendors that do not supply this level of teamwork and service are eliminated from the plan as soon as possible, although this has happened only rarely.

"When we first started down this path, I was not enthusiastic about it. I thought it would just be another layer of something, and it was going to disrupt my whole world," said Melody Morrison, special education chair at Mooresville High School, who retired in 2012.

"But as I saw my students grow, I became a huge advocate. Last year, one of my students who is dyslexic and has significant learning challenges was not getting started on his senior project. I suggested he do a presentation of how to build an engine—I knew he had old cars around his home and that he loved working on engines. He came back to class a few weeks later, after a little direction, with an 82-slide presentation with photos of every part of a car engine. It was a stellar presentation. I'll never forget that."

REFLECTIVE QUESTIONS

1. What are your digital conversion planning objectives?
2. How do you select your pilot school or schools?
3. Who is involved in your planning decisions?
4. How far ahead do you plan for infrastructure needs?
5. Who evaluates your digital resources and against what criteria?

REFERENCES

Fullan, Michael. (2008). *The Six Secrets of Change: What the Best Leaders Do to Help Their Organizations Survive and Thrive.* San Francisco, CA: Jossey-Bass.

Lambert, Linda. (1998). *Building Leadership Capacity in Schools.* Alexandria, VA: Association for Supervision and Curriculum Development.

Chapter Five

Evolutional Capacity Building

"Individual and team effectiveness are both essential to capacity building, and both are works in progress, as teachers and staff learn right along with students."

A common lament at MGSD in the early stages of digital conversion was along the lines of, "I know how to teach but not with all this computer focus." Mooresville High School principal Todd Wirt liked to respond by holding his arms wide apart and saying, "We're from here to here on our range of skills in using technology, but as long as we're all moving forward and understanding that we have a responsibility to learn and grow, we'll be just fine."

At MGSD, we have embraced what we call "evolutional" capacity building as a major component of our digital conversion initiative. We believe we have to focus every day on building the capacity of teachers, administrators, teacher assistants, support staff, and ultimately every staff member. We are all well prepared with college degrees, certifications, and varying amounts of experience, but we also acknowledge the need to change our practice and improve our skills on an ongoing basis.

PD **◯** TOOLKIT™

Listen to the author explain why ongoing professional learning is essential to digital conversion success.

To live up to our district motto of *Every Child, Every Day*, we believe it is absolutely essential that we as educators evolve and learn right along with students. Students' needs and realities morph almost daily, it seems, as the competitive world we are preparing them for calls for more and more relevance and applied learning. To make change real, our work in schools and classrooms must have an organic, underlying commitment to ongoing professional learning and "maximum efficacy," or impact on the needs of every child.

Online resources, assessment, and collaboration opportunities have radically changed the learning process, so that evolutional capacity building is a long-term commitment that requires time and patience, as well as clear expectations. At MGSD, we started with baby steps, celebrated when they were successfully completed, and kept our focus on growth and improvement.

Our work on building the capacity of all employees has built a high level of synergy among team members, which has led to more effective teaching and academic improvement, as we have gradually moved from a didactic whole-group instructional focus to highly differentiated teaching.

Our teachers are becoming more and more invested in self-improvement and are better prepared to teach in our ever-changing world. As Roland Barth writes in *Learning by Heart*, "In times of change, learners inherit the earth, while the learned find themselves beautifully equipped to deal with a world that no longer exists." We view the need to grow and learn as the responsibility of both the school system and the individual, and we approach this responsibility with vigor, while understanding that individuals and teams will each grow at their own pace.

Building Momentum for Change

In a quarterly data meeting at Mooresville Middle School, principal Carrie Tulbert was able to demonstrate to Bill Parker, our executive director for secondary education, how she had responded to his growth plan for her. Bill had encouraged her to be more assertive with faculty members who were not performing as well as they could.

Mrs. Tulbert was crisp and articulate. "This meeting gives us an opportunity to review how we're doing as individuals and as teams and to plan for the next quarter," she said. Every attendee reported on strategies and plans to meet student needs. Every department chair reviewed the quarterly benchmark data and the alignment of resources to support areas of need. The consensus was that we were not where we wanted to be, but we were ahead of last year—and optimistic. Bill Parker had helped Mrs. Tulbert to grow, she had helped her staff to grow, and they were clearly responding.

We provide the time, the funds, and the attention to individual and team growth to create the momentum for change. In doing so, we send a clear message to everyone, including students, about the need to keep on learning, while also communicating that the pace of change will depend on the individual.

Students get a kick out of seeing that their teachers and principals are also learning and improving, while a wave of evolving teacher capacity lifts up both students and teachers and moves them forward. In the words of Allen Stevens, science teacher at Mooresville Middle School, "My students are always pushing me to move faster in using our digital resources, and they are encouraging all of us to stretch ourselves."

Personal Development Plans

Growth plans for principals, administrators, teachers, and grade-level and department chairs, like the one mentioned on the previous page, were a change that some employees found challenging in the beginning. However, growth plans, or professional development plans, are an essential component of capacity building. In many school cultures, staff and leadership growth is not emphasized and is therefore minimal. But in a digital conversion initiative, growth is a must and often has the effect of rekindling everyone's enthusiasm for education.

Outline: Teacher Personal Development Plan

- Identify areas where you want to improve.
- Identify skills you want to consistently practice.
- Meet with the technology facilitator bi-weekly to co-plan lessons that will help you practice the skills.
- Use your time appropriately to collaborate on how to become a more accomplished teacher with 21st-century skills.
- Identify what other support we can give you as we move forward with 21st-century learning tools.

Outline: Principal Personal Development Plan

- Identify areas for personal growth.
- Identify areas for school improvement.
- Establish goals for personal and school improvement.
- Identify strategies for growth, such as reading, increased collaboration, and workshops.
- Engage with central office staff and your director for support and feedback.

Additional Planning Time

In the past, our teachers were not nearly as inclined to collaborate as they are today. A major barrier was the lack of time, since planning together, sharing, and building relationships are time-consuming. Because we wanted to create the conditions to develop teamwork and collaboration, in our second year of digital conversion, the MGSD school board approved early release days eight times a year, whereby students are released at noon. These afternoons are now used for professional development, collaboration, reflection, planning, and data analysis at the school and district levels.

The early release day concept was presented at a parent advisory council meeting, where parents acknowledged the need for teacher growth during the digital conversion process, and their support encouraged the school board to move forward. Our parents have helped build our collective capacity by allowing for a redesign of the calendar that clearly signaled the importance of adult learning in our emerging culture. We provide childcare for K–6 students on early release afternoons, along with tutorial support for some students.

Students and Teachers Learning Together

PD **pd** TOOLKIT™

Listen to teacher Samone Graham talk about learning from students and colleagues.

As part of the change process, teachers had to learn to accept what they didn't know, develop the patience to learn new things, and be willing to learn alongside students. It took time for some teachers to learn how to deal with a slow Internet connection or presentation software not working the way they wanted. It also took time for some teachers to accept that they could learn about technology from our digital-native students.

But joint student-teacher learning experiences became the norm over time and are now enthusiastically embraced. Frustration with hardware or software has evolved into opportunities for collaborative troubleshooting, and our teachers have found to their delight that students are patient, nurturing, and supportive of their efforts to learn about digital resources.

Julie Buda and her third-grade class at Park View Elementary learned together how to use Skype and Edmodo, a networking site similar to Facebook, to connect with students in China as part of the Flat Classroom Project and to share movies, audio, and pictures. "My students are always ready to learn something new," says Julie.

STUDENT FEEDBACK   *"I learned that students in China watch the same TV shows as us. But some said they wished they could wear any kind of clothing to school. One girl said she had to wear a uniform."*

"My topic was housing and transportation, and I used a program called Glockster to make a poster showing different types of vehicles and houses in the U.S."

"We got to learn about many different styles of clothing. I thought it was cool."

"I put up pictures of food from school and home and talked about them. I also put up pictures of our Halloween party at school and some Thanksgiving pictures."

"I posted pictures of different sports teams."

—Park View Elementary School students

Steady Progress and Constant Effort

Unfortunately, a few teachers were truly resistant to change. But, with the support of the school board and the community, we recognized the challenge and implemented an approach that called for steady progress and constant effort, to set the tone we wanted. Our approach reflected the sentiment of Keith Krueger, CEO of the Consortium for School Networking (CoSN), which he expressed to me in an email conversation:

"The greatest challenge we face in powerfully leveraging technology in schools isn't technical or technological. The biggest challenge we face is human capacity. In other words, the problem is us. We are talking about a cultural shift that is as major as the industrial revolution, and it is going to be very disruptive. But is also the most exciting time for learning since we can focus on personalizing instruction."

The message to our instructional staff was supported by our planning and policy documents and clearly reinforced by our evaluations, which focus on growth, especially in using digital resources and data, collaborating with peers, and, above all, demonstrating pervasive care for students.

Our strategic plan makes specific reference to digital conversion goals and measures. For example, it requires that teachers demonstrate the capacity and competency to use digital resources in all aspects of instruction. The North Carolina Technology Standards and Performance Indicators for Educators, which are aligned with the state evaluation program, include detailed requirements for the integration and use of technology in the classroom. And MGSD school board policies mirror the state requirements and the strategic plan.

A handful of teachers who did not meet the requirements for steady progress and constant effort were put on a growth plan with a timeline for improvement. Lack of progress meant nonrenewal or dismissal. However, 95 percent of our teachers understood from the beginning that digital conversion was the right thing to do—our moral imperative—and we in turn recognized that their rate of progress would vary. Looking back, many of our staff members recognize what a serious transformational change we went through. They realize that we had a lot to learn about using data and creating a student-centered culture, and it took a while.

Change Management Strategies

We used a range of change management strategies—including training, constant encouragement, calm leadership, candid feedback, and emotional intelligence— to build momentum for change. We also relied heavily on veteran and respected staff members to train others. Many books that we discussed together provided ideas about the need for change, and we didn't just read them. We took books such as Michael Fullan's *All Systems Go* to heart and tried hard to translate their ideas into practice.

For example, the concept of transparency in *All Systems Go* represented a major cultural change for us. It took time for our teachers to adjust to and ultimately embrace a new policy of disaggregation of student performance data, by teacher, on end-of-quarter exams and state tests. In the beginning, asking teachers to look at their names up on a screen next to their students' numbers required some serious change management attention. In *Leadership for Learning,* Carl Glickman offers a reality check on the topic of change management: "Those educators who can't publicly practice the act of continuous improvement over time must leave on their own accord or be terminated. Clearly this is not easy work."

We focused on support and collaboration, and as our teacher leaders emerged and grew, the process of discussing systemic school improvement data provided an ongoing constructive reference point for what we were trying to do. We all began to sense that the confluence of adult learning and new teaching goals was starting to change our world, and our discussions increasingly led to emotional reaffirmation of the moral imperative to improve the achievement of all students.

Candid Feedback

After visiting every classroom in every school every semester, I sent summary comments to all staff in the district, expressing encouragement and confirming expectations. Other district leaders did the same, and the feedback was always candid. We have continued this practice ever since, as an ongoing part of our leadership team change management strategy.

The Long View

We all learn and grow at our own pace—teachers as well as students. It is important to be candid and persistent, but it is equally important to balance candor and persistence with patience. In the words of Carol Ann Tomlinson and Susan Demirsky Allan, who discuss cultural change in schools in *Leadership for Differentiating Schools and Classrooms:*

> "The knowledge and skills required for change must be developed within teachers. Teachers must own knowledge and skills, not simply receive them from or borrow them from colleagues. Coming to own new ways of teaching, thinking, and collaborating is a slow process."

Different schools, teachers, and departments build capacity at their own pace, and it is essential to take a long-term view regarding their evolution. Major changes require a developmental approach, and good things take time, as my mother always told me when I was waiting for something delicious to come out of the oven. It can take time for serious momentum to kick in, but a determined commitment to capacity building will get results in the long run. Our evaluation standards focus on

Sample Summary Comments

From: Mark Edwards
To: All MGSD Schools
RE: **Progress/Challenges**

Having had the pleasure of visiting MMS yesterday, I wanted to share some observations. I truly believe the MMS leadership team (Mrs. Tulbert, Mr. Stewart, and Mrs. Gloster) is going to have a hugely positive impact on students and staff. I saw a significant increase in the work with digital conversion. The decorum of the students was outstanding, and the early return on Capturing Kids' Hearts was obvious. So many teachers said that the students are just great, and I really believe that when students hear their teachers say this, they live up to it.

I do want to challenge several MMS teachers to step up their work with digital conversion. Parents have asked me to look at the contrast between MIS and MMS regarding digital conversion. I have, and we have to step it up. Thanks, MMS staff!!! Let's go get "90" [MGSD goal of 90 percent district achievement].

From: Mark Edwards
To: All MGSD Schools
RE: **MHS and N.F. WOODS are taking it up!**

I had the great pleasure of visiting MHS and N.F. Woods last week, and both schools' faculty and staff are taking it to the next level. N.F. Woods looks great (Mr. Norman and the bus drivers and custodians are on it!), and the faculty, as always, are positive about their students and the work they are doing. I really believe Mr. Gibbs and the N.F. Woods team can be the best technical center in NC, and that is the immediate goal for this year. The Mi-WAYE team is moving forward and making a difference for students. N.F. Woods faculty have really got it together, and I am very proud of them. MHS students and staff are on their way to honor school designation.

I was very impressed with several teachers who have taken digital conversion to the next level. The foreign language department has truly moved to the next level, integrating current events into language development. I was impressed with the focus of students and staff and the overall work effort and attitude. A student from Mr. Bost's class shared that Mr. B's participation in the Capturing Kids' Hearts training had a profound impact on her class. She was living proof that relationships set the tone for all classes.

I deeply appreciate the MHS media specialists who have transformed the MHS media center into a research center teeming with activity. At MHS and N.F. Woods the office staff are making a difference, the child nutrition staff at MHS deserve a big shout out for doing a super job, and I am so proud of the work effort and leadership by the counselors. We have serious early momentum at both schools! *Every Child, Every Day*!

teacher growth, as do our strategic plan goals, but we look for growth over time in order to balance our expectations for change with our commitment to the long view.

For example, in the first few years of digital conversion, East Mooresville Intermediate School lagged behind in student performance, partly because it got started a year later than Mooresville Intermediate School. Robin Melton, who moved from assistant principal to principal in the summer of 2010, used our concept of evolutional capacity building to see where her staff needed to improve and find ways to help. "We're going to leverage our use of the tech facilitator, and I'm going to get more specific with expectations for teacher growth, as outlined in their evaluations," she said at a principal meeting.

Mrs. Melton went on to hire a new technology facilitator, previously a grade-level chairperson, and began to talk to teachers about how they could be more effective in using laptops, digital resources, and differentiation. She brought in some new grade-level chairs and worked with them on growth plans based on student data and differentiated instructional approaches. She also scheduled weekly meetings with teachers who were under-performing, to provide direction and support. It took time and a clear focus on capacity building, but East Mooresville Intermediate made huge strides and received the North Carolina School of Distinction Award at the end of the year.

Similarly, the foreign language department at Mooresville High School did not integrate digital conversion as quickly as some other departments, and I adjusted my expectations accordingly. However, one day, during a classroom visit, I saw students going online, pulling up newspapers from other countries, and using the articles in individual and group assignments. One student showed me her report about Santiago, Chile, that incorporated information from a local newspaper.

When I asked the teacher what had been the catalyst for this change, she said that the new department chair, Tracey Waid, had shared the practice of online research from her French classes and that all the foreign language department teachers were now running with it. The capacity of our foreign language department as individuals and as a team evolved rather slowly. But now they are taking off. The synergy of the department chair's new ideas and the principal's focus on steady progress and constant effort eventually got them moving in the right direction and turbo-charged their growth.

It's generally worth the wait. We have seen some reluctant teachers emerge as digital conversion superstars over time. One of our middle school teachers made an amazing transformation. "She didn't start moving until year three, and then in year four—boom," the principal told me. "She's just been selected to be a Rising Star in the DEN for Discovery Education. She's super pumped."

Team Building

PD **TOOLKIT**™

Listen to the author talk about the importance of working on teamwork.

After our chief technology officer, Dr. Scott Smith, visited East Mooresville Intermediate School a few years ago, he sent me the following email: "The EMIS team has taken off like a rocket with digital conversion. Our tech facilitator, Ms. Gander, is working with individual teachers and grade-level groups to support their needs. The team capacity has been leveraged up by Mrs. Melton's [the principal's] leadership. She is very supportive and caring, but she expects teachers to step up their game every day, and they do."

Individual and team effectiveness are both essential to capacity building, and both are works in progress, as teachers and staff learn right along with students. As our teams work at working together, we see their capacity evolving and their collective awareness of the importance of team growth translating into greater success for students. Michael Fullan explains this well in *All Systems Go*:

> "The power of collective capacity is that it enables ordinary people to accomplish extraordinary things—for two reasons. One is that knowledge about effective practice becomes more widely used on a daily basis. The second reason is that working together generates commitment. The speed of effective change increases exponentially. Collective capacity, quite simply, gets more and deeper things done in shorter periods of time."

We think it is important to reflect on individual and team performance on a regular basis and to use those reflections as part of instructional planning and resource application. We also think it is essential to work on being a "school family," caring for each other and connected to each other through personal and professional bonds. MGSD staff work together in a variety of teams to ensure continued progress.

MGSD Teams

- Grade levels
- Curriculum departments
- Schools
- District administrators
- School leaders
- Teachers

- Principals
- Assistant principals
- Tech staff
- Maintenance staff
- Office professionals
- Custodians
- Food service workers
- School board
- Parents and the community

Executive Team Meetings

Our executive leadership team is made up of our executive directors of instruction (elementary and secondary), executive director of human resources and student services (one person), director of operations, chief financial officer, chief technology officer, public information officer, and myself. This team is responsible for all aspects of our school system, and we focus all our efforts on the needs of students and teachers.

In our weekly meetings, each member updates the team on the past week and on any upcoming activity. We discuss how we can leverage resources to best serve students, as well as the needs of each school and the district in the short term and the long term. The ongoing dialogue has created a sense of team and collegiality. We debate, and sometimes disagree, but we always strive to arrive at a place where we can meet our standard of *Every Child, Every Day*. We believe in Margaret Wheatley's ideas about team dynamics in *Leadership and the New Science*:

> "When organizations are willing to give public voice to information . . . to listen to different interpretations and then to process them together . . . the information becomes amplified. In this process of shared reflection, we grow and creative responses emerge."

Principals' and Faculty Meetings

In our monthly principals' and faculty meetings, we discuss what's going on in the different schools, share solutions and ideas, and watch presentations by peers. We use this time to try to become a better team and understand each other better. At almost every meeting, we blend in a teamwork activity, enjoy some refreshments, acknowledge special occasions in each other's lives, or just laugh out loud as a team.

As the dynamics of our school system constantly change throughout the year, month, week, or day, we respond to evolving phenomena and adjust our goals, plans, and aspirations accordingly. We often incorporate reflective discussion or comments from each team member to personalize our collective commitment as educators.

We talk about the importance of teamwork at every meeting. Caring for each other, sharing with each other, and cheering each other on are leadership norms in Mooresville. At a recent principals' meeting, each leader was asked to discuss how we are improving our work as a team of leaders. Carrie Tulbert, principal of Mooresville Middle School, asked the group to acknowledge the work of our director of operations, Mr. Mauney. "He's worked with us to make sure we have optimal conditions for testing time. He's coordinated the mowing schedules and made sure transportation staff are dialed in and ready to provide help as needed," she said.

"Who has good news to shout out?" someone asked at a high school faculty meeting last year. Hands popped up all around the room. "I think we owe a big thank you to Eddie Karriker for doing such a great job rounding up judges for the senior projects," said Nancy Gardner, the English department chair. Spontaneous applause erupted as Eddie stood up. "It's a team effort, and thanks to everyone for pitching in," he said.

Meetings reflect culture. If meetings focus on sharing and growing, chances are the culture is one of sharing and growing. Teams grow together when they do meaningful work together and recognize the contributions of all.

Department and Grade-Level Meetings

In the early days, many teachers joined online professional learning communities (PLCs), but our grade-level and department teams have since evolved into MGSD PLCs that we see as more organic and valuable because they focus on MGSD goals, such as learning how to use new digital resources or enhancing data skills to fine-tune the instructional efforts of individuals and teams.

We have moved away from a meeting format in which the chair disseminates information and work requirements. Our chairs now focus on improving the team, fostering discussion around the use of data, and sharing strategies that are working, so that all can learn and benefit from each other. New teachers are given special support, as is anyone who is dealing with challenges.

Not all teams function as well as others, but we are seeing a consistent level of synergy from the focus on improvement and the powerful impact of teacher leadership. Most grade levels and departments now have several teacher leaders who lead by example and demonstrate true respect and care for their colleagues.

The selection and development of teacher leaders—grade-level and department chairs—is vitally important work, for which principals receive coaching on how to be both thoughtful and strategic. All our principals have made changes in teacher leader assignments that have led to improvement on the part of teachers and students.

Articulation Meetings

Articulation meetings are designed to check for alignment and articulation, usually by content area. Teachers who serve the same age group in different schools get together to compare notes and make sure they are on the same page. For example, teachers from Mooresville Middle School meet by content area with teachers from Mooresville Intermediate School and East Mooresville Intermediate School to analyze successes and areas of need.

A few years ago, the Spanish teachers at Mooresville High School noticed a growing disconnect between their program and the one at Mooresville Middle School. The teachers from the two schools got together to develop a new plan for student expectations and curriculum design. The first meetings were challenging, but with the support of principals, assistant principals, and the executive director of secondary instruction, a sense of common direction and expectations slowly emerged. An ongoing goal is to build team capacity and maximum efficacy so that the articulation meetings are more organic and self-sustaining.

Other teams get together to discuss the needs of students as they move from one school to another. Elementary teachers meet with middle school teachers, and middle school teachers meet with high school teachers to help students make the transition. Counselors at Mooresville Middle School and Mooresville High School actively map out course and schedule pathways and look at the needs of students as they transition from middle school to high school.

Teacher Advisory Committee Meetings

Our teacher advisory committee (TAC) meetings focus on information sharing and dialogue, the goal being to hear from teachers how things are going and how morale is faring. Teachers are encouraged to share concerns and constructive criticism at every meeting, and we act on many of their suggestions. Teachers are not excluded from administrative decisions.

For example, when Kitch Deaton, kindergarten teacher at South Elementary School, told us in a recent TAC meeting that she needed more in-class planning time, we listened. "We need time in our classes during some of the early release days," she said. "We know the professional development is important, but we also have student planning and data analysis and team planning we need to do." We used Kitch's input to schedule individual teacher planning time on certain early release days.

We have also used TAC meetings as a forum to discuss tough budget cuts, so that everyone has a clear understanding of the trade-offs involved in difficult choices. This has been a learning experience for all concerned. Teachers have grown in their ability to work together for the common good, and they have grown as leaders by participating in planning and prioritization decisions.

Parent Advisory Committee Meetings

PD **TOOLKIT**™

Listen to parent Leon Pridgen describe the role of PACs.

Team building must involve parents and community leaders as well as teachers. We hold parent advisory committee (PAC) meetings several times a year and use them as a forum for communication and information sharing. These meetings have gradually allowed parent leaders to emerge and built support for system growth. We believe in transparency in our interactions with parents, just as we do among MGSD employees. This has worked well and has been invaluable in building trust and buy-in.

PARENT FEEDBACK *"My son, just yesterday, completed a multimedia project about the Sahara Desert, working together with another student. They created a video imagining themselves driving a vehicle through the desert while reciting facts about the desert and incorporating pictures and graphics about what they were describing. It was as if they were taking me on a virtual tour of the desert. This is the way we communicate now."*

—Parent of Mooresville High School student

For several years, we have used PAC meetings, as well as TAC meetings, to share information about pending budget cuts. Three years ago, when we anticipated that we would need to cut 10 percent of the MGSD workforce, a father's hand shot up at one of our PAC meetings. "I sure hope we don't backtrack on the digital conversion," he said. "I know these cuts are tough, and we have had to make cuts at my work, but the digital conversion was a major reason we chose to live in Mooresville." Several other parents commented along the same lines. We believe that openness about challenges as well as successes is the best recipe for the across-the-board relationship building that is key to a successful change effort.

Student Advisory Committee Meetings

I learned about the value of a formal program of student input when I was superintendent in Henrico County, where we also had a student advisory committee (SAC). At MGSD, we have student advisory committees in two schools, Mooresville High School and Mooresville Middle School, to promote dialogue with students and hear their viewpoints. We have often incorporated their suggestions into our school programs.

The SACs are also helpful in developing student leaders and addressing challenges. For example, we have had great discussions about bullying at both the high school and middle school level, with students quick to recognize that they can have a positive impact on the problem. It is exciting to see student leaders emerge with the ability to use their talents for the benefit of all.

Community Involvement

Our education foundation, made up of parents, business leaders, and community leaders, holds regular meetings. I am an ex-officio member, as is our school board chair. Our chief financial officer, public information officer, and director of operations represent district employees. The sole purpose of the education foundation is to support the district and advocate for our needs, including to our elected officials. When we had to brainstorm new funding strategies in light of the ongoing budget cuts, one of our former school board members was very clear on the strategy. "We need to make it clear that we expect our elected officials to step up and support our schools, and we mean it," he said.

At a recent school board meeting, parents, grandparents, the mayor, business leaders, and Chamber of Commerce executives voiced their support for a five-cent school tax levy to deal with looming state funding cuts. The board passed the levy, and the room erupted in cheers. "This is all about a synergy to build a better community, attract economic development, and prepare our workforce," said our new mayor, Miles Atkins.

Our parents and community members have come together to support important issues. We use PAC and PTO meetings, booster clubs, civic clubs, and other organizations to participate in the community and build relationships. If our band or choral group can help support a community event, we are there whenever possible. Our ROTC color guard was asked to present the colors at 83 different community events in 2011.

We have active partnerships with organizations that support families in need, including the Mooresville Soup Kitchen, the Mooresville Christian Mission, and the Mooresville YMCA. One of our high school students spearheaded an effort to provide meals to some of our students over the summer, by partnering with the Mooresville Christian Mission. All our schools and students support food drives and other efforts to benefit the needy and homeless.

Teamwork with other organizations works—and is viewed very favorably by the community. Several new community and collaborative projects are currently under way in Mooresville:

- We are working with the town to develop after-school and summer programs in a neighborhood with a high density of English learners and African American students and a significant level of poverty. Our plans include enrichment and academic programs for both students and parents.

- We have engaged in extensive discussions with the town and the community college about the possibility of pooling resources to build a performing arts center to be shared by all three organizations.

- We have submitted an Innovation Race to the Top grant application to the U.S. Department of Education in partnership with several other school districts. The focus is on digital innovation and teacher and administrator collaboration aimed at improving student achievement.

Powering Professional Growth

After a visit to Mr. Bost's AP chemistry class at Mooresville High School, a student, clearly excited, came up to me and said, "We just had an amazing class! Mr. Bost was sharing what he'd learned, and it's changed our whole class about how we work together, and it's going to be great." Mr. Bost had just attended a two-day district professional development program called Capturing Kids' Hearts, which focuses on building relational foundations among students and respectful and purposeful classrooms.

Before we began our digital conversion initiative, our professional development program, as in many other school districts, relied on state-initiated activity or was organized by content area, course, or textbook. Our elementary teachers did have a solid foundation in how to use data for reading and math, and our career and technical education (CTE) classes were also using data to some extent. However, our graduation rate was 64 percent, and our overall performance left much room for improvement.

Professional learning is key to promoting growth, increasing confidence and competence, and getting teachers on board with digital conversion. Despite our early release days, professional learning time is always limited, so we try to maximize the benefits as much as possible. Recently we have worked together on implementing the new Common Core Standards, and we are currently developing new teacher effectiveness criteria that will include student achievement.

Second-Order Change: Evaluating Progress

In 2012, we participated in National Digital Learning Day, led by Bob Wise, former governor of West Virginia, and sponsored by the National Learning Alliance, co-chaired by Bob Wise and Jeb Bush, former governor of Florida. Much of the discussion focused on second-order change. The event was broadcast from the Newseum in Washington, DC, and included a downlink to two Mooresville classrooms.

We sent teams to each classroom to take a quick snapshot, using a rubric to determine progress toward second-order change, and we observed several bright spots, such as a Skype conversation between a social studies class at Mooresville Middle School and a professor of international studies in Pakistan about the relationship between our two countries.

Another example of learning that could not have taken place in the old world was provided by two art students at Mooresville High School, who were working on a collaborative project with students in Pennsylvania, in which they were sharing their work to create a digital photo mashup.

We have changed our professional development format to focus on hands-on activities, in which individuals and teams work on plans or analyze data together. We meet as grade levels and as departments, with an evolving agenda grounded in second-order change, aiming for a deep level of transformation enabled by today's technologies and guided by the demands of the 21st-century workplace.

To support our expectation for growth, we provide and fund a strong program of school- and district-level pathways designed to build individual and team capacity, and the pathways are always evolving, along with our staff.

MGSD Professional Development Goals

We have tied continuous growth in student achievement to each of the following professional development goals:

- Growth toward excellence for teachers, students, and staff
- Collaborative relationships based on commitment, focus, and maximum efficacy
- Efficient use of technical and instructional resources
- The ability to use data to improve student performance and teaching skills
- Commitment to self-improvement

School-Level Professional Learning Pathways

PD **rd** TOOLKIT™

Listen to technology facilitator Tara Gander speak about integrating technology into staff development at her school.

Leadership teams meet at each school with principals and assistant principals to develop plans, review progress, and build capacity by working together. Teacher leaders have become mentors, coaches, and cheerleaders, with a huge impact.

Each school has several ongoing professional development programs and activities, aligned to its school improvement plan. Some take place on early release days, some during weekly department and grade-level meetings, and others at monthly faculty meetings. Occasionally we hire substitutes so that we can engage in special activities or professional programs. School-level sessions focus on the following topics, differentiated according to developmental needs:

- Creating a positive culture
- Building positive student behavior
- Building relationships with students

- Using software tools effectively
- Integrating online content
- Using data to improve student performance
- Collaborating with colleagues
- Building teams
- Scheduling articulation meetings
- Integrating the Common Core Standards

PD **[ ]** TOOLKIT™

Watch the
Capturing Kids'
Hearts program
in action in
Chris Gammon's
seventh-grade
class.

Capturing Kids' Hearts Professional Development

The Capturing Kids' Hearts program aims to help teachers build positive and productive relationships with high school and middle school students. It is based on the following tenets:

- Every student is valued.
- Adults are responsible for identifying and meeting individual students' needs.
- Student needs may be social, emotional, physical, or educational.
- Secondary-level students are greeted by name and with a handshake as they enter each classroom.
- Positive behavior and good decisions are affirmed and rewarded.
- Students are given the chance to correct or reframe their mistakes.

District-Level Professional Learning Pathways

We have sent a clear message that adult learning is serious business and essential to living up to our motto of *Every Child, Every Day*. We provide many ways for our staff to grow together at the district level, with learning opportunities for individual teachers, grade levels, departments, schools, and ultimately the entire MGSD team.

Early Release Days   Eight days a year, students are released at noon to provide time for professional development, planning, data analysis, and collaboration by grade level, department, school, and district.

Annual Summer Institute   This is a three-day, voluntary professional development institute on digital conversion, offering sessions led by teacher leaders and designed around differentiated needs according to content area, grade level, and technology skills. Attendees were initially compensated at $50 per day, and after a couple of years, we increased the rate to $100 per day. The number of attendees grew from 225 in 2008 to over 300 in 2012, representing over 90 percent of teachers. We are now channeling our training to the Common Core Standards and will soon incorporate our new teacher effectiveness criteria.

Graduate Programs   In partnership with local universities, we have initiated master's degree and doctoral cohorts, made up of MGSD administrative leaders and teacher leaders, with a focus on school leadership. In the spring and summer of 2012, 10 administrators and teacher leaders completed their doctoral cohort programs, and another 10 completed their master's degrees in school leadership. A new doctoral cohort began in fall 2012.

Annual Summer Institute, 2012

Tuition Reimbursement   Every employee has access to tuition reimbursement of up to $1,000 a year. Courses must be approved and must relate to improving employees' ability to help students.

Teacher Leader Workshops   We provide quarterly leadership development workshops for MGSD teacher leaders. Grade-level and department chairs attend, along with other selected teacher leaders. About 50 teacher leaders study books and articles and work in school teams to develop strategies for improvement. Our central office administrators and principals, and sometimes our teacher leaders, lead these discussions. I have led sessions on occasion, and I try to attend as often as possible to affirm and encourage the effort.

Principals' and Faculty Meetings   These monthly meeting are focused on capacity building and collaboration, and they are structured to offer growth experiences as part of the meeting culture. After we take care of routine school business, we use our time together to keep on learning. We frequently discuss books and articles to extend our understanding and mutual growth.

Content and Grade-Level Workshops   The focus here is usually on specific courses or content areas. Our central office administrators provide coordination services and work with service providers. North Carolina Department of Public Instruction staff, university staff, and other organizations provide support and resources.

Leadership Retreats   Each year, we take a day and a half to focus on leadership team capacity, collaboration, synergistic focus, and relationships among district administrators.

Summer Connection Institute   We run a three-day professional development institute every summer for districts from around the country that are interested in digital conversion. In 2010, we had 250 participants, and this number grew to over 400 in 2012, with requests exceeding capacity. Our teachers and administrators develop and staff the institute, which gives them many excellent learning opportunities and the chance to network with like-minded educators from all over the United States.

Service Provider Training Sessions   We invite many of our service providers, such as Apple, Discovery Education, Blackboard, Pearson, and netTrekker, to provide training on their solutions, sometimes using a train-the-trainer model, and we provide feedback to make sure the information delivery is aligned with our needs.

Hosting Visitors   Each month, 50 or 60 guests visit our classrooms and attend information sessions on digital conversion. It takes preparation and work, but demonstrating digital conversion in action is a great growth opportunity. Staff and students alike thrive on the regular experience of teaching others about our program. Visitor days are like game days, and both students and teachers enjoy the opportunity to showcase their work.

Teacher Leaders

We have used the work of Linda Lambert, in *Building Leadership Capacity in Schools*, to develop our model of teacher leadership. Our principals dedicate a substantial amount of time and energy to selecting and cultivating these leaders. As outlined earlier, we conduct a district-level teacher leader workshop each quarter, in which about 50 teacher leaders study a relevant book or article and work in school teams to develop strategies for improvement.

The focus is on sharing successes and challenges and identifying ways to help every teacher grow and be successful. The school teams integrate what they have learned into their individual school improvement plans and model best practices for their colleagues in data analysis, instructional planning, and use of digital resources. The teacher leaders appreciate our investment in building their professional capacity, and we see them as a major factor in the success of the digital conversion initiative since they influence each other's growth and the overall growth of the district.

> **STUDENT FEEDBACK**   *"I like how we can see animations to explain things, such as a couple of days ago my teachers showed us an animation explaining how to find the area of parallelograms and trapezoids."*
>
> —Mooresville Intermediate School student

Personal Reflection

In *Learning by Heart*, Roland Barth says that personal reflection on our experience is how we learn. At MGSD, along with our focus on teamwork, we also emphasize the importance of personal reflection in refining our professional craft. As part of the moral imperative to do the best we can for our students, every teacher and administrator needs to make a personal commitment to grow and learn.

When I visit our classrooms, I notice that our teachers are attentive to their own learning as well as that of their students. Teachers often tell me, "We're trying something new today, but we're not quite there yet. We're learning our way through it." This is a pattern I am always happy to see. When teachers are learning their way through a new instructional strategy, they are modeling what we are trying to do district wide for our students and staff members. They are reflecting on their own work and trying to grow and improve, showing students every day that learning is "where it's at."

Employee Evaluations

Our employee evaluation system focuses on personal growth as the primary requisite for all members of the MGSD team, as do our school improvement plans, school board policies, and strategic plan. A rubric of teacher effectiveness and data-driven assessments inform our teacher evaluations and identify precise areas for growth.

Conferences discuss the growth of individuals and teams, providing a framework for reflection. Our principals meet with each teacher to develop his or her personal growth plan, focused on student achievement data and instructional effectiveness with regard to digital resources, collaboration, communication, and leadership. This process requires a high level of attention and follow-through by principals and other administrators. We want our teachers to know that we expect to see evidence of growth, whether in using new software. employing a new student collaboration model, or improving achievement.

At a recent information meeting, Cindy Dunagan, Mooresville Middle School technology facilitator, spoke about her own growth. "We've learned to collaborate much more effectively this year, and we see the benefits," she said. I was delighted to hear it, but I also knew that Principal Carrie Tulbert had given Mrs. Dunagan feedback about the need to move her level of support up a notch. Mrs. Dunagan had risen to the occasion, and she received and deserved our heartfelt applause for her effort.

New Teachers

Our capacity-building strategy has naturally influenced our requirements for new hires. At a principals' meeting in 2012, Dr. Danny Smith, executive director for human relations and special education, explained our evolving approach to recruitment as follows: "Now, we are primarily looking for eagerness to learn, strong technical foundation, collaborative team spirit, a huge work ethic, and, most of all, efficacy for all students. Just having experience doesn't cut it. We're looking for excellence!"

Each new teacher is assigned a mentor selected by the principal, and all mentors receive training on roles and responsibilities and how to communicate the "all in" spirit. The teacher and mentor work together for a year, and in many cases, they establish a lasting collegial and collaborative relationship. A combination of instructional support, collegial advice, and moral support are at the heart of this program.

The Impact of Adult Empowerment and Growth

Our ongoing effort to help all employees grow in their jobs is tightly connected to student improvement goals at MGSD. The willingness of our teachers to change and improve has been a critical factor in successful digital conversion and student performance. Teachers' ability to use digital content and tools and their embrace of a culture of caring and growth are at the heart of our student learning gains.

At a data meeting at Park View Elementary School, Michelle Robbins, the third-grade department chair, reported that 25 out of 26 students had passed or were proficient on their state end-of-grade math and reading tests but that she was not pleased with herself. We told her that she had performed extremely well, but she said, "I just can't accept that I let that one student down. It's my job to guarantee success for every child, and I'm not at all happy about it."

STUDENT FEEDBACK   *"When we had paper and pencil, the teacher would talk to the class and we would write. Now we can do interactives and do it our own way, and we can understand it better."*
—Mooresville Middle School student

In *Change Forces*, Michael Fullan writes, "Teachers who want to improve their practice are willing to be self-critical. They accept that they can and should improve, even though they may feel threatened at times by change." Digital conversion requires that teachers and principals become comfortable with a constant state of flux and a lot going on at all times in every classroom.

In the words of Todd Wirt, principal of Mooresville High School, "Teachers must learn to trust kids like we never have before. The scary thing is giving up control." The transition away from traditional teaching modes can be challenging, but the reward is a fantastic opportunity for teachers to connect with students and to connect students to their future like never before.

As adult learning has become the norm in our district, our teachers have become more thoughtful about and committed to their work. Our efforts to reflect individually and together and search for best practices are building a powerful adult learning community that has expanded beyond our district to include other school systems and even educators from overseas—from South Korea, Singapore, and Canada—who are also ramping up efforts to extend the use of digital resources in schools.

Along with more personal investment on the part of teachers comes more love for their profession. "The only way to do great work is to love what you do," said Steve Jobs in his 2005 Stanford University commencement address. At MGSD, we have many employees who love what they do, and improved academic achievement for students follows as a natural consequence.

Dr. Crystal Hill has been a mentor to Mr. Mark Cottone since she served as the principal at Park View Elementary when Mr. Cottone was assistant principal. He has since become the principal, and I asked her a few years ago how he was doing. She replied that he still had a lot to learn.

Six months later, in a principals' meeting, I asked each attendee to share how someone had inspired them in their work. "Dr. Hill has been a huge source of inspiration for me," said Mark, with visible emotion. "She works incredibly hard and leads by example. She's been patient with me while I'm learning how to do my job. I know she gets frustrated, but she sits down with me and gives me feedback, and I'm improving." I shared Mark's comments with Dr. Hill the next time I saw her and commended her for her leadership in building Mark's capacity.

Three years later, Mark Cottone is still learning and growing—and succeeding. At a recent MGSD school board meeting, he shared the Park View improvement plan and convincingly demonstrated that the school was very close to achieving the North Carolina School of Excellence designation (a 90 percent composite score based on all end-of-grade exams). Over the past few years, the school's collective capacity—made up of Mark's leadership, teacher leadership, collaboration, teamwork, data use, methodical instructional focus, and maximum efficacy—has become a powerful force.

REFLECTIVE QUESTIONS

1. What are the barriers to change in your school or district?

2. What are your professional learning goals?

3. How important are teams in your school or district?

4. How do your students know that teachers are also learning and growing?

5. How can you increase the time available for professional learning?

REFERENCES

Barth, Roland S. (2001). *Learning by Heart.* San Francisco, CA: Jossey-Bass.

Fullan, Michael. (2010). *All Systems Go: The Change Imperative for Whole System Reform.* Thousand Oaks, CA: Corwin.

Fullan, Michael. (1993). *Change Forces: Probing the Depth of Educational Reform.* Bristol, PA: Falmer Press.

Glickman, Carl D. (2002). *Leadership for Learning.* Alexandria, VA: Association for Supervision and Curriculum Development.

Lambert, Linda. (1998). *Building Leadership Capacity in Schools.* Alexandria, VA: Association for Supervision and Curriculum Development.

Tomlinson, Carol Ann, & Allan, Susan Demirsky. (2000). *Leadership for Differentiating Schools and Classrooms.* Alexandria, VA: Association for Supervision and Curriculum Development.

Wheatley, Margaret. (2006). *Leadership and the New Science: Discovering Order in a Chaotic World.* San Francisco, CA: Berrett-Koehler.

Chapter Six

Instructional Transformation

"Relevant, personalized, collaborative, and connected learning experiences drive student engagement, which in turn drives student achievement."

One day, as I walked down the hall at Mooresville Intermediate School during recess, I heard a loud commotion. I turned and saw three sixth-grade boys running toward me as fast as they could. The running immediately kindled the principal in me, and I said, in a firm and fairly loud voice, " Whoa, slow down, gentlemen! What's going on?" They all talked at once in excited and urgent tones. "We've been monitoring earthquakes, and we think one's going to happen! Can we go in our classroom and show you?" "All right," I said. "Let's take a look."

Once in the classroom, one of the boys opened his laptop, went to a web site that tracks seismic activity, and clicked on a link to a map of Southeast Asia. "Everywhere you see a light blinking shows an earthquake," he told me. Then, as a light suddenly started blinking, they yelled, "It's happening right now!" All three boys were incredibly excited, "high-fiving" and congratulating each other. The boys explained that they had been tracking seismic activity in Southeast Asia for several days and that they had permission to come in early from recess because they thought an earthquake might be imminent. In my over 30 years in public education, I had never seen kids come in early from recess.

As the rest of the class filtered in, the boys started sharing their news, pointing at the still-blinking light. Comments like "Darn it, I should'a come in early," "That's not fair," and "Lucky" burst from the other students, as they crowded around to take a look. Once the students had returned to their seats, their teacher, Maureen Tunnell, showed me how the earthquake-tracking activity aligned with the North Carolina Standard Course of Study for Science and then moved on to a class discussion about earthquakes, scientific data, and the meaning of real time.

Several drivers of student engagement—relevance, personalization, collaboration, and connectivity—had come together to energize these students and transform their learning. Over the past four years, we at MGSD have seen and felt what we call an instructional "boom," or uplift, from the interplay of these factors, as they have stimulated students and teachers in positive ways and created a dynamic instructional whole that is greater than the sum of the parts.

Key Drivers of Student Engagement

In 2001, the first year of the Teaching and Learning Initiative in Henrico County, Virginia, I visited a middle school science classroom with the principal, Ann Poates. The students were tracking a winter storm on www.weather.com, still a novelty at that time. A young man whom I recognized called out that the class knew when it would start snowing and that I would definitely have to call off school the next day. Several other students joined in with supporting comments. Even as I laughed out loud, I was impressed and told them their input would be considered.

We ended up announcing that school would be closed early that evening—a rarity in my 17 years as superintendent. The next day, I saw the young man sledding in my neighborhood. He waved, and I said, "Great advice!" He replied, "Excellent decision, Dr. E."

We believe that relevant, personalized, collaborative, and connected learning experiences enhance student engagement, which in turn drives student achievement. Although these learning experiences were available in a more limited way before the advent of technology, digital conversion has taken them to an entirely new level.

Relevance makes school more interesting because it connects students to life outside of school, now and in the future. *Personalization* means that school speaks to each student because each works according to his or her own interests and skill levels. *Collaboration* builds motivation and engagement because students enjoy working together and learning from each other. *Connectivity* creates a vibrant pulse of inquiry-based learning, as students access online resources and enjoy the discovery process. These engaging learning modalities are entwined throughout our approach to instruction.

VISITOR FEEDBACK   *"Mooresville actively measures engagement as it is clearly a prerequisite for improvement."*

—Karen Cator
Director of Educational Technology,
U.S. Department of Education

Relevant Learning

There is a great deal of discussion these days about the need for relevant instruction, so that students can see the value of school. In the past, instruction has generally not connected students to the world outside of class, now or in the future, and many students have felt bored or disconnected. Digital conversion addresses this issue and allows educators to bring relevance into daily teaching and learning.

When students are using digital resources, building multimedia projects, collaborating and connecting online, and conducting online research, they are more interested in their schoolwork today, and they feel more connected to what their future holds tomorrow. Most of today's students expect that, as a matter of course, they will be using technology after high school—in college, in their future occupations, and in their personal lives—to work collaboratively, research, create, and solve problems.

The ability to connect life in school with life outside of school has a huge impact on students' "learning disposition." It allows learning to be personally centered. It helps students feel that school has meaning and purpose, which can make a world of difference in their level of engagement and achievement. When students do work that is relevant to the real world, their current lives, and their future plans, they become more curious about learning, show more initiative, and improve their analytical skills.

An important byproduct of the relevance factor is that teachers and staff also feel more connected to the world outside of education and to their own future lives, creating a kinship with students in which both parties are experiencing the same thing.

STUDENT FEEDBACK   *"The laptops prepare us, the students, for a future filled with technologically advanced jobs and societies. Getting the experience now can only help us."*

—East Mooresville Intermediate School student

Personalized Learning

PD TOOLKIT™

Listen to technology facilitator Tara Gander talk about using digital resources to differentiate instruction.

When teachers harness formative data to teach with precision, differentiating learning to meet both individual and class needs, great things can happen. Personal focus is an absolute power driver for student development. The availability of real-time data permits the laser focus on personalization that we see now in our schools. The differentiated instruction that technology enables allows struggling students to learn at their own pace and helps gifted learners advance more quickly.

Real-time data gives teachers precise information to provide personalized interventions, to extend help to individual students, and to assign students to work in flexible collaborative groups—groups that can change as students progress at different rates or redirect their learning focus. Teachers can personalize group instruction for optimal productivity and to avoid any matches that may be problematic.

VISITOR FEEDBACK   *"Mooresville has given me the best example of differentiation I've ever seen. In class after class, I saw individual and group work going on, with students highly engaged and teachers working with small groups as the norm."*

—June St. Clair Atkinson
State Superintendent of Public Schools, North Carolina

Collaborative Learning

Several researchers have found that the digital environment allows a collective of students and talents to come together with an enhanced impact on learning. Thomas and Brown, in *A New Culture of Learning,* say that learning communities facilitated by technology allow students—both individuals and groups—to deepen and broaden their conceptual understanding of curriculum topics. And the 2010

Project RED research study found that online collaboration was one of the key factors in improved student performance: "Online collaboration contributes to improved graduation rates and other academic improvements."

STUDENT FEEDBACK   *"In my French class, we are partnering up with students in CANADA who are also learning French! We are interacting with students all over the world!"*

—Mooresville High School student

We work with students on developing their collaboration skills both online and offline. Learning to collaborate as a team—using blogs, discussion boards, wikis, and more—is engaging for young learners. It also prepares them for their future, and they know it. But people often make the mistake of assuming that kids know how to collaborate from day one. They do not. Developing team skills in collaborative working groups has to be part of the curriculum.

Students in our district hear about sharing, caring, and working together from kindergarten on, but they still need to practice these skills every day. Just as sports teams and orchestras practice together, our students learn to work together and take collective as well as individual responsibility for the outcome of a project by practicing the following skills:

- Giving and taking
- Being flexible
- Sharing
- Understanding roles and responsibilities
- Working with deadlines
- Allowing for strengths and weaknesses

The process takes practice, patience, and planning, and our teachers now use a rubric that spells out collaboration roles and evaluation criteria. But the effort is worthwhile: When students acquire collaborative skills, they thrive. Collaboration adds new vitality to the learning experience for students and teachers alike and builds the communication skills they need for the world of work. Today, even very young students at MGSD see collaboration as the norm. At Park View Elementary, our third graders have been working with students in China. To them, collaboration is part of school and part of life, and they want it.

Connected Learning

Digital resources have had a significant impact on our instructional program, and the impact has grown as connected learning has become more integrated into our curriculum. Search tools and reference engines catapult students into an environment of daily research while connecting them to people, places, information, and tools, to stimulate learning and the pursuit of knowledge.

Kindergarten student at Rocky River Elementary School

Teachers make sure that online assignments are aligned by course objective while allowing students to select from several topics, all of which include online formative assessments, so that personal interests and data points are combined. Discovery Education Science, for example, provides many great opportunities to put this practice into action.

STUDENT FEEDBACK   *"Why would I need to feel a bump on a globe to know that mountains are high when I could video chat with someone who lives on that mountain and learn not only about its height but its climate, economic opportunities, and indigenous animal species?"*

—Mooresville High School student

Information Literacy   Our media centers have become research centers, and our media specialists now design their work to fit the needs of the inquiry-based, exploratory environment. They review and vet online resources, work with teachers and students on a variety of online reference tools, and teach digital citizenship and research skills. To help students learn how to determine the validity of online information, they also conduct information literacy sessions that include the following practices:

- Review credible articles in online encyclopedias and databases linked to district, school, and state web sites.

- Steer students to these resources early on to discourage quick Internet searches that lack relevancy or accuracy.

- Demonstrate the difference in quality between built-in source citations in credible resources and web resources found via search engines.

- Allow students to use search engines but teach them to phrase searches well and to limit their visits to the domain extensions .edu, .gov, and .org.

- Help students look at the author of a web site or articles to evaluate credibility and suitability for their research needs.

Dialogical and Dialectical Thinking   Today's students are connected to a wide variety of online opinions and information, and these connections facilitate two important kinds of thinking in our classrooms. It is vitally important to promote *dialogical thinking* by students—to familiarize them with the diversity of views on a particular topic and help them understand where the different views are coming from. It is equally important to promote *dialectical thinking*—to help students realize that what is true today may not be true in the future.

When students' perspective grows, they become more capable of formulating opinions, more adaptable to different circumstances, more understanding of complex issues, and more able to find realistic solutions to problems.

FIGURE 6.1

Key Drivers of Student Engagement in Action:
Relevance, Personalization, Collaboration, and Connectivity

Grade Level	Classroom Activity
Grade 3	• When our third graders are studying weather, they watch online videos about current and future weather patterns in our area that will affect their lives. They also research tornadoes and other extreme weather events that are taking place in other parts of the world at the same time, using vibrant, real-time imagery that promotes discussion and learning.
	• One of our third-grade teachers gave an overview in which she asked students to do online research for their team projects on famous Americans. Students worked together on personalizing their projects by selecting a subject to study; researching photographs, video, and audio passages; and developing group presentations. The teacher conferred with individual students, and directed, encouraged, or monitored.
Grade 5	• A couple of years ago, our fifth graders worked via Skype with a group of students from Illinois. Our students were studying the Midwest, and the Illinois students were studying the South. Students took turns sharing information about their respective states and finding similarities and differences. When our teacher announced that it was time to go to lunch, an immediate cross-state groan arose, followed by both teachers quickly assuring students that they would reconnect in the near future.
	• One year, a group of fifth-grade science students created a movie about cloud formations, a topic that is included on the state end-of-grade test. Each student selected a cloud formation and developed a digital presentation to be shared with the class. The movies were entertaining and varied in quality, but all reinforced the concepts students needed to learn about cumulus, stratus, and cirrus cloud formations.
	• When the two fifth-grade classes at East Mooresville Intermediate School finished reading a chapter of *The Lion, the Witch and the Wardrobe* by C. S. Lewis,

Continued

Grade Level	Classroom Activity *(continued)*
	students in each class got together for about 15 minutes to discuss what the chapter meant to them. Then the two classes connected via our LMS chat to compare notes. It was interesting and exciting for students to see how two classes reading the same chapter came up with different ideas and interpretations.
Grade 6	• One day, a student from a sixth-grade gifted class came out into the hallway to look for me and asked me to come and look at the "humongous" project his class had been working on. Jodi Salmon, the AIG (academically or intellectually gifted) teacher, explained that she had asked the class to develop a social studies project that included individual and collaborative digital presentations. "And then I basically got out of the way," she told me.
	The students were gathered around the interactive whiteboard, which displayed a spectacular array of buttons below the heading "Marvels of the World: Modern, Ancient, and Beyond." I chose Grand Coulee Dam, and up popped a page with other buttons on a dozen topics related to the dam. I tapped the virtual tour button, and an HD video started to play, with the sound of roaring water and mist and spray that made me feel like I was right there. Each student had worked on one "marvel of the world" as part of a multimedia research project that was appealing to gifted students and that allowed for personalization to individual interests.
Grade 7	• At half time at a recent basketball game, a parent came over and proudly told me that his daughter was studying the relationship between the United States and Pakistan and looking at all sides of the issue. Her class had Skyped in a teacher from Pakistan, who explained the Pakistani view and answered students' questions, and she had researched a huge variety of sources to put together a presentation. In this parent's view, his daughter's presentation was better than the research papers he had written in college.
Grade 9	• The ninth-grade English curriculum requires that students read *Romeo and Juliet* and write a book report. Students are given a rubric that indicates what needs to be included—thesis, theme analysis, etc.—but they can also choose how to create the report. One student developed an iMovie with the help of her classmates, in which they acted out her modern-day interpretation of the play. Another student used GarageBand and set his report to music. Some chose the more traditional path of typing their reports. Each student was able to personalize the report in a way that made it relevant to him or her.
Grade 10	• In tenth-grade biology, students use online software to practice frog dissection as many times as they wish, without the smell of formaldehyde. This digital resource is common in operating rooms and medical schools and helps prepare students for the world of work in which digital support is now the norm.

Continued

Grade Level	Classroom Activity *(continued)*
	• A tenth-grade algebra student explained to a group of visitors that she liked to watch online math videos over and over because she found math difficult. "I watch the videos at home," she said. "Sometimes I watch the teacher do the problem three or four times, but then suddenly I get it. And it gives me another problem like the one I just finished, to make sure I understand how to do it." This girl was a special needs student whose teacher was able to select the right kind of help for her, monitor her work online, and tailor the interventions to her needs.
Grades 9–12	• Students studying French and Spanish publish their own blogs as part of our world languages program. The blogs serve as a mini digital portfolio, allowing students to share their work products with parents, teachers, classmates, and others beyond the school community. Students also continue class discussions in student learning communities by responding to classmates' posts and encouraging debate.
	The blogs serve as a form of personal expression, increase literacy skills, and provide a place to reflect on struggles and successes in the learning process. Students can also connect with other learners and speakers from around the country, and sometimes the world, as they share their work.

Teaching in a Digital Learning Environment

At Rocky River Elementary School one day, I saw a group of first graders making valentines by cutting out red, pink, and white paper and pasting in personalized messages they had each written and designed on the computer. The class was also working on the concept of symmetry, and one boy was studying an online math game that combined math terms with cartoon-like examples. "Symmetry means when it looks the same on both sides if you cut it down the middle," he told me quietly, quickly refocusing on the screen to signal that it was time for me to move on. Other students were using a digital art tool to design portraits. The teacher, Lori Dunbar, had set up her classroom so that each of these children could learn through personal, inventive, exploratory experience.

Listen to three principals discuss how digital conversion has changed teaching in their schools.

Success in a digital conversion classroom depends more than ever before on the talent, initiative, and skills of the teacher. Many of those skills and talents are the same as in traditional classrooms, but many are new and different. To ensure successful implementation of the digital learning key drivers, we took a careful look at the role of the teacher.

Our goal was that our teachers would no longer be lecturers surrounded by books but would become "roaming conductors" of learning. We began to transition from having the teacher stand at the front of the class to our current teacher-as-facilitator model. We began talking about "teaching from the inside out," or from the center, and made sure that classroom layouts would allow teachers to move around easily among tables and desks.

VISITOR FEEDBACK   *"In several classrooms, I couldn't tell where the front of the classroom was. The whole space was a learning environment, and the technology was just part of the infrastructure."*

—Karen Cator
Director of Educational Technology,
U.S. Department of Education

This has led, over the last four years, to innovative yet structured teaching—two adjectives that may appear incompatible. However, that is exactly what we are seeing. I believe that this is the power of the digital learning key drivers. They energize students and teachers while at the same time helping them organize, plan, record, and report.

Visitors from other school districts frequently ask, "Is teaching easier now?" I'm sure that most of our teachers would say, "Absolutely not." However, I think most would also say that, although it took time, they are now more effective, successful, and excited about the kind of teaching they are doing and that they are growing and learning exponentially.

Third-grade class at Park View Elementary School

Teaching in our digital conversion initiative requires a significant evolution in design methodology and pedagogy. Teaching students who have a portal to the world at their fingertips and want to use exciting tools and work on personal interests requires teachers to make significant changes. They must move away from whole-group didactic-static sets to directing and assisting individuals and small groups, interspersed with presentations, discussions, and teacher-directed activities.

STUDENT FEEDBACK   *"We know much more than what's on the tests—not only the 'what' but the 'why.' We get many perspectives on whatever it is that we are learning, and this 'why' knowledge seems to stick better than simply memorizing the facts."*

—Mooresville High School student

Teachers need to orchestrate a variety of activities and use a variety of digital resources. This takes time and practice, but today most of our teachers are happy to have left the old ways behind. "After a couple of years, it was completely natural, and I could not imagine teaching now without these resources," says Katie Higgins, an English teacher at Mooresville High School. "I really think I'm much more effective in this environment, being more of a facilitator, where I can give students individual attention," says Brenda Martin, a fourth-grade teacher at Mooresville Intermediate School.

Kellie Thompson, fifth-grade chair at East Mooresville Middle School, was asked by a group of visitors about the transition to a new kind of teaching. "It took some time and some trial and error," she replied. "But we took the steady-as-she-goes approach in our first couple of years, and then we all started taking off, learning from each other and sharing, and now we're all over it. In fact, I don't know how I could ever go back to the old world now that I've lived in this environment."

Evolving Instructional Methods

It is impossible to be an effective teacher in today's digital age without being a voracious learner. Software and applications are constantly evolving and improving, and online resources continue to expand. Teachers must study, practice, and analyze in order to ensure effective use. Effective teachers take full advantage of digital resources and customize them to pull students into the content, using multimedia elements that students respond to and also expect in this digital age.

Digital conversion is driving several new approaches to classroom instruction in our schools that incorporate the key drivers of student engagement and support our goal of improved academic performance.

Intentional Design   The key drivers discussed earlier in this chapter must be infused with intentional design in order to be meaningful. Although creativity and innovation abound in our school culture, intentional design must guide the work, and the intent of project-based activities and research assignments must be clearly understood.

For example, teachers must create collaborative learning goals in which students take individual and collective responsibility for the outcome. They must connect their work to exacting detail about individual students, broken down by content objectives and underscored by opportunities for creativity, collaboration, and personal learning interests.

> **STUDENT FEEDBACK**   *"The interactives that my teacher provides help me see and understand the subject better than if I read it out of a book."*
> —East Mooresville Intermediate School student

PD **TOOLKIT™**

Watch a seventh grade class work on a group geography activity.

Individual and Group Work   Teachers generally articulate their expectations to the whole class, but, more often than not, after the initial direction, the work is done individually and in small groups. Teachers may utilize a station format, particularly in the elementary grades, but groups are the norm for discussion, project design, and research. We still use whole-group instruction on occasion since it is useful for discussion purposes, as well as for presentations by individual students and groups.

Group work varies somewhat from teacher to teacher, but most of our staff draw from the following strategies:

Keys to Successful Group Work

- Model group interactions at the start of the school year.
- Get to know personalities and skill sets to create a good balance.
- Experiment early in the year to find a good mix.
- At some times, group students with similar strengths and weaknesses together.
- At other times, mix up the groups to create student leaders.

- Clarify goals, expectations, and the need to be kind at all times.
- Assign roles such as recorder, timer, illustrator, leader, or reader.
- Occasionally allow students to choose groups or assign roles.
- Listen to student concerns and offer strategies for support.
- Implement peer review.
- Use open-ended questions for exploration and dialogue.
- Assess progress and adjust groups if needed.
- Observe and facilitate.

Robin McElhannon, fifth-grade teacher at Mooresville Intermediate School, describes her group work strategy as follows: "On day one, I begin getting to know the different personalities of the students and their modality of learning. My groups usually consist of four people—someone visual, someone auditory, someone kinesthetic, and someone who is a high-level thinker—and will utilize each modality and help the group maintain focus. I walk around constantly to observe if the students are comprehending and communicating. This aspect can be the hardest for teachers to understand, and yet it is the most important factor to successful group work."

Roaming Conductors   Success in the productive digital hum is more dependent than ever before on good classroom management. To orchestrate several work groups, teachers have to be roaming conductors, deftly moving between tables, intently listening and observing, and engaging as needed with groups or individuals. This approach is part of our instructional design, included in our professional development sessions, and modeled in the classroom for new teachers.

Several teachers have emerged as expert roaming conductors, and principals provide many opportunities for other teachers to observe them, as they orchestrate multiple work groups at once and switch focus from groups to individuals and back again—a form of artistry in itself.

Teaching from the Inside Out   Rather than stand in front of the class, our teachers have moved to the center because many students work better, with more focus, when the teacher is standing beside them. This gift of proximity allows teachers to be close to student computer screens, advise individuals or groups, monitor, and provide direction. When teachers stay close to students by constantly moving around the room and teaching from the inside out, they can achieve impressive results.

Physical Teaching   Tactile cuing—touching a student on the shoulder, standing close behind, or placing a hand on the table near the student's laptop—typically helps students refocus and increases their productivity. "Please show me what you are working on" is one of the most frequent requests from teachers.

Teachers monitor students in a proactive and preventive manner since many students, particularly those with ADHD or similar learning challenges, need some cuing or prompting to maintain their focus. Good teachers maintain a good ratio of proximity to mobility.

Power Teaching   With our focus on evolutional capacity building, over the past four years, our teachers have embraced the online resources and assets available to them. As a result, they have become much more knowledgeable about their subject areas, and this greater depth of teacher knowledge is helping to drive student interest and achievement.

Fourth-grade student and teacher at Mooresville Intermediate School

Teachers have also brought the outside world into the classroom and learned new ways of using online information, with instructional tactics and lesson designs that focus on individual student needs while addressing a broad range of learning levels. Individual student data from assessments embedded in our online software allows them to create work groups, make assignments, and accelerate or slow down the pace.

These changes add up to what we call "power teaching"—teaching that is turbo-charged by the digital environment, our culture of caring, our relentless focus on student achievement, and our commitment to evolutional capacity building. Teachers are creating learning environments that hum with the interactive engagement of students and a new flow of energy.

Student Choice   Students are given a lot of opportunity to move about the classroom. They can finish up an individual assignment and move to a group project if they wish, or they may join another student sitting on the floor in the back of the class or out in the hall. They can move from task to task, just as most of them will in the world in which they will eventually live and work.

STUDENT FEEDBACK   *"Digital conversion means more resources at my fingertips at the same time. I have more choices for projects and assignments, which makes learning more fun."*

—Mooresville Intermediate School student

Students at Mooresville High School

Sharing and Privacy   When students work in small groups, they are allowed to look at each other's laptop screens because seeing each other's work is a significant part of the digital conversion instructional design. We sometimes create privacy with tabletop space dividers for testing or for a particular activity, but the best way to ensure privacy and test security is to have a roaming conductor moving around the classroom.

Learning from Students

Listen to seventh grade teacher Chris Gammon talk about how he learns more from students all the time.

I love Roland Barth's work on school culture in *Learning by Heart* and often quote his tenet that only a school that is hospitable to adult learning can be a good place for students to learn. It took time, but we have now reached the point where most MGSD teachers are perfectly comfortable asking students for help navigating a web site or figuring out a new piece of software. Once teachers have the confidence to say "I don't know" and are willing to reveal themselves as learners, a new symbiotic classroom culture develops that is empowering and energizing to students and teachers alike.

"Who knows how to use this?" and "Who knows how to do that?" are questions our teachers commonly ask. They have come to understand and embrace the fact that several students in every class have an advanced aptitude for technology, know how to troubleshoot software, and are great resources for the teacher and other students.

We learn from our students every day and adjust our thinking and our teaching strategies accordingly. Last spring, I toured our high school with a group of visitors from a university. We entered a senior English class, where the students were working in groups on their senior projects and sharing and critiquing each other's work. When a visitor asked if she could see one of the projects, the teacher said that unfortunately they were not ready, but one young lady volunteered to show hers. The teacher was a little hesitant but agreed that the student could go ahead.

> **PARENT FEEDBACK**   *"These children are learning more than I ever learned through a book. They are still required to write papers. However, their projects go further in depth than just writing words on a piece of paper. They are forced to use more of their understanding of the material to produce projects and papers for grades."*
>
> —MGSD parent

We huddled around the student's laptop, and she ran through her project. Then as we proceeded down the hall, the teacher ran after us to explain the reason for her hesitation. This was the girl's first year in a mainstreamed class, the teacher explained, and she had struggled at times. The teacher shared how proud she was of the young woman's self-confidence and communication skills and how much she had learned from her that day.

Student and Teacher Mobility

Our goal is to allow teachers and students to move easily around the classroom, but our classrooms are normal rectangular spaces that are fairly cramped, with class sizes of about 30 students. We have had to think carefully about how to utilize the space to facilitate mobility. We stopped buying student desks three or four years ago and now use tables and chairs as much as possible. The placement of tables and chairs allows teachers to continuously move around the classroom to help students with their individual and group work, monitor their progress, view individual student laptops, and provide physical cuing or prompting to enhance focus.

Online Daily Plans

Teachers post the plan for each day on our LMS, and plans may include a whole-class discussion, individual work on projects, practice assessments, video viewing, comprehension quizzes, or group work and reporting to the rest of the class. Most teachers use the brief individualized assessments in our online software that give students instant feedback before they continue on with their work. Students access the LMS regularly to see their assignments and check on grades.

Lesson Planning

Since we started our digital conversion initiative, lesson planning has changed dramatically at MGSD. Researching, using, and aligning digital resources take time, thought, and collaboration with colleagues. We have used our early release days and the Summer Institute to provide time for designing lesson plans, aligned to the North Carolina standards, that are highly engaging and offer personalized experiences for students.

Teachers and tech facilitators get together to design lesson plans, and the tech facilitators then help troubleshoot and develop rubrics. Tara Gander, formerly a teacher and now the tech facilitator at East Mooresville Middle

PD TOOLKIT™

Listen to technology facilitator Tara Gander describe her changing role.

FIGURE 6.2

LMS Student View

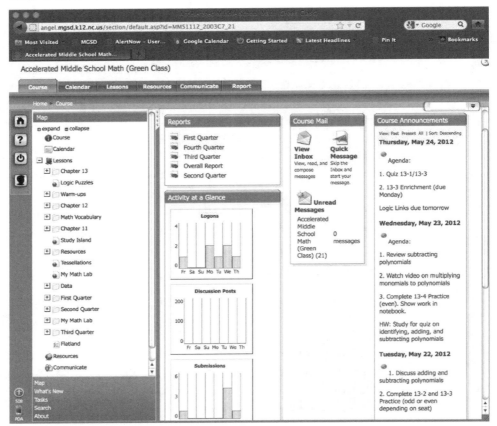

School, described how she developed a lesson plan with sixth-grade teacher Jill Conley:

> "We met to brainstorm how we wanted to teach a certain objective and decided on our course of action—to use a Google presentation and have students work collaboratively on a project, create their slides, and then create a crossword puzzle to test their presentation. I created the Google docs, set up the project with the class, and came in each day for a week to help troubleshoot. Afterward, I helped Mrs. Conley work with students to create their crossword puzzles. Then I came in for two days during Mrs. Conley's planning time to help her develop and grade a rubric and input the grades into the LMS."

Extended Learning Time

Although teachers often say that they could not imagine going back to the "old world" of teaching, finding enough time to accomplish curriculum goals in MGSD schools is still daunting, as it is in most other schools. In our digital conversion initiative, we have found ways to extend time for learning.

Teachers often engage with students in online discussion boards at night, as part of a homework assignment. A couple of years ago, when I heard my son laughing in the kitchen one evening, he called out, "I'm on a discussion board with Mrs. Gander, and Thomas just made a really funny comment." I went into the kitchen, looked at the discussion board, and saw that 25 students were logged on, continuing the work they had done at school that day.

Teachers also use online collaboration to prepare for tests. One winter we had a lot of snow, for North Carolina, and right before semester exams, we were hit with several inches. We were concerned that this interruption would hurt student performance because we feared there would not be enough time for exam review.

Several high school teacher leaders enlisted digital resources to address the challenge. They sent out emails to students, alerting them that they would be conducting online discussions and exam review sessions at different times during the snow days. They reported excellent student participation in the review sessions, and student performance showed significant gains across all content areas.

Jim Farster, a math teacher at Mooresville High School who recently retired after teaching for 44 years, said that after his students finished their assignments, they did other purposeful things on their laptops, like getting ready for a quiz the next day, finishing up a report for another class, or taking an online assessment for another class. As a consequence, they were not bored, less likely to get in trouble, and positively engaged. We have seen in our schools that the availability of digital tools extends student engagement beyond their assigned tasks and helps them keep on learning.

Online Assessment

All our students receive immediate feedback via formal and formative assessments, and this infusion of real-time data has greatly influenced our teaching and learning. Our online content includes assessment tools that give instant feedback and provide teachers and students with vital information about next steps, customized to each learner. Detailed reports cross-reference differentiation by content objective, group, or individual student.

It has taken time to build the capacity to integrate real-time data into teaching and learning, but as we are hitting our stride, we see students monitoring their progress right along with their teachers. Students are now able to share details about their grades and project how they will do on their next test.

VISITOR FEEDBACK   *"One young man showed me his grades on the LMS and said if he could make at least a 90 on his next test, he would have an A for the course. He had taken a practice assessment and said he knew exactly what he needed to study. Needless to say, we were blown away."*

—Diane Robertson
Superintendent, Community Unit School District #4, Mendon, Illinois

Students from elementary through high school like to know how they are doing, and in our digital world, they want to know now, not next week. Report card days are old news in our district. Parents and students receive online grades and progress reports on an ongoing basis, an important factor in improving student performance.

Digital Citizenship

Digital conversion brings with it new challenges, since students may be exposed to online threats, inappropriate content, or cyberbullying, and all schools must address safety and privacy issues, cheating, and Internet surfing. Daily vigilance is required. Teachers must constantly monitor online material to ensure that it is age appropriate, as well as verify the intellectual integrity of web sites and programs for classroom use. Protocols for online etiquette and civility of online exchanges and conversations must be established.

Although we filter out social networking sites on student laptops, online bullying is a concern at MGSD, as it is in all other school systems. At a ball game in the early days of our initiative, a clearly distressed father shared with me that some of his son's classmates were calling the boy names and making fun of him on a well-known social networking site. He asked for my help because he was afraid the situation was heading toward a fight.

Digital citizenship is part of our curriculum at every grade level and a vital part of our code of student conduct in light of the tragedies in the news related to online bullying. We must be ever vigilant in educating students, teachers, administrators, and parents about our standards of behavior, online and offline.

Frequent monitoring by parents and staff is essential. Working closely with parents and creating trust and confidence in each other is a big part of this work.

MGSD students learn that online bullying is still bullying, online plagiarism is still plagiarism, and online cheating is still cheating. They learn how to use digital resources responsibly and conduct themselves with decorum on blogs and discussion boards, as part of an ongoing dialogue about personal responsibility and treating others with respect. They learn that their digital footprint will always be with them and that appropriate behavior is no different in a digital conversion initiative from the days when the pencil was the primary tool.

> **PARENT FEEDBACK**   *"After four years of this initiative, our help desk and IT department have it all locked down. The system has a lot of red flags built in and a plan as far as security and monitoring. As a parent, I remember this being one of the first things discussed at the initial meeting."*
>
> —MGSD parent

We have developed two programs to promote appropriate behavior within a caring and supportive environment—the Positive Behavior Program, at the elementary, intermediate, and middle school levels, and Capturing Kids' Hearts, at the middle and high school levels. Both include guidelines for online and offline behavior and are grounded in genuine respect for students.

Visitors often ask if students surf the Internet instead of working on schoolwork. We explain that, as our digital initiative has evolved, teachers have learned how to monitor student behavior in a digital environment and transitioned to a guide-on-the-side role that involves walking about the room and observing student work constantly throughout the day. There are also times when teachers say "lids down."

Many challenges still remain, but teaching appropriate use every day, combined with thorough monitoring by teachers, has led to an environment where the vast majority of students observe the rules, behave responsibly, and use digital resources productively.

Effective Teaching

Our teachers have grown in so many ways. They have modeled working with "calm urgency," showing students how to use their time in a worthwhile manner but with a calm demeanor. They have learned to use data about individuals and groups to make precise interventions that were previously impossible. In the words of Maureen Fitzsimmons, Mooresville Middle School math department chair and 2010 MGSD Teacher of the Year, "I'm doing the best work of my career because I have daily detail on my classes and students, and I can zero right in."

VISITOR FEEDBACK   *"I was fortunate to work with Mark Edwards when I was a principal at Deep Run High School in Henrico, Virginia, and I had the chance to implement his vision for one-to-one laptop teaching and learning. We were not far into implementation before we realized that this is how our kids want to engage with their world and their learning. More important was the impact this had on our culture."*

"Much of the conversation was about what we were teaching. When we put these engaging tools in the hands of our kids and our teachers, we started talking more about how we were teaching. It was a real paradigm shift and ultimately a game changer. We learned that students will master what we want them to learn if we can engage them in the process in an authentic and exciting way, and technology gave us the medium to do just that. Now I have the good fortune of being in the same state again as Mark."

—Aaron Spence, Ed.D.
Superintendent of Schools, Moore County Schools, North Carolina

Teachers have learned how to work with students to find answers online. "My kiddos and I are like on a treasure hunt, and we have fun discovering things we didn't know," says Michelle Izzo, sixth-grade team reading chair at East Mooresville Intermediate School. And teachers have also learned how to use digital tools and resources to address the skills Tony Wagner identifies, in *The Global Achievement Gap*, as essential for success in today's world— problem solving, collaboration, agility and adaptability, initiative, accessing and analyzing information, effective communication, and curiosity and innovation.

In fourth-grade teacher Vicki Brawley's social studies class recently, I saw hands flying up all over as she asked questions and students searched online and found the answers. "Okay, we're going to have some fun today with search engines and research," she said. "What's the biggest city in the world? What's the tallest building in the world? What's the smallest state in our country? Where is Justin Bieber from?" The reward for our work on instructional transformation is seeing our students enjoying research and engaged in learning.

Impact on Students

In a high school social studies class I visited, I watched students giving presentations of their individual projects about the Revolutionary War. I asked one student, whose iMovie included historical text, archival photos, video vignettes, and period background music, how long it had taken her to put it all together. She explained that she had spent many hours on it and that one evening she worked through dinner up until 11:00 PM, and that she was so into it, she didn't want to stop.

It is a life-changing experience for students to become so absorbed in their work, and it is wonderful for teachers to see students so energized. Student engagement is one of the hallmarks of digital conversion because digital tools provide the transformative opportunity for students to research and explore curriculum topics that interest them. As students and teachers connect every day to online resources, each other, and the world outside school, a vibrant new teaching and learning energy results from the "confluence of connectivity" in every classroom.

Purposeful Engagement

When visitors describe what they see in our classrooms, they consistently remark on the active engagement of our students and the "productive hum." Although the digital world is highly engaging for young learners, our view of student engagement is that it must be purposeful and supportive of instructional goals.

Second-grade students and teacher at Rocky River Elementary School

Our teachers monitor student activity to ensure that:

- All projects connect to grade-level work.
- Online searches relate to curriculum goals.
- Activities connect tightly to content.
- Activities align to the state course of study.
- Activities are personalized to student learning needs.
- Practice assessments provide immediate feedback and personalized direction.

Cognition Ignition

We constantly observe our students leaning into their work, as they create, research, and collaborate. This reflects what I call the "cognition ignition" factor. When students are deeply involved in their work, encouraged to be creative, and have tools available to them—whether audio, movie-making, or research tools—a cognitive process kicks in that not only engages them but also helps them truly understand what they are learning. When students are able to touch multiple modalities such as audio, visual, and text and employ a variety of experiential activities, they are intrigued and attracted by the fresh and dynamic approach to instruction.

STUDENT FEEDBACK   *"In my honors chemistry class, we do a virtual lab online before moving to our lab tables and doing it hands on. Why do it both ways? Because it is important to have the hands-on work of measuring, etc., but by also doing it virtually, we are able to not only see a general chemical reaction, i.e., a color change, but we also see the actual breakdown of the molecules and how that causes the reaction. This would not be visible to the naked eye, but it is visible on the computer, creating a whole new understanding for me."*

—Mooresville High School student

According to noted educational technology researcher Tom Greaves, one of the co-authors of *Project RED*:

"So often, students I meet will say they are doing an 'assignment,' often a worksheet. But Mooresville students talk about doing 'their work' and seem to have a cognition level about the purpose of the work. I believe they are rapidly moving into second-order change work—that means they are doing things using digital tools that they could not do with the old world toolset."

Support for Struggling Students

Listen to third-grade teacher Heather Graham talk about how she supports young Spanish-speaking students.

Digital resources support struggling and at-risk students every day at MGSD. Mooresville High School English teacher Mary Magee shared a compelling story about an EL student who came to Mooresville having previously spent only one semester out of a self-contained, Spanish-only speaking classroom and was immediately mainstreamed in all regular classes at MGSD.

Although this student's English was less than proficient, digital resources helped him rise to the occasion. Using Google Translate, he was able to do assignments and communicate with his classmates and his teachers. Mrs. Magee and our EL teacher coordinated vocabulary support and coaching. The student eventually used Google Translate to develop his senior project, which was judged one of the very best of 2012, the year he graduated.

As in many other districts, helping struggling readers is a major goal at MGSD, and it can be challenging to increase students' confidence levels and build their desire to read. However, digital resources have had a major impact in this area. Tonya Mays, second-grade teacher at Park View Elementary School, shared the following story with me:

> "In my class, the key to helping one child increase her confidence and start to enjoy reading was her excitement about using the computer. With the technology at her fingertips and the immediate feedback from our software, she set out on a beautiful journey. Seeing her success as she got closer to each of her reading levels and surpassing them was a marvelous experience for her and for me. Using the program, I was able to send her messages of encouragement, and when she walked into the room in the morning, thanked me for my messages, and told me that now she loved reading, it was so rewarding for me to share her success and feel her excitement. Her ability to use the reading program at school and at home helped her reach her goals faster. Technology was the 'something that was missing' for her."

Organizational Skills

Another very real benefit of digital conversion is that it helps students with their time management and organizational skills and provides a user-friendly online "storage space" for their work. With our LMS, students can easily find all their assignments and class materials in one place and refer to the daily calendars, organized by course and by teacher, to keep up with what's due. They use online desk folders organized by course or class for ongoing work, and they use dropboxes to turn in assignments.

> **STUDENT FEEDBACK**   *"I have a much more organized life now with these laptops, which makes school a lot more stress free. Rather than searching desperately through my bag for an assignment, I can just swipe my fingers and have it right in front of me in an instant!"*
>
> —Mooresville High School student

The central source of information and storage provided by the LMS has been of particular value to students who struggle with ADHD and other learning issues that impact organizational skills, but we have found that all students—and parents—appreciate the availability of management tools and the convenience of "everything in one place." No more lost homework—assignments are always right there online. And students are taking more responsibility for their own learning thanks to the availability of online reports in the LMS.

Creativity

The hallways of our schools are lined with student projects, developed with digital tools, that illuminate the space with examples of creativity, research, and collaboration.

Walking down the halls of Rocky River Elementary, I saw math projects displaying vibrant charts, graphs, and data, connected by name to each student, collected from class polls, and personalized by color and style. I also saw poems about family members, illustrated with digital photos; historical biographies with archival photos, maps, and diagrams; and student-made marketing brochures promoting various topics. When elementary students have access to graphics, photos, and other digital resources, their work resembles the work of high school students.

STUDENT FEEDBACK   *"The possibilities were endless to what we could achieve and produce in and outside of the classroom: iMovies, Keynotes, songs on GarageBand, superior note-taking (very helpful in college), an unlimited amount of information through the Internet, etc. The list could go on and on."*

—Mooresville High School graduate

Having Fun

When a CEO from a prominent educational publisher visited MGSD, we stopped by a fourth-grade class where a little girl dressed in pink and with a big ponytail was working with great intensity. She explained to our visitor that she was finishing up a project about the history of female candidates for president of the United States and asked him if he knew who was the first.

He asked if it was Shirley Chisholm. The little girl said that was a good guess but that the first female candidate was Victoria Woodhull in 1872, and then she spouted off a stream of details. Clearly impressed, the CEO told her he thought she would get an A on her project. "I won't get a grade," said the little girl," because I'm just doing this for fun." Our students have done some amazing "school work" in their spare time in the past few years. Why? Because it's fun. When students have the opportunity to build their own creations, and include real-world assets to enhance and add texture, good things can happen.

I still love to watch an iMovie on the Apollo moon landing that one of our students created in our first year of digital conversion. She included an array of archival photos and other references, with a captivating audio background and superb narration. It was put together well enough to air on the *PBS NewsHour*.

The student told me she had *loved* working on this project. Love is a powerful thing, and kids love to have fun. I believe that learning is catapulted forward when students are having fun as they work. Of course, it is essential to align assignments tightly to standards, but when students love what they are doing—and when teachers smile and open up to students—the result is improved learning.

Academic Success

Our test scores have grown over the years, and our graduation rate has improved dramatically. We have significantly narrowed achievement gaps, and more MGSD graduates are receiving college scholarships than ever before. We have excellent athletic, music, drama, and ROTC programs in which our emphasis on teamwork plays an important part. In 2012, eight students from our N.F. Woods Advanced Technology & Arts Center, which serves all Mooresville High School students, made it to national competitions, and 28 students placed among the state championships.

Our students have greeted and interacted with visitors from all over the country for several years, developing their communication skills and impressing visitors with their attitudes toward school. They are part of a high-performance culture where expectations of hard work, sacrifice, teamwork, and mutual respect are taught, coached, and fostered for life.

On a visit to a fifth-grade science class on force and motion, I watched students taking turns to show their iMovies or slides. One young man showed a funny, goofy iMovie that had us all laughing. He had enlisted his entire family in the project. He had them all standing close together in the backyard and waving at the camera, while, off camera, he yelled at them that he was on his way.

He ran into view, right into his dad, who fell over on to his mom, who fell over on to big sis, ... you get the picture. His classmates laughed, clearly understanding the concept. The fifth graders in this class are more likely to retain their understanding of force and motion because they will associate it with a fun, real-life, and communal experience, not to mention the impact of this project on the young man himself.

REFLECTIVE QUESTIONS

1. How has technology changed your approach to teaching and classroom management?
2. How do you differentiate instruction for all students?
3. What learning modalities are driving student engagement in your schools?
4. How do you extend learning beyond the school day?
5. Beyond test scores, what is the impact of your instructional approach?

REFERENCES

Barth, Roland S. (2001). *Learning by Heart.* San Francisco, CA: Jossey-Bass.

Greaves, T., Hayes, J., Wilson, L., Gielniak, M., & Peterson, R. (2010). *The Technology Factor: Nine Keys to Student Achievement and Cost-Effectiveness.* Sheldon, CT: MDR.

Thomas, D., & Brown, J. S. (2011). *A New Culture of Learning: Cultivating the Imagination for a World of Constant Change.* Lexington, KY: CreateSpace.

Wagner, Tony. (2008). *The Global Achievement Gap: Why Even Our Best Schools Don't Teach the New Survival Skills Our Children Need—And What We Can Do About It.* New York, NY: Basic Books.

Chapter Seven

InfoDynamo:
A Daily Date with Data

"The data always show room for improvement, but the daily analysis fuels our commitment to improving student achievement and teacher effectiveness."

On a visit to Mrs. Ferguson's second-grade class, I asked one little boy to show me what he was working on. "I'm working on my math, and I just moved up to the next level. We take the test, and it tells us how we did right away," he said. He opened up his profile and showed me a chart with a trend line pointing upward. "Here's where I was, and I've moved to here, and here's where I am going to be. It's my trajectory," he explained matter-of-factly.

One of the many advantages of digital conversion is ubiquitous access to formative student data. Student achievement is our major goal, and clear expectations for all students and employees are part of our culture of personal and professional responsibility. At MGSD, daily information in the form of performance data, organized by student, teacher, department, and grade level, helps everyone focus on improvement and increase the likelihood of success. We call the dynamic infusion of data into the instructional process "infodynamo," because it drives personalized learning and tailored intervention on a daily basis.

We have refined our ability to analyze and use data, providing an ongoing catalyst for improvement. We systematically align student data with instructional planning to provide for precise intervention, for both acceleration and remediation purposes. We include student performance goals in our district strategic plan, school improvement plans, department and grade-level plans, and individual teacher plans, and we gather data on the impact of our district, school, and teacher culture. The data always show room for improvement, but the daily analysis fuels our commitment to improving student achievement and teacher effectiveness.

Listen to Director of Elementary Education Carol Carroll describe the impact of data analysis on daily instruction.

Accountability

Ginger Huffstickler, MGSD accountability director, who is responsible for testing and reporting data to the state, often clarifies for the team that our emphasis on data, which might be misconstrued as a test fixation or an all-business focus, is really all about students and their welfare. Ginger's mantra at our meetings is always, "Behind every number there is a child."

Educators need state accountability tests, despite their limitations. We need a reasonable way to assess the achievement of students and determine by teacher, school, and district where we are successful and where we need to improve, as discussed by Scheurich and Skrla in *Leadership for Equity and Excellence*. Bethany Smith, the English department chair at Mooresville Middle School, expressed our philosophy very well at a 2012 information meeting:

> "The kids like knowing how they're doing. They monitor their progress, and we discuss it. They've embraced their own accountability, and we have to embrace ours. If anyone is not up to where they need to be, we can get the job done by analyzing our data together and helping each other. We're a no-excuses team, and we know it."

STUDENT FEEDBACK   *"Teachers are always working to utilize the rich resources available through our laptops and other learning resources to help us become critical thinkers and problem solvers. However, we also live in a world where the educational system is judged using multiple-choice tests. The laptops allow us to navigate both worlds in a much more flexible way than we could without them."*

—Mooresville High School student

However, we must always keep in mind that the objective of testing is to shine a light on what we need to do next to help students progress. In the words of Keith Krueger, CEO of the Consortium for School Networking (CoSN), in an email conversation with me:

"Our U.S. policy framework has focused on using data for accountability, and that is important and has its place. But the real power of data is around informing instruction, giving the learner and teacher the ability to constantly know what students have not yet mastered and keeping them on task until they understand the concept. Formative data is the 'secret sauce' for 21st century learning, and it will empower personalized learning."

An In-Depth Picture

To build an in-depth picture of every student and every class, we look at the North Carolina state assessment program—end-of-grade exams in grades 3–8 and end-of-course exams in grades 9–12—as well as data on graduation rates, attendance, discipline, dropouts, scholarships, college entrance, and participation in honors and AP classes.

We use released items from the state to develop an item bank that we update every summer. We have also contracted with experts on North Carolina formative assessments and conducted training sessions for our teachers on test item writing. We review and update the benchmark assessments every year, constantly checking to see if we need more items related to objectives on the state tests and benchmarking against student performance to see if we need to bolster our efforts in any areas.

MGSD Keys to Data-Driven Decision Making

Our commitment to data analysis is informed by the following ongoing activities:

- Collection and analysis of student data, using end-of-quarter tests and other common formative assessments.

- Updating of department, grade level, and individual teacher plans to reflect changes in data.

- Teacher review of daily data to adjust instructional planning for individuals and groups.

- Involvement of colleagues, grade-level and department chairs, and principals.

- Monitoring of online assessments by teachers and students to map toward the next objective or assignment.

- Individualized assessments within adaptive software that tailor assignments to student needs.

- Rubrics to record performance scores for project-based learning, including critical thinking and problem-solving skills.

Transparency and Openness

"This is my first year as grade chair. I knew you put up our names and talked about us, and I thought it would be pretty intimidating, but now I can see it's about helping kids," said Jemma Conley, a new grade-level chair at Rocky River Elementary School, after her first information meeting. Transparency can be challenging at first, but as staff listen and learn, a dynamic culture of sharing and support, focused on student achievement, emerges.

We have worked on building a culture of transparency among our staff regarding student performance, embracing what Michael Fullan, in *The Six Secrets of Change*, calls "transparency rules." This means that teachers, grade-level chairs, departments, schools, and the district understand and accept that being open about the constructive use of data is a fundamental part of our culture of caring and our pedagogical approach.

As Michael Fullan says, confidence in U.S. public schools depends on openness about student and school academic performance. In order for individuals and teams to improve, it is essential to have exact information about how they are performing and to engage in thoughtful and purposeful analysis. In our district, quarterly information meetings at each school, formerly called data meetings, have kept us focused on actual student progress and needs.

Building Confidence

In the first stages of digital conversion, I have to admit that our data meetings were pretty tense and uncomfortable. Projecting results on a screen for all to see—by teacher, grade level, school, or department, and then by subgroups such as gender, ethnicity, special needs, or poverty—is a powerful process but one that can be very scary at first.

It took time and patience to build the understanding that student improvement is everyone's responsibility. Our goal was that every team member would come to realize, when the team reviewed his or her student performance data, that overcoming fear or awkwardness would lead to greater student learning in the end. We made sure the meetings were constructive in nature, with a focus on support, assistance, and problem solving.

Now, after four years of digital conversion, the nervousness has largely dissipated. Our school-by-school improvement and overall rise in student achievement have contributed to a new level of comfort because staff can see that their work on data analysis gets results. In the words of Maureen Fitzsimmons, the math chair at Mooresville Middle School, "We used to collaborate, but it was casual. Now we collaborate with a focus on students, and we're all learning together and seeing the results."

Data Analysis Categories

PD **pd** TOOLKIT™

Listen to the author speak about meeting the needs of individual students with data.

We aim for a level of detailed knowledge that is unique in my career as an educator. This allows us to know how every child is doing every day and plan together for the next days and weeks. We attach names of teachers, departments, and grade levels to individual and class student performance and analyze data in each of the following categories:

- Student
- Subgroup
- Content area
- Objective
- Grade level

- Department
- Teacher
- School
- District

Information Meetings

Some time ago, we changed the name of our data meetings to *information meetings.* We made this change after the executive team, reflecting on a recent round of meetings, observed that we had expanded from reviewing achievement data against our quarterly benchmarks aligned with the North Carolina accountability program to include both helpful strategies for teachers and the realignment of financial and human resources.

Each school's leadership team—grade-level and department chairs, principal, and assistant principals—holds a quarterly information meeting with the instructional directors, myself, and other district administrators, as needed. Principals lead the meetings with a digital presentation of the past quarter's data by grade level, content area, and teacher, broken out into subgroups. They also call on the department and grade-level chairs to review their data. The data are developed locally but with online professional assistance.

We look first at a group report and then drill down to individual teachers and content areas, and the teacher leaders comment on areas of concern and share positive results. "We've seen growth in every subgroup, and we're way ahead of where we were last year at this time. We're on track to pass 90 percent for our composite, and we're all so proud of our students," said third-grade chair Tracy Pratt-Dixon during our South Elementary School information meeting in March 2012.

VISITOR FEEDBACK   *"Although there is a concerted focus on data and discreet elements of learning, Mooresville has also embraced larger projects and challenges for students. These projects keep student and teacher voices and spirits alive, amidst the constant emphasis on improving test scores."*

—Karen Cator
Director of the Office of Educational Technology,
U.S. Department of Education

Principals and assistant principals provide school-wide focus and direction, and teacher leaders, grade-level chairs, and department chairs provide the local detail and texture. Principals and assistant principals share other data points, including student attendance, tutoring plans, and discipline issues, to augment the teacher grade-level and department plans.

"We're starting our after-school help sessions earlier, and we're really working hard to make sure the students stay for them. We're offering snacks, calling parents, and setting up transportation, and we're seeing results," said LeTrecia Gloster, Mooresville Middle School assistant principal, at the March 2012 information meeting.

After the meetings, principals continue the work with their leadership teams, and teachers review data with students on a daily basis, fueling a dynamic process of data review and improvement strategy development. Principals and assistant principals meet with grade-level, department, and school improvement teams on a monthly basis or more often, as needed, to continue the focus on data. Assistant principals at Mooresville Middle School and Mooresville High School are responsible for certain departments and provide leadership and support in planning and implementation, while assistant principals at the intermediate schools work in support of all grade levels.

Teacher leaders and other staff members have stepped up at every school and championed the ongoing critical analysis of student performance and the use of the data to drive instruction. "Our morale is good because we're being successful with more students, and that's why we're here," said Tara Gander, technology facilitator at East Mooresville Middle School, in a recent information meeting.

Reflective Advancement

Our information meetings have become a catalyst for what we call the "reflective advancement" of individuals and teams. Three researchers we have studied in our district stress the value of this concept. Roland Barth, in *Improving Schools from Within*, has said that teacher improvement starts with the practice of reflection. Michael Fullan, in *The Six Secrets of Change* and *All Systems Go*, and Linda Lambert, in *Building Leadership Capacity in Schools*, both talk about the need to be open about results and practices in order to identify problems and spread success.

A team approach to analysis and planning stimulates individual and team reflection and advances professional growth. Our information meetings have become a powerful resource for sharing best practices and leveraging the strengths of individual teachers to the benefit of all. Now our highest-performing teachers are eager to help their colleagues improve, teacher leaders are lead learners, and listening and sharing are part of our daily work experience. The enthusiastic integration of data into classroom experience has become the norm.

Resource Alignment Decision Making

Data analysis has huge implications for resource alignment. Our information meetings give leadership teams the information they need to plan for funding and resources, ensuring that our limited funds are used as effectively as possible.

Principals and teachers schedule lessons and tutorial assistance based on daily and weekly data reports to optimize the use of resources. District administrators and principals use student performance data to make financial decisions regarding part-time tutorial assistance and staffing allocations. With today's increasingly dismal forecasts regarding education funding, it is more important than ever before that we use our available resources as best we can, to maximize the benefit for every child every day.

"Doc, we have got to find the funds to help with transportation costs for the Mooresville Middle School after-school help sessions. The students we need to be there are exactly the ones who need help with transportation. I know funds are tight, but we need to step up here," said Bill Parker, executive director of secondary education, at an executive meeting following an information meeting. I looked at Terry Haas, our chief financial officer. "I think we can find it, but we'll have to watch the budget like a hawk for the remainder of the year," said Terry.

We use our weekly executive team meetings—which include the executive directors of instruction and human resources, the chief financial officer, the chief technology officer, the public information officer, and the director of operations—to review the work of the district and follow up on other meetings to provide support. In May 2012, when Mooresville Middle School requested substitute teachers in order to focus more resources on remediation, it took just a couple of quick emails for our CFO, executive director of secondary education, and myself to agree that we should go forward. We notified the principal within a few hours. "Student and teacher success takes priority over everything else," said Terry Haas, our CFO.

Precision and Speed

A group of visiting school superintendents asked Mrs. Thompson, fourth-grade chairperson at East Mooresville Intermediate School, if digital conversion had helped her improve as a teacher. "I'm doing the best teaching I've ever done," she said. "We've learned to use digital resources to pinpoint intervention, so accuracy and precision have become a huge means for improvement. I could never go back to how I used to teach. It was a bunch of guessing and hoping."

"Precise intervention" is how we describe our instructional process, now that we rely on digital formative data. In my past experience as an educator, re-teaching to the whole class was a very common way to try to make sure that students were learning. This time-consuming and teacher-intensive process had little impact on student improvement since it did not take into account individual differences. Similarly, hand grading was the norm, often delaying the feedback process for weeks and having minimal effect on student performance.

Now everyone at MGSD is using data to inform what they do every day. Students and district administrators use data to chart out their work. Teachers use data to construct lesson plans. Principals use data to align resources, depending on changing areas of need. Our culture has become dependent on data and information for planning and improvement.

FIGURE 7.1

Math Overview Report

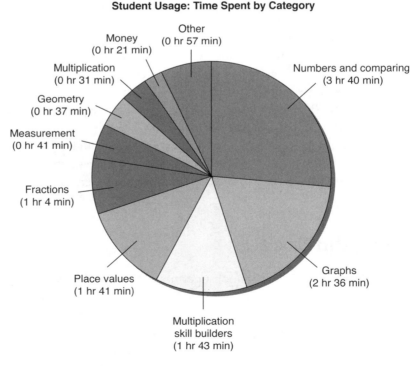

Student Usage: Time Spent by Category

Other (0 hr 57 min)

Money (0 hr 21 min)

Multiplication (0 hr 31 min)

Geometry (0 hr 37 min)

Measurement (0 hr 41 min)

Fractions (1 hr 4 min)

Numbers and comparing (3 hr 40 min)

Graphs (2 hr 36 min)

Place values (1 hr 41 min)

Multiplication skill builders (1 hr 43 min)

Courtesy of IXL Learning

Students can log in to our LMS at any time to see their grades and assignments. They can access feedback on assessments and a variety of classes and see the results of formative assessments immediately after taking a test. Visual dashboards, trajectory displays, and trend lines all help them see how they are doing and where they need to go. Students are literally charting their education, informed by real-time data. (See Appendix D for a sample report.)

No More Guesswork

PD TOOLKIT™

Listen to department chairs Sharon Markowski and Scott Bruton discuss online formative assessment and instant remediation.

Digital conversion brings with it an array of tools and resources that give students and teachers personalized, immediate feedback on online quizzes, practice drills, tests, benchmark assessments, and other assignments. This takes the guesswork out of who needs help on what and for how long. It replaces the shotgun approach to remediation with precise intervention that changes daily, depending on the most recent data.

Our teachers can now look at digital reports by content area, objective, individual student, or subgroup—and all within an instant. This immediate feedback has had a huge impact on teaching and student self monitoring since most of our digital content includes assessments that students can see immediately.

Students Informed to Succeed

We have seen a remarkable impact on students as a result of the immediate feedback on tests and assessments that digital tools provide, as well as the grade information available in our LMS.

Students at all grade levels, including at-risk learners, pay attention to how they are doing and monitor their own progress—much as they will need to do in college—taking much greater responsibility for their own learning than in the past and using their time more productively. They spend less time waiting for grades and more time focusing on what they need to do next. They often show visitors their grades and test scores and describe how they are doing.

STUDENT FEEDBACK   *"It helps in being able to check your grades. You drop below a 70, and you know what you need to do to get it above a 70."*

—Mooresville Middle School student

Tom Greaves, one of the authors of the *Project RED* study of technology use in schools, commented to a group of fellow visitors:

> "I'm impressed with how knowledgeable Mooresville students are about what they're doing and why they're doing it. They're very willing to discuss their grades, progress, and projects and seem to have a clear sense of purpose and direction."

Keeping Parents in the Loop

Digital conversion has hugely influenced our communication with parents. Teachers encourage parents and students to monitor progress so that everyone is informed and working together on a very regular basis. The convenient availability of grades and assessment reports has led to improved communication between teachers, students, and parents, and the constant flow of information has created tighter connections between home and school.

At back-to-school meetings, parent conferences, and on technology nights, we train parents on how to go to the LMS and check grades and assignments, which are updated weekly and even daily. They can also look at the assessments in many of our software programs, including IXL, Discovery Education, Study Island, My Math Lab, NovaNet, and Waterford, and review their students' work by course, content area, and even objective.

> **PARENT FEEDBACK**   *"As a parent of students in Mooresville district, I can attest that the laptop initiative has resulted in tremendous teacher accessibility."*
>
> —MGSD parent

Data Charts by School

Listen to teacher Jemma Conley speak about evolving student achievement strategies for third-grade students.

At a recent data meeting at South Elementary School, kindergarten teacher Kathi Pickard summed up our thinking: "We bought into the concept of every child every day, but these meetings have really brought it home to us that every teacher here has to accept responsibility for every child in this school."

Third Grade Schools

All three of our third-grade schools have achieved North Carolina Honor School of Excellence status, the highest honor awarded to North Carolina schools. Rocky River Elementary received this designation three years ago and continues to

FIGURE 7.2

MGSD Third Grade Schools

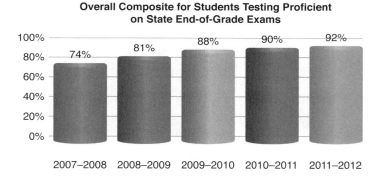

Overall Composite for Students Testing Proficient
on State End-of-Grade Exams

perform with excellence. Park View Elementary jumped up three points in 2012 and epitomizes the MGSD caring culture every day. South Elementary embodies our "all in" philosophy and willed its way across the 90 percent composite mark in 2012. All three schools made 100 percent of AYP targets and have erased any achievement gaps, with all subgroups performing at 90 percent or higher.

East Mooresville Intermediate School

East Mooresville Intermediate School is a North Carolina School of Distinction, having made a four-point gain on the composite in 2012. This school has an end-of-grade composite score of 89 percent, is well positioned to reach 90 percent

FIGURE 7.3

East Mooresville Intermediate School

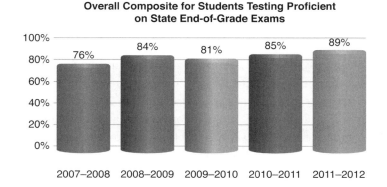

Overall Composite for Students Testing Proficient
on State End-of-Grade Exams

very soon, and has met 100 percent of AYP goals. Although we do not formally note the differing digital conversion implementation levels of individual schools, informally it is safe to say that East Mooresville Intermediate School has moved into the lead. Collaboration and capacity building have been the catalysts for strong, consistent growth.

Mooresville Intermediate School

Mooresville Intermediate School is a North Carolina School of Distinction, having made a four-point gain on the composite, 100 percent of AYP goals, and ongoing rock-steady improvement. This school has been a leader of the digital conversion initiative for four years. The school has focused on *Every Child, Every Day,* gained momentum over time, used data to turbo-charge teaching and learning, and closed all achievement gaps.

FIGURE 7.4

Mooresville Intermediate School

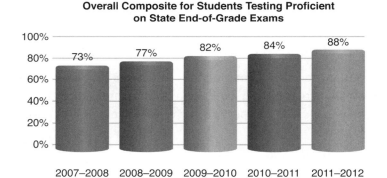

Overall Composite for Students Testing Proficient on State End-of-Grade Exams

Mooresville Middle School

Mooresville Middle School is a North Carolina School of Distinction, having made a three-point gain on the composite, met 100 percent of AYP goals, and achieved steady forward progress. In the 2011–2012 school year, the school took off like a rocket with digital conversion, and the faculty exemplified evolutional capacity building, showing tremendous growth as a team. You can see and feel the momentum in this school.

FIGURE 7.5

Mooresville Middle School

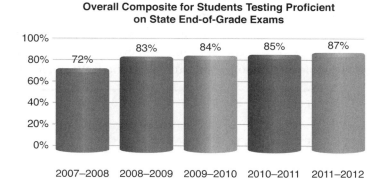

Overall Composite for Students Testing Proficient
on State End-of-Grade Exams

Mooresville High School

Mooresville High School is a North Carolina Honor School of Excellence, with 100 percent of AYP goals met, a 23-point gain on the composite over five years, and the emergence of leaders all over the campus. The faculty, staff, and teacher leaders have attached their performance trajectory to daily effort and catapulted achievement up to 90+, which is North Carolina Honor School of Excellence territory. Their caring, loving, focused attitudes are exemplary, and they go above and beyond the call of duty every day.

FIGURE 7.6

Mooresville High School

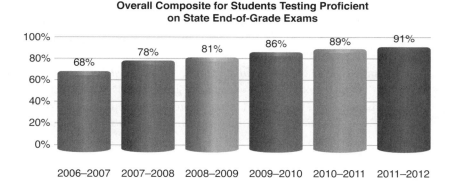

Overall Composite for Students Testing Proficient
on State End-of-Grade Exams

In 2011, the third quarter benchmark data, measured by content area aligned with North Carolina state end-of-course tests, looked very promising. Scott Bruton, the science department chair, said his team was confident that 90 percent or more of students could achieve a passing grade on the upcoming biology end-of-course exam. "But even if we reach 90 percent, we still have a lot of work to do," he added. "What about the other 10 percent?"

REFLECTIVE QUESTIONS

1. How do you share student performance data among colleagues?
2. How long does it take to give feedback to students?
3. Do you use data to allocate resources?
4. How do students monitor their own progress?
5. How do you incorporate data analysis into your regular meetings?

REFERENCES

Barth, Roland S. (1990). *Improving Schools from Within: Teachers, Parents, and Principals Can Make the Difference*. San Francisco, CA: Jossey-Bass.

Barth, Roland S. (2001). *Learning by Heart*. San Francisco, CA: Jossey-Bass.

Fullan, Michael. (2010). *All Systems Go: The Change Imperative for Whole System Reform*. Thousand Oaks, CA: Corwin.

Fullan, Michael. (2008). *The Six Secrets of Change: What the Best Leaders Do to Help Their Organizations Survive and Thrive*. San Francisco, CA: Jossey-Bass.

Greaves, T., Hayes, J., Wilson, L., Gielniak, M., & Peterson, R. (2010). *Project RED, The Technology Factor: Nine Keys to Student Achievement and Cost-Effectiveness*. Sheldon, CT: MDR.

Lambert, Linda. (1998). *Building Leadership Capacity in Schools*. Alexandria, VA: Association for Supervision and Curriculum Development.

Scheurich, J. J., & Skrla, L. (2003). *Leadership for Equity and Excellence: Creating High-Achievement Classrooms, Schools, and Districts*. Thousand Oaks, CA: Corwin Press.

Chapter Eight

Resource Alignment

"Funding digital conversion is mostly about prioritizing and repurposing, not about finding new or more monies."

In our first year of digital conversion, a less-than-enthusiastic teacher asked MGSD school board member Larry Wilson, "Why did you spend all that money on computers when you could have given us a bigger raise?" Larry responded, "We spent that money directly on the students, and it was the right thing to do."

It is essential to remember that students are always the number-one priority when making financial as well as other decisions. We were fortunate at MGSD to have school board members who were on board with this thinking, and we aligned our funding from the start with our priority of serving every child every day.

Many visitors ask, "How could you afford to do it?" The question is not surprising, given that educators are currently in deep despair about the cuts in education budgets across the country. Our answer is that we established priorities and aligned resources to match our goals—a chapter of our story that we enjoy sharing with others. The trick is to change the thinking, thoughtfully repurpose funds, and look for cost-efficiencies as well as productivity gains. Second-order change management impacts financial decisions, as well as what takes place in the classroom.

During the third and fourth years of digital conversion, we received budgetary cuts from the state and county that totaled 10 percent, forcing us to reexamine every expenditure. We realized that digital resources would allow us to maximize cost-efficiencies, so we stopped buying textbooks, with a few exceptions. We found digital content much less expensive and vastly superior in value, with a huge range of embedded assets, such as formative quizzes, games, links, and interactive activities that include audio and video support.

We had limited funds available for field trips, so we moved to virtual tours. We also began to save money by offering some staff development and holding some meetings online. Now we regularly participate in webinars and web-based meetings at the state, regional, and local level.

VISITOR FEEDBACK   *"Mooresville's digital conversion has provided the rest of the country with a clear, concise blueprint of how to use technology to transform the way students learn and teachers teach. The concepts of leasing versus purchasing hardware, using laptops to replace textbooks, focused teacher/staff development, student empowerment and accountability, common teacher planning time, hardware repair centers at each campus versus huge district technology repair staff, and student responsibility encouraged by allowing computers to be taken home are among many lessons that can be learned by other educators."*

—Terry Grier
Superintendent, Houston Independent School District, Texas

MGSD is not the only school district to align resources differently. As more and more districts transition to one-to-one computing, the mystique around funding is rapidly giving way to a more pragmatic sense of how to approach the budget issue and the development of new and very do-able funding strategies.

Establishing Priorities

At one of our first planning meetings, Chief Technology Officer Scott Smith explained the importance of our bandwidth strategy. "We have to have a network infrastructure that can support huge usage. Kids couldn't care less whether they're downloading a 4KB email or a 25MB video. Kids and teachers just want it to work, period," he said.

As districts consider the cost of digital conversion, they need to maximize the available dollars by deciding what is essential, what they can do without, and what they can repurpose. They also need to take a long-term view and look at the investment in digital tools and resources as part of the financial plan for years to come.

Despite the severe budget cuts schools face today, a school or district network needs to provide all the bandwidth students and teachers need today and tomorrow, and hardware choices need to be made carefully in terms of reliability, durability, and support and with an eye to the future—or there will be a negative impact on both budgets and instruction. So it is important to make a long-term commitment to quality and productivity while looking to fund that commitment through the creative repurposing of resources.

TCO and ROI

We took a hard-line cost–benefit analysis approach that included estimated total cost of ownership (TCO) and return on investment (ROI). We examined the major recurring costs—hardware, software, warranties, maintenance, and staff development—as well as the infrastructure costs—wireless networks, routers, switches, and servers. However, we viewed the infrastructure costs primarily as start-up costs and also as costs that would, to a great extent, have been necessary even without digital conversion, since we would still have had multiple computer labs, networks, servers, and so on. We used the following criteria to evaluate the ROI of every purchasing decision:

- Academic return regarding student improvement
- Improved instructional experience for students and teachers
- Support for key drivers of student engagement
- Financial savings from reduced textbook, classroom space, and paper costs
- Laptop costs
- Other efficiencies, such as web meetings and online grades

Infrastructure

Investing in a robust network is absolutely essential to digital conversion since the entire instructional program becomes dependent on digital resources. I like to say that network infrastructure is like plumbing and should be viewed similarly in terms of budgeting. The network infrastructure pipes the data around the school and the district, just as plumbing pipes the water. In education today, on-demand Internet access is just as important as on-demand water.

Today, most schools have computer labs and some desktops in classrooms, so the foundation of the network is generally in place. As districts build out their networks to support digital conversion, I recommend that they fund the infrastructure in the same way that they fund the plumbing—with capital dollars, construction funding, E-Rate, or state technology funding.

I clearly remember back in Henrico County, in the first year of the Teaching and Learning Initiative, waking up night after night, worrying about the network. If the pipes are blocked and you have everyone ready to turn on the water, the challenges of change management are quickly compounded by frustration, cynicism, and doubt. On numerous occasions in our first year as a pioneering district, network outages and overloads meant that we had to expand our bandwidth "on the fly."

We made the necessary adjustments, but frustration with the network and the laptops—with issues such as battery life, durability, and software compatibility—created significant tensions as we worked through the challenges. Fortunately, digital conversion at MGSD has largely been a smooth ride from a technical standpoint, thanks to vast improvements in hardware, infrastructure, and content.

At MGSD, our negotiated infrastructure cost ran just under $1.9 million for eight schools. This included the Cisco 802.11n wireless network, 1252 N access points in each classroom, the ACE Application Control Engine working as a load balancer, and Cisco Catalyst 3560-E and 3750-E switches. To help fund this cost, we received a one-time grant of $250,000 from Lowe's Home Improvement, headquartered in Mooresville. In addition, the Town of Mooresville provided a $50,000 grant to fund other wireless costs in our pilot year. Many of our infrastructure costs (for example, the cost of switches) were one-time costs or have extended life cycles of eight to 12 years. The rest of the funding came from our local operating budget, as well as our capital outlay budget that includes all sources of revenue—local, county, and state funding.

Hardware

The major expense of digital conversion is the student and teacher laptops. We worked with an estimate of $850 per student, which included the hardware, software, maintenance, backpack, and warranty, and this turned out to be an accurate figure. We funded the laptop cost out of the operating budget and signed up for a four-year lease program, which spread the $850 expense over four years, for $212 per student per year.

Digital Resources

We spend on average less than $40 per student per year on digital content. This includes a variety of offerings from Pearson, Discovery Education, Study Island, IXL Math, BrainPOP, Angel Learning, and netTrekker by Knovation. We also take advantage of open source software and free content.

Professional Development

We have negotiated initial training from most of our content providers, including Apple and Cisco, as part of the base cost. Much of our staff development funding has been lost in recent budget cuts, so our staff members train each other, with our early release days as the primary time for teacher training. Teachers who attend our Summer Institute for two or three days each summer are paid a $100-per-day stipend.

Affordability for Families

Making sure that students from low-income families could benefit from 24/7 access to technology was a major priority. We negotiated a lower monthly rate with our local ISP for families without Internet access at home, and our education foundation covers the laptop maintenance fee of $50 a year for any family that cannot afford it. Currently, only 26 percent of families have asked for this assistance, although 40 percent of our students receive free and reduced lunch.

Several families pay the fees in installments, and some families have offered to pay for other families. Bob Gates, president of the Mooresville Education Foundation, said at the 2011 fall meeting of the foundation, when funds were approved for the families who had requested assistance, "This is one of the very best ways we can support MGSD, and it sends the message that our community cares about all students."

Our digital conversion is also helping family budgets in other ways. For example, the laptops include both graphing calculators and plain calculators, which parents previously needed to purchase for their students. In addition, many more graduating seniors receive college scholarships now than in the past.

Repurposing Resources

"We're in good shape in terms of classroom space at the intermediate, middle, and high school levels, but we're going to need a new elementary school sooner than we expected—within three or four years. We used to think it would be five or six years, but growth is picking up, and we'll have our largest kindergarten class ever this coming year," said Steve Mauney, director of operations, reporting on a facilities study at the June 2012 school board meeting. Despite this unavoidable expense, the repurposing of computer labs across the district has bought us much extra time and space over the years. Fourteen computer labs have become regular classroom space, saving at least $250,000 per classroom, for a total of $3.5 million saved.

Most often, when districts look into providing students with laptops, they think they will need to pay for the devices on top of their current budget items. But that is not the case. Before any district CFO fires up his or her calculator for the first time, it is important to understand that funding digital conversion is mostly about prioritizing and repurposing, not about finding new or more monies.

PD TOOLKIT™

Listen to the author describe some of his district's successful repurposing strategies.

Instructional Materials and Supplies Monies

One of the major elements in our funding strategy has been the reallocation of monies in our instructional materials and supplies budget, by means of a steady transition to digital resources as the primary instructional tool set. This

Third-grade student at South Elementary School

may sound like a simple change, but in reality it involves a huge adjustment in pedagogical and instructional practice and requires everyone to embrace the new digital world and, for the most part, leave behind the old world of print materials.

At MGSD we had no choice. We could not afford to live in both worlds, and, having made the commitment to the digital world, there was no going back. In the words of Chief Financial Officer Terry Haas, "Once you dive into the digital river, you have to swim, and you can't afford to go back. Of course, you don't want to go back anyway."

We have purchased no textbooks for grades 4–12 in three years, except for AP classes. This represents a considerable savings that has funded our purchase of online content. We no longer buy workbooks, calculators, maps, globes, dictionaries, thesauruses, encyclopedias, or periodicals. These resources and many more—even frogs for dissection—are available online for every student as part of our online content budget. Whereas previously students could access reference materials and dictionaries only in the media center or in certain classrooms, now every student has the reference equivalent of the Library of Congress in his or her backpack.

With daily and weekly grades available to students and parents online, we no longer have hard copy interim reports, and although we still make report cards available quarterly, their function is now largely obsolete.

Print materials and even live frogs are still available in our schools, but digital resources provide, in most cases, far more and far better tools than we could ever provide when we relied solely on print—and at lower cost. We have achieved a cost savings of approximately $40 per student per text, based on an average textbook cost of $80 and an average digital content cost of $40 per student. And that savings is for just one textbook. At MGSD, as in most other school districts, the number of textbooks purchased was considerably higher in the past than it is today.

STUDENT FEEDBACK   *"In my biology class, we had to make a rap about the cell cycle. It was actually so much fun, it didn't feel like work, and I felt like I learned a lot from that project."*

—Mooresville High School student

Computer Labs

Back in Henrico County, when we issued laptops to every student in grades 6–12 in the fall of 2001, we repurposed more than 40 computer labs as classroom space, for an estimated savings in construction costs of $175,000 per classroom, which helped to fund the Teaching and Learning Initiative. On average, we eliminated one computer lab per school. Today, the estimated savings per classroom has risen to $250,000.

We were dealing at the time with a rapidly growing student population— approximately 1,000 new students a year in a district of more than 45,000 students. We opened 12 new schools between 1994 and 2004 and built new additions on over a dozen existing schools. Repurposed computer labs allowed us to reduce the number of new classrooms that had to be built.

We have continued this strategy at MGSD. At Mooresville High School, with 1,600 students in somewhat cramped quarters, we have repurposed three computer labs, representing a return of capital resources back to the district and the school as a result of digital conversion. We have also opened two new schools and built one major addition on another school in the past three years—and saved the cost of computer labs.

The average cost of a new computer lab today—including construction, wiring, furniture, and air conditioning—is $250,000, but at MGSD, new computer labs are no longer needed. Now that students have their own laptops, they can easily transform the cafeteria, hallway, or media center into an online learning lab.

Staff

PD **id** TOOLKIT™

Listen to CTO Dr. Scott Smith describe how roles and responsibilities have been redefined to support successful digital conversion.

At MGSD, we have managed digital conversion without adding new positions, and we have improved productivity in the process. We have also repurposed a variety of staff positions to support our new work because much of the old work has gone away.

We used to teach keyboarding, but when students have their own laptops, they teach themselves to type. Our courier used to deliver instructional CDs to each school, but now we pull up the content online. Lab techs used to run our computer labs, but now most of them have become tech facilitators, offering greatly increased value to students and teachers by troubleshooting problems and advising on professional development. Other lab techs have become help desk facilitators. Media specialists and librarians no longer just catalog and check out books. They also support students and staff with curriculum research and online resources, as well as managing a hub of student collaboration in the media centers.

Cost Savings and Cost Avoidance

"I'm loving the new online EOQs [end-of-quarter tests]. They're saving us money and saving wear and tear on me and my car," said Carol Carroll, MGSD director of elementary schools. "We used to run off the test booklets for each student, and I used to deliver them in my car to each school and lug them into the office. Now we do it all online. We save paper, copying costs, and my time to make them and deliver them. And now we get instant data back, so we also save the time of scanning and returning the tests to the schools."

Our digital conversion has led to significant cost-efficiencies in many areas. This experience matches the findings of the 2010 *Project RED* research study of properly implemented one-to-one computing. According to *Project RED*, similar cost-efficiencies at the national level could represent savings in the billions of dollars.

Project RED found three main areas of cost-efficiencies resulting from what the study calls "technology-transformed learning," all of which have been realized in our district and in our community:

- *Cost savings.* Cost savings result when technology provides a less expensive way to perform a function, such as when parent newsletters are sent out electronically rather than on paper.

- *Cost avoidance.* Cost avoidance savings result when a current practice ceases, such as when free online primary source materials replace purchased materials.

- *Revenue enhancements.* Revenue enhancements are additional tax revenues that result when students are better trained and enjoy higher incomes.

Project RED has developed interesting estimates of the digital conversion savings experienced by a sample district and how those savings could be extended nationwide (see Figures 8.1 and 8.2).

Dropout Prevention

Digital conversion has allowed our teachers to provide precise, personalized intervention for struggling students, along with effective remediation and support, in a much more timely manner than was possible in the past. As a result, our graduation rate has increased from 64 percent to 90 percent over the past four years.

FIGURE 8.1

Project RED: Implementation Cost Comparison

What Is the Cost to Move to a One-to-One Environment?

Traditional Classroom (3:1 Ratio)		1:1 Classroom (1:1 Ratio)	
HARDWARE			
$1,000	Cost of student computer with 4-year warranty	$900	Cost of student computer with 4-year warranty
$1,100	Cost of teacher computer with 4-year warranty	$1,100	Cost of teacher computer with 4-year warranty
$7,600	Total cost of 1 printer per classroom plus 2 for common areas (20 b/w lasers and 2 color lasers)	$9,200	Total cost of 1 printer per classroom plus 4 for common areas (20 b/w laser printers and 4 color laser printers)
$202,100	Total cost over 4 years	$509,200	Total cost over 4 years
$101	Cost per student per year	$255	Cost per student per year
SERVERS, ROUTER, FIREWALL, AND RELATED SOFTWARE			
$25,000	Cost of servers, router, firewall and software	$50,000	Cost of servers, router, firewall and software
$13	Cost per student per year	$25	Cost per student per year
ANNUALIZED SOFTWARE COSTS			
$50	Cost per student per year for instructional software	$50	Cost per student per year for instructional software
$13	Cost of productivity tools per student computer	$40	Cost of productivity tools per student computer
$25	Cost for LMS, assessment software, etc.	$25	Cost for LMS, assessment software, etc.
$8	Installation and customization costs per student	$13	Installation and customization costs per student
$96	Cost per student per year	$128	Cost per student per year
WIRELESS NETWORK			
$2,000	Cost per classroom/common area, includes POE	$3,000	Cost per classroom/common area, includes POE
$50,000	Total infrastructure	$75,000	Total infrastructure
$14	Cost per student per year	$22	Cost per student per year
TELECOM			
	10 Kilobits/sec/student average		*50 Kilobits/sec/student average*
$75	Cost per megabit at 5 megabit/second rate	$50	Cost per megabit at 25 megabit/second rate
$225	Cost per month	$1,250	Cost per month
$2,250	Cost per year (10 months)	$12,500	Cost per year (10 months)
$5	Cost per student per year	$25	Cost per student per year
TECH SUPPORT			
(0.25 dedicated tech support person, presumes 4-year hardware warranty)			
	0.25 dedicated tech support person		*0.5 dedicated tech support person*
$75,000	Cost of tech support person plus overhead	$75,000	Cost of tech support person plus overhead
$38	Cost per student per year	$75	Cost per student per year
PROFESSIONAL DEVELOPMENT			
	0.25 trainer year 1, 0.125 trainer years 2–4		*0.50 trainer year 1, 0.25 trainer years 2–4*
$100,000	Cost of PD person, fully burdened	$100,000	Cost of PD person, fully burdened
$62,500	Total cost	$125,000	Total cost
$31	Cost per student per year	$63	Cost per student per year
$298	**Total cost per student per year**	**$593**	**Total cost per student per year**

www.ProjectRED.org · 877-635-4198
©2012 Project RED. All rights reserved.

N.B. Costs for most areas listed above have decreased approximately 15% since the time of publication. The only area of substantial increase is in Internet Access due to increased usage.

Used by permission of the authors.

FIGURE 8.2

Project RED: Potential Savings from Technology-Transformed Learning

1:1 Cost Savings Calculator

Category	Traditional Costs				Potential Cost Reduction			
	National Average Cost per Student	Your Cost: Current Cost per Student	No. of Student	Gross	Savings per Student	Gross Savings	Pct. Savings	New Costs
Student data mapping	$50		500	$25,000	$11	$5,500	22%	$19,500
Online professional learning	$23		500	$11,500	$12	$6,000	52%	$5,500
Teacher attendance	$65		500	$32,500	$13	$6,500	20%	$26,000
Space savings	$15		500	$7,500	$15	$7,500	100%	$0
Power savings	$27		500	$13,500	$16	$8,000	59%	$5,500
Digital core curriculum saving	$438		500	$219,000	$17	$8,500	4%	$210,500
Disciplinary actions	$200		500	$100,000	$20	$10,000	10%	$90,000
Post-secondary remedial education	$302		500	$151,000	$30	$15,000	10%	$136,000
Digital supplemental materials vs. print	$65		500	$32,500	$31	$15,500	48%	$17,000
Copy machine cost calculations	$80		500	$40,000	$40	$20,000	50%	$20,000
Online assessment	$44		500	$22,000	$44	$22,000	100%	$0
Dual/joint/AP course enrollment	$145		500	$72,500	$58	$29,000	40%	$43,500
Paperwork reduction	$480		500	$240,000	$60	$30,000	13%	$210,000
End-of-course failure	$533		500	$266,500	$107	$53,500	20%	$213,000

Used by permission of the authors.

Dropouts have the highest impact on the community, as well as on the individual's chances of happiness, of any of the variables discussed by *Project RED*, primarily because students who do not stay in school or who do not go on to college have substantially decreased earning power and consequently pay much lower taxes. *Project RED* estimates the numbers as follows:

> "The greatest financial benefit results from the difference in lifetime tax revenues between a dropout, a high school graduate, and a college graduate. On average, these additional tax revenues range from $448,000 (females) to $874,000 (males). If 25 percent of those dropouts graduated from high school and 25 percent of those graduated from college, the increase in tax revenues would be $77 billion per year per graduating class."

STUDENT FEEDBACK   *"Our school has increased academically since the laptops were put into order. Less dropouts, better grades, and much more has been the outcome of this. My brother is a Morehead-Cain Scholar, and another person in our high school became one as well last year. These laptops led them to success just like for everyone in this school."*
—Mooresville High School student

Online Assessment

Online formative assessment provides real-time feedback that helps drive student improvement, and it also offers significant financial advantages. *Project RED* estimates the savings as follows:

- Test printing costs three to four cents a page. Tests run from one to 10 pages, and students often take one test a month in each of five classes, or 50 tests a year. At nine pages a test and three cents a page, the cost is $13.50 per student per year.

- Manual scoring takes one to three minutes per multiple-choice test. If teacher time is worth 30 cents to 60 cents per minute, the cost is roughly 30 cents to $2 per test, including recording in the grade book, returning tests, etc. Assuming 50 tests a year and 50 cents a test, the cost is $25 per student per year.

Our experience at MGSD supports these calculations, with additional savings accruing from the staff time saved.

Paper and Copying

Project RED estimates that a high school with 1,500 students spends $100,000 in paper and copy machine costs a year, and schools with an LMS save 20 percent in copy machine expenses. At MGSD, we are excited to see a reduction in our paper and copy costs really start to kick in.

Paperwork Reduction

Teachers nationwide complain about excessive paperwork that consumes far too much time. Because digital conversion reduces their paperwork burden, our teachers can spend more time with students, improving performance and reducing dropouts and disciplinary actions, which in turn reduces expenses.

Our teachers have experienced another huge time savings because assessments are now graded electronically, recorded for later use, and sorted by groups and by areas. And because we no longer use worksheets—having replaced them with online quizzes and activities—more teacher time is available for the important work of differentiating instruction.

Disciplinary Actions

Disciplinary actions cost schools money and take staff away from instruction. Some schools need full-time police presence or security guards, at a cost of approximately $50 per student per year, and suspensions frequently result in legal fees of $250,000 or more, according to *Project RED* estimates.

At MGSD, short-term suspensions and expulsions have dropped more than 50 percent compared with the year before digital conversion, and long-term suspensions and expulsions have also declined—thanks, we believe, to our caring and engaging culture. This impacts both student success and cost savings.

Online Professional Learning

As the price of gasoline continues to go up, along with the cost of travel in general, we are migrating to web-based interactive broadcasts with a wide range of meeting functions. The cost savings are significant. Principals, teachers, administrators, and other staff now regularly engage in online meetings for training, information, and discussions.

End-of-Course Failure

End-of-course failure can be devastating to students and increase the likelihood that they will drop out. When students fail a course, reteaching can cost over $1,300 per student, according to *Project RED*. At MGSD, thanks to our focus on daily data and intervention, we have cut back on the reteaching of courses significantly. We have seen 15 percent more students pass the end-of-course and end-of-grade exams, improving both budgets and morale.

The End Result: $1.25 per Student per Day

When I was preparing to speak to the Missouri Association of School Administrators in April 2012, I knew that they would really want to know in detail how we had paid for digital conversion. Within our district, we had used the figure of $1.25 per student per day for digital conversion for some time. But I looked at our figure for annual funding for each student, $7,463, and did another calculation. I divided that figure by 200 days—180 instructional days and 20 weekend days—and saw that we spend about $37 per student per day overall. $1.25 is about 3.5 percent of our daily expenditure for each student—for the huge resources and benefits of digital conversion— leaving 96.5 percent of the daily expenditure for everything else. What a bargain!

The end result of all our prioritization efforts, repurposing of resources, and cost-efficiencies is that digital conversion costs only $1.25 per student per day at MGSD. The cost of hardware, software, digital content, professional development, and backpacks is $200 per student per year, based on 200 days a year and a four-year hardware lease.

As discussed earlier, we separate the infrastructure costs out of this analysis, since these are capital costs and should be aligned with capital funding sources and because much of the infrastructure is required anyway, with either computer labs or digital conversion.

Money is not the biggest hurdle for school districts looking at digital conversion. If districts can carve $1 to $2 per student per day out of their budget, they can cover everything in a laptop program except infrastructure.

We are not a wealthy school district. As of 2012, MGSD ranks 100th out of 115 school districts in North Carolina in per-pupil expenditures. Our figure of $7,463 per student per year includes all funding sources—the county, the state, the federal government, and the Town of Mooresville, which contributes a small city school tax. So for little more than three percent of the daily budget, we are able to provide students with a portal to the world, cutting-edge creativity tools, and a reference library larger than the Library of Congress.

FIGURE 8.3

North Carolina District Rankings, 2012				
Compared with Per-Pupil Expenditures				
	District	Percent Proficient using EOG Reading, Math, Science; EOC	Per Pupil Expenditure (state ranking)	District Enrollment Numbers
1	Camden County	90%	7989 (73)	1891
2	Mooresville Graded School District	89%	7463 (100)	5622
	Polk County	89%	9604 (22)	2363
3	Chapel Hill Carrboro	88%	8979 (39)	11,504

Formula: Number of proficient test scores on reading grades 3–8, math grades 3–8, and EOCs, divided by the total number of tests taken in school year 2011–2012.

"That help desk operation just blew me away," said Leslie Winner, Executive Director of the Z. Smith Reynolds Foundation, on a 2012 visit to Mooresville High School. "What a fantastic opportunity for the students to manage real-world work and challenges. And the teacher is running a business and is really, really good at it!" We had realigned resources to make this happen, moving funds from a software lab teaching position to a help desk teacher/coordinator position—for a much bigger bang from the buck!

REFLECTIVE QUESTIONS

1. What priorities impact the cost of your digital conversion effort?

2. What are the results of your TCO and ROI analysis?

3. How can you achieve cost-efficiencies?

4. What monies can you repurpose?

5. What is your estimated digital conversion cost on a per-student per-day basis?

REFERENCE

Greaves, T., Hayes, J., Wilson, L., Gielniak, M., & Peterson, R. (2010). *Project RED, The Technology Factor: Nine Keys to Student Achievement and Cost-Effectiveness.* Sheldon, CT: MDR.

Chapter Nine

"All In": Collaboration, Synergy, and Momentum

"'All in' means that every adult and every student counts in a major way and every adult and every student is counted on in a major way—and we want them to know it."

Lynn Miller, an MGSD bus driver for over nine years, called out to the K–3 students on her bus, "All right, boys and girls, let's get out your books and start reading! You all have been doing real good, and I told Mr. Cottone, and he's very proud of you." Mrs. Miller had asked Mark Cottone, principal of Park View Elementary, if she could implement a program she called Read on the Ride, in which students would be asked—or strongly encouraged, knowing Mrs. Miller—to read each day as they rode home. With support from Mark Cottone and the teachers at Park View Elementary, students are now accustomed to reading as they ride home each day.

Mrs. Miller has been recognized by Mr. Cottone for her initiative and "all in" attitude. She is making a difference as she goes about her work as a bus driver. She hasn't had a raise in three years, but she is a prime example of the "all in" culture that most MGSD employees exhibit every day. "All in" means that every adult and every student counts in a major way and every adult and every student is counted on in a major way—and we want them to know it.

I strongly believe that when all participants are valued and when the culture emphasizes appreciation as a major construct of the work of education, people are inclined to come together as a team, pitch in to take their effort to the next level, and work together for the greater good, as discussed by Roland Barth in *Improving Schools from Within*. In our schools, a culture of both formal and informal collaboration creates a powerful synergy and momentum that drive student performance every day.

Everyone Counts!

When I entered a fifth-grade classroom at East Mooresville Intermediate School with the principal, Robin Melton, teacher Sarah Dillard walked toward us and exclaimed, "You're a godsend!" I extended my hand and thought, "I've never been called a godsend before in my life." Then she walked right by me, beaming at the technology staff member standing behind us who was returning her laptop.

PD **pd** TOOLKIT™

Listen to department chairs Sharon Markowski and Scott Bruton describe how the "all in" philosophy has impacted teaching, learning, and school culture.

At MGSD, we look for a commitment by each employee to each student, a commitment by each member of the district and administrative staff to create the conditions for success, and a commitment by each student to do his or her best. Our "all in" collaborative approach to solving problems, working toward goals, and pulling for each other has a daily impact on students, who recognize our high expectations for them and our determination to make sure they are successful.

It takes time, but we have seen the number of employees who are "all in" increase each year. We still have a few who are not quite there, but the strong pull of the majority has left very few on the fringe. The success factors that we work hard on every day—attention to the moral imperative, the culture of caring, evolutional capacity building, data-driven decision making, digital resources, and the belief in every child—come together synergistically to motivate more and more teachers, students, and staff to be "all in."

Students In

Just as we have asked teachers and principals to work hard and learn together how they can support every child, we have also asked students to work hard and learn how they can support their own achievement, because an "all in" attitude has a huge impact on their performance. "Students in" means that each student takes responsibility for his or her performance and also contributes to the success of others and the community at large.

STUDENT FEEDBACK   *"Having the laptop makes you feel responsible. There are community groups, so it brings the whole school together. In the community, you can get everyone's ideas and can communicate with other people. Everyone has the opportunity to work and learn."*

—Mooresville Middle School student

Leaning In   On a visit to a seventh-grade math class in Mooresville Middle School with the principal, Mrs. Tulbert, I observed some very intense dialogue among the students at each table. The teacher, Mr. Piper, explained, "We're reviewing each student's quarterly assessment, and I've assigned an honors student at each table to coach other students on any problems they've missed. This is the first time I've tried this, and it's going really well."

Seventh-grade students at Mooresville Middle School

At each table, students were "leaning in," a physical and symbolic term I use to describe student engagement, as they worked out problems together using online math review assessments. They were absorbed in the task at hand and eager to accomplish it successfully, both as individuals and as a group. They demonstrated their "all in" attitude by:

- Leaning forward
- Listening intently
- Participating
- Helping each other
- Collaborating
- Giving their best
- Monitoring their own learning
- Focusing on their work

Extra Help Sessions   Very often, if you walk through the Mooresville High School media center just after dismissal, you are likely to see as many as 100 or 150 students working at tables as individuals or in groups. These extra help sessions are voluntary and last an hour or more. Teachers elicit parental help to encourage students to attend and are present to help with coordination. Many of the students who attend are not there to receive help but to offer help. Some of the peer tutors come back after the state test scores are released, over the summer, to see how "their" students have done. They care and want to know. And of course their "all in" attitude benefits them also, in many ways—through repeated practice and exposure to content, as well as through a boost to their self-esteem.

I recently visited an algebra extra help session and observed the student tutors working with great intensity, leaning in toward the students they were helping, and I saw those who were being helped leaning in and listening. As they worked together, these students were demonstrating the emergence of a "student in" culture, in which students are willing to both give and receive help.

Community Support   Mooresville High School students have started an organization called Reach Club that provides support for diversity in the school and the community. Members volunteer at various events, including serving at a community dinner to raise funds for homeless families. Year after year, the Mooresville High School Naval ROTC program receives the highest ranking in its formal Pass and Review by the Navy. In 2011, the Mooresville Color Guard provided support and service at more than 80 community events, including Chamber of Commerce, Rotary Club, Town of Mooresville, and Lowe's corporate events.

The award-winning Mooresville High School band and a variety of music ensembles are always on call to support community and school events, and the Band Boosters is an active and vibrant parent group. These groups clearly demonstrate to the community our students' "all in" attitude in action.

Teachers In

If we are asking students to work collaboratively, to care about all members of the community, and to support the "all in" philosophy, teachers need to model these important responsibilities and attitudes. In our culture, everyone needs to be "all in," sharing and working together. "All in" collaborative teacher teamwork has impacted student achievement, as teachers have learned together how to support areas of deficiency, identify strategies and tactics around content objectives, and integrate digital resources.

VISITOR FEEDBACK *"[MGSD] teachers actually talked to each other and planned together. The old isolationist attitude of 'leave me alone and just let me teach' mentality that is found in too many schools across the country has been replaced by a 'together we can, whatever it takes, no excuses' culture."*

—Terry Grier
Superintendent, Houston Independent School District, Texas

Almost all our teachers have committed to the "all in" spirit with great enthusiasm, but a couple of years ago, a teacher resigned rather than move to another grade level. The grade-level chairperson shared with me that, unfortunately, this teacher's departure ended up being a blessing in disguise because she was not a team player and did not work well with others. Just as positive attitudes, a collaborative spirit, and a willingness to work through tough situations can promote the "all in" philosophy, the opposite is true. Negativism and an unwillingness to commit to problem solving can affect collaborative success.

Extra Time with Students   We know that, in order to meet our goals, we have to spend some additional time with our students, and more and more of our faculty step up each year and do a little more. "We have so many teachers who go above and beyond on a regular basis that if you don't, you stand out. We're seeing great pride and high expectations from our teachers about and for each other," commented Lenoa Smith, curriculum resource teacher at Park View Elementary, in a recent meeting.

Our high school teachers have decided that the after-school extra help sessions are important enough that they stay after school with no additional pay. The English teachers divide up the extra help sessions so that each teacher contributes one day a week. "We are 'all in' as a department and as a team," said Nancy Gardner, Mooresville High School English department chair.

Attention to Students' Perspective   In our teacher and culture training, we have studied the research on student perspective, particularly "Students' Perspective on School Improvement," by Ruddick, Day, and Wallace. As part of our "all in" philosophy, we expect teachers to reflect on and take to heart these characteristics of a good teacher, as defined by students:

- Enjoys teaching the subject
- Enjoys teaching students
- Makes lessons interesting and relevant to the real world
- Will laugh but still keeps order
- Is fair
- Talks to students
- Doesn't yell
- Explains things as much as needed
- Never gives up on students

Beyond the Classroom   "All in" extends beyond daily instruction and into other school and district activities. For example, Mooresville Middle School faculty and staff support Race for the Cure every year, along with their students. The entire faculty and student body have taken on Race for the Cure as a school mission. And at a recent musical performance of *Grease*, our students, directors, and community all pitched in to make it a huge success. The Mooresville High School head football coach gave a cameo performance with some impressive acting, playing a football coach yearning to win, and an assistant principal had her own cameo role with some excellent dancing. Seeing these staff members step up and participate, out of their normal comfort zones, brought cheers from the audience for their "all in" attitude.

Support Staff In

When I was principal of Northfield Elementary in Murfreesboro, Tennessee, I worked with an outstanding custodian, Michael Jennings, a super-hardworking guy. At an academic pep rally in 1989, we called Michael up on stage and presented him with an "attitude pin." Students were generally given these pins as awards. Michael received a standing ovation, with all the kids yelling, "Mr. Jennings! Mr. Jennings!" I think it's safe to say that Northfield was the cleanest school in Tennessee for the rest of the year. When people feel appreciated, they often take their work to a higher level, and when they know they are making a difference in the lives of students, they become important ingredients in the "all in" recipe for success.

ABCD Awards   At our monthly MGSD school board meetings, we present ABCD (Above and Beyond the Call of Duty) awards to maintenance workers, food service workers, bus drivers, custodians, and clerical workers. Nominated by principals, assistant principals, teachers, and central office staff, 20 to 30 individuals are honored each year. We also hold a luncheon for support staff each spring, attended by all school board members and administrators. We recognize individual teamwork and collaboration, along with the outstanding performance of our support staff teams, with special awards.

For example, in April 2012, Chuck LaRusso, East Mooresville Intermediate School assistant principal, nominated a custodian, Dennis Jones, saying,

> "East Mooresville Intermediate School has the extreme good fortune of having terrific support staff. One shining example of this commitment to exceptional work and service is Mr. Dennis Jones. Along with a terrific work ethic and knowledge of the job, Mr. Jones has a keen understanding of leadership and its effect on people and performance. Mr. Jones is just as likely to be found hand-cleaning a spot on a rug or polishing the glass on a clock as he is cleaning the main hallway. He understands that all jobs, big and small, are a reflection on his custodial team and have a direct impact on what happens in the classroom with students and teachers."

ABCD award recipient Dennis Jones with School Board
Chair Karen Hart and myself

We make an effort to help everyone, including students, parents, and the
community, understand the important role that every employee plays every day,
and our students are on board with this thinking. Every year at our high school
graduation ceremony, the student speakers enthusiastically recognize the head
cashier in the Mooresville High School cafeteria, who not only greets every
student personally every day but also knows his or her preferred cookie choice!

A Sense of Accountability   Because they feel valued, our support staff have
stepped up to the plate with a terrific sense of accountability. A huge number of
them are taking their game to the next level. Bus drivers take pride in knowing
our students by name. Custodians are lauded for our incredibly clean schools.
Office staff are proud to be frontline communicators with the public.

Recently, an assistant principal from Alabama commented as we made our way
down the fourth-grade hall at Mooresville Intermediate School that he could not
believe how clean the school was, late in the afternoon on a Friday. He asked me

how old the school was. "It's four years old, but we have a custodial team that's next to none," I replied. "Kathy Everhart, the lead custodian here, is our Custodian of the Year. She's also a great vocalist, and she sang a solo at our convocation this year."

Last year, we had just finished a presentation at Mooresville High School to over 70 guests, and as I was leaving the building, I stopped to thank the custodian, Wayne Robertson, who was mopping up some spilled coffee in the hallway. I shared with him that several guests had commented on how clean the school was, and he said, "These kids know we care about them. They need to have a clean school, and we aim to keep it that way."

Both of these employees are great examples of "all in." Every MGSD employee realizes that he or she is a difference-maker in the lives of our students, and their commitment and positive attitudes have resulted in improved services at all levels. Caring for and recognizing all team members bolsters morale throughout our schools, which translates into a positive impact on students.

Administrators In

Leadership development—a shared task—is always on the agenda at our principals' meetings. Our annual leadership retreat also focuses on learning together, "all in," and following the same guiding star. And we encourage leaders to learn from each other every day. Leadership must recognize the need for help and be willing to ask for and accept it.

Support for Each Other   When Robin Melton was promoted from assistant principal to principal at East Mooresville Intermediate, a school that had lagged behind on digital conversion and dropped slightly in student performance, she immediately asked our accountability director to provide staff development on how to use data and asked our chief technology officer to provide guidance. Mrs. Melton saw the need to seek help and laid out a clear picture for staff: "We're not doing as well as we could, and it's time to step up. We're going to look for help so we can improve." Her decisive leadership and willingness to work with her colleagues toward a common goal led to increased collaboration among teachers, greater use of digital resources, and significant progress in student achievement.

Similarly, we have seen a new level of collaboration between our high school and our tech center, N.F. Woods Advanced Technology & Arts Center, which also houses our Mi-WAYE alternative program for struggling students. Several years ago, the faculty in these two schools barely communicated with each other, although they serve the same students. But when the two principals started demonstrating and cultivating collegiality and teamwork, the department chairs, counselors, and teachers followed suit. Teachers, counselors, and staff in both schools now engage in regular communication and planning. Both groups are "all in," working to share expertise, better address student issues, and give life to our motto *Every Child, Every Day.*

Sandy Fowler, special populations coordinator, always receives support and admiration from her colleagues at Mooresville High School when she talks about her students' progress. "I was so proud of our Mi-WAYE students who attended the community symposium sponsored by the Career Bridge Advisory," she said recently. "We used some of the funds the foundation provided to get new outfits for students who did not own a dress shirt, or a tie, or dress pants. They were so proud of themselves, and they looked so sharp. One young man who is a tough customer even wore his new clothes the next day, and no one gave him any flack about his 'dress duds.'" Her colleagues were "all in" in their support for Sandy's effort to make a difference in the lives of a group of struggling kids.

Administrator "All In" Initiatives   Our executive director of elementary education, Bill Parker, who retired in 2012, started many "all in" initiatives over his last four years with MGSD, creating opportunities for teachers, community members, and others to be part of the "all in" equation. On our MGSD cable access show "School Talk," I shared a few of his initiatives with the audience:

- The Change a Life mentoring program now has 200 active mentors serving MGSD students.
- Career Bridge Advisory is a program in which local business leaders work directly with N.F. Woods Advanced Technology & Arts Center students as supporters and sponsors.
- The Minority Student Law Conference involves eight to 10 MGSD minority students traveling to an intensive week-long law seminar at Southern University.
- Mr. Parker led our systemic effort to close achievement gaps.

Parents and Community In

Parent and community leaders are a major part of our momentum and provide tremendous support for our work. Our teacher and parent advisory committees foster a sense of team spirit, and community and business leaders work closely with principals and teachers—via the Mooresville Education Foundation; parent/ teacher organizations; and band, choral, and athletic booster clubs—to boost morale and provide financial and organizational support.

Listen to parent Lisa Gill talk about the importance of parental involvement in the digital age.

As active members of MGSD affiliate organizations, these individuals share their time and talents on an ongoing basis and play a huge part in our success. They organize events, raise money, and provide leadership for our education foundation, career and technical advisory committee, and other support groups.

Tanae McLean, MGSD public information officer, often helps coordinate the work of community groups and participates in the planning and implementation of events. Tanae has helped organize events in partnership with the Mooresville Christian Mission and the Williamson Chapel West Methodist Church, whose Back-to-School Bash provides hundreds of students with an array of services and goods from haircuts to shoes. Many teachers and staff also jump in to assist at community service events.

PARENT FEEDBACK   *"The laptops have helped to create a true community of parents, administrators, teachers, and students. It is the future, and the future is now in our town."*

—MGSD parent

At our January 2012 school board meeting, several members of the Mooresville Education Foundation spoke about a small property tax increase that Chief Financial Officer Terry Haas and I proposed in light of the additional cuts in state funding. "We recognize that the economy is tough, but we as a community must stand together to support our children," said George Brawley, foundation member and retired bank president, who expressed his appreciation for the wise use of funds in the district.

Kirk Ballard, the CEO of the Mooresville South Iredell Chamber of Commerce, also supported the measure and recognized the achievement of the district. These comments led to a vote in support of the tax increase. Public support from community leaders in making difficult decisions in tough financial times is a good example of the "all in" attitude we have experienced in our community.

Feedback on programs and policies is valuable, but nothing is more important than a sense of "we're in this together," where parents and community members become part of the synergy, part of the "all in" culture. When they step up to provide support, it sends a powerful message to students, teachers, and all employees.

"All In" Success Factors

At one of our principals' meetings, Mark Cottone, principal of Park View Elementary, told the group, "Our specialist teachers—art, music, PE, media specialist, and tech facilitator—are taking on small-group tutoring, beyond their normal responsibilities, to focus on some immediate needs as quickly as possible. Our media specialist and I were talking about it, and everyone else jumped on board."

Several factors come together to create a culture of "all in," in which individuals and teams consistently strive to pull together and pitch in to do the best job possible. Every school, department, grade level, and work group is responsible for making sure these factors are in place:

- Clear goals and expectations for individuals and teams
- "Signposts"
- Mutual respect
- Mutual support in day-to-day work
- Fairness
- Open communication
- Teamwork and collaboration
- Willingness to work through tough situations
- Ability to construct pathways for success
- Commitment to problem solving
- Strong work ethic
- Flexibility and understanding
- Modeling
- Team spirit

Signposts

Chip Heath and Dan Heath, in *Switch: How to Change Things When Change Is Hard,* write about the need to highlight individuals, teams, and successes as a way to demonstrate what needs to be done. To support the "all in" philosophy, we at MGSD talk about "signposts" as examples of excellence, initiative, effort, sharing, and caring. These signposts—people, teams, or programs—are cultural indicators that point us in the right direction and illustrate the type of behavior and leadership we want to see from our employees. Highlighting outstanding efforts, early adopters, and an emerging commitment to "all in" created signposts at MGSD that helped illuminate the path and the potential ahead for everyone.

Many transformational teachers function as signposts, leading the way for others. We recognize them by means of our Teacher of the Year and Beginning Teacher of the Year awards and by selecting them to serve on interview committees, as grade-level and departmental leaders, and to lead professional development sessions. The veteran teachers who stood out in the first months of digital conversion in terms of attitude, effort, and personal change management were also signposts, showing their colleagues by personal example how to navigate serious change in pedagogical methods and accountability.

I recall that three years ago, we fell short of our goals and expectations at one school. A new process regarding a particular section of the curriculum was challenging for some teachers, and student performance varied significantly from class to class. "We have to be more directive, if necessary, to make sure we all get the job done," said Sharon Markofski, the department chair. The next year, everyone followed the game plan and met his or her performance goals. When teacher leaders take a leadership role in working through issues, they are cultural signposts, making clear that the path ahead is for everyone.

Principals and assistant principals are the primary leaders of the "all in" effort. They are purveyors of expectations and support for teachers and students, and they function as signposts for their teams through personal example, guidance, evaluative feedback, professional dialogue, and collaborative planning. District administrators can light the way and push the process forward by acknowledging and highlighting individuals, special effort, and teamwork. The winners of our ABCD awards also function as signposts for the rest of the support team and the school community in general.

One super-signpost that guides us every hour is our motto *Every Child, Every Day*. Fulfilling this vision is a never-ending path, but we talk about our motto at almost every meeting in order to keep the vision front and center at all times. The result of this constant focus is that over time, most teachers and staff members have become living signposts.

Modeling by Principals

Our principals model the "all in" concept in their daily work with teachers and students, team spirit, and convictions. If you walk through any MGSD school with

PD [◉] TOOLKIT™

Listen to three principals discuss how their roles and viewpoints have changed in the digital conversion initiative.

any principal, you will see students waving to principals, talking to them, asking for help, and smiling. It's clear that students know the principal and the principal knows them. Our principals know the names of hundreds of students—which is one of their most important responsibilities, in my view. The *Project RED* research study of almost 1,000 schools supports our belief in the importance of modeling by principals:

> "The principal's ability to lead change is critical. Change must be modeled and championed at the top. *Project RED* analysis shows that within the school, the principal is one of the most important variables across education success measures."

One result of this modeling is that our teachers have grown in their ability to care for each student and take personal responsibility for his or her achievement. This has led to an increase in our overall rates of job satisfaction, teacher self-confidence, and academic success. Every MGSD principal leads by example, with vigorous involvement in classrooms, hallways, and events, clearly illustrating for all to see that we need to focus on every child and believe that we can improve with daily effort.

Modeling by Teachers

When students put their hearts into their work, caring, and taking responsibility for their learning, they are frequently responding to the role model in front of them. I have often observed that students seem to have an innate awareness regarding the authenticity of the care that teachers offer. I have also noted that teachers who truly care about their students usually receive it back two- or three-fold. We all need and want to be cared for, to be looked out for, to be respected and appreciated— children especially so. When students receive caring, appreciation, and respect from their teachers, they copy this behavior as a matter of consequence.

When our teachers jumped into the digital conversion initiative, despite some fear and uneasiness, students saw them as role models. Teachers and students together developed a mutual sense of discovery, pioneering, and destiny, and the resulting "all in" synergy and momentum have become a source of power every day.

Countering the Counterproductive

In our schools, teacher leaders and administrators take collective responsibility for dealing with recalcitrant or underperforming colleagues. "Don't put up with it!" is the mantra. They challenge the negaholics and don't let them mess up the positive energy. They address counterproductive tendencies and any "glass half empty" responses to daily challenges. Their collective energy and influence has created a positive sense of belief and determination that can be felt by every student.

At a Mooresville Intermediate School information meeting, one of our fifth-grade teachers, Jody Cohen, put the topic of negativity squarely on the table for discussion. "We have to pitch in to beat back the inclination to get into a whine party," she said. "Over time, we all know what it takes to get the job done, and we're going to do it, so we don't have time for any negative stuff."

Team Spirit

When the "all in" key factors are in place, we have seen great team spirit develop—a huge factor in the success of our digital conversion effort and one that visitors often comment on. Team spirit manifests itself when people help others, even if it is not part of their job, when teams solve problems that require sacrifice and change, when people and teams cheer each other on, when allegiances are strong, and when collaboration moves every team to improve its performance.

As in many other school districts and other organizations, at MGSD it can be difficult to build and maintain team spirit, mutual caring, and collective commitment. Change is always a work in progress. However, districts and schools that persevere, working on an "all in" culture every day, have a distinct advantage over those that do not.

Respect and Communication

The impact on our "all in" culture of how we treat each other every day cannot be overstated. Showing respect and support for all employees, by recognizing their work, who they are as individuals, and the challenges they face, is a foundational element of our culture. We want everyone to know that they matter and can make a difference. Communicating with all employees about expectations, which also includes listening, creates a flow of team focus and builds strong cultural foundations that stand us in good stead when challenges come up, as they always do.

Problem Solving with Flexible Teamwork

You really find out what kind of team you have when you hit bumps in the road, and leaders often emerge during tough times. Back in Henrico County in 2001, during the most challenging phase of our massive one-to-one laptop initiative for 26,000 students, the assistant superintendent for instruction, Dr. Vicki Wilson, was relentlessly positive about overcoming the obstacles. "We're going to need everyone to be flexible and show great teamwork as we work through this," she explained to our principals when we had to take back all the laptops mid-year to address hardware, software, and networking problems. The Henrico team, led by Dr. Wilson, responded with teamwork and perseverance. Similarly, the MGSD team has risen to the occasion many times, to the benefit of students, with dedication to student achievement and an "all in" attitude.

"All In" in Action

Jean Millsaps, my administrative assistant, stood in the doorway of my office and told me she had a call on line one from a parent who wanted to share some good news. "Well, that's always a fun call to take," I replied. A parent had called to say that his son, who has some special learning needs, had passed the retest of the third-grade reading end-of-quarter exam after some focused tutorial support from the Rocky River Elementary third-grade chair, Jemma Conley. "Mrs. Conley gave him the extra tutoring help and also let him know how much she believed in him," he said. "She even came in when she wasn't feeling well because she knew he was counting on her. I want you to know how much that means to me and my wife and our son!"

We have many great examples of "all in" in action, where employees have gone above and beyond the call of duty, but here a few that have had district-wide impact on our work and our students.

The Change a Life Mentoring Program

When I signed up for the MGSD Change a Life mentoring program, Bill Parker, then executive director of secondary education, told me, "Doc, you'll get far more out of this than the student will." And he was right. Bill took the initiative for this program and managed recruitment, training, assignments, marketing, and budgeting, with the support of a few other volunteers.

Bill Parker grew up in southeastern Washington, DC, in a challenging environment, and he has always had a special relationship with students in need. He saw the mentoring program as a way to reach a little further to help them. We believe that the Change a Life program is a key component of our dropout prevention strategy and that when we give students personal care and attention, everyone benefits—both students and mentors.

By the end of the first year, Bill and his team had recruited and trained more than 50 volunteer mentors, who were working with students from every MGSD school. By the end of the second year, the number of mentors had grown to over 100, and now we have around 200 volunteers. Mentors include teachers, coaches, teacher assistants, maintenance staff, custodians, bus drivers, clerical staff, local business owners, clergy, and Mooresville Police Chief Carl Robbins.

According to the *Mentoring Makes a Difference* survey, eight out of 10 young people in mentoring relationships have one or more challenges that can jeopardize their success in the areas of school, health, or development. The survey reported that the most prevalent problems facing these young people are negative feelings about themselves, poor relationships with family members, poor grades, hanging out with the wrong crowd, and getting into trouble at school. The Change a Life program was developed to address these issues, with positive, caring adults taking the time and taking an interest in the lives of young people at risk.

Goals of the Change a Life Mentoring Program

- Build one-to-one caring, supportive relationships between adults and students, based on trust.

- Support students in structured mentoring programs to help them become successful academically, personally, and socially.

- Focus on the needs of the young people and encourage them to develop to their fullest potential, based on their own vision for the future.

- Strive for early intervention.

- Seek support from the business community, faith-based organizations, social agencies, service institutions, and schools.

Technical Crisis Management

One night around 8 PM, our chief technology officer, Dr. Scott Smith, sent me a text: "Give me a call asap, we may have a major prob." I called him back right way, and he explained that our antivirus software had malfunctioned and was now working like a virus, causing our laptops to shut down and malfunction to such an extent that our machines were inoperable. "We're not sure yet, but probably hundreds of machines are affected, and we don't have a fix, though we're working on it," said Scott.

This was on a Wednesday evening. By the next morning, Scott and his tech team of eight people had worked through the night, talking to technical support staff from the antivirus software company in India and finally finding a fix around 5 AM. I went by the tech office early that morning, where a tired, bleary-eyed team was eating some breakfast biscuits delivered by a sympathetic spouse. Scott Smith gave an update: "Well, we found a fix that we're testing now. If it works, we're going to have to collect all the machines and work the fix, which we can do in about 15 to 20 minutes per machine. We're talking about probably 1,500 to 2,000 machines, and we'll need to coordinate with students and staff to collect them."

Public Information Officer Tanae McLean and I spoke to the editor of the local newspaper and gave him a straight-up review of events and the potential disruption. The headline in the paper on Friday morning was accurate but alarming: "Software Problem Causes 700 Laptops to Crash." We began collecting the affected machines and transporting them to the tech office. Scott called to tell me that the tech team and other volunteers would work on Saturday and Sunday and try to get most of the machines back online and returned by Monday.

Tanae used our automated phone messaging system to let parents know what to expect. Principals worked with teachers to adjust assignments, since hundreds of students would not have their laptops. On Saturday morning, Scott sent me a text: "We have all tech team here and around 20 volunteers—teachers, tech facilitators, and principals—and we're making progress. MGSD rocks!"

They worked all day Saturday and Sunday, well into the evenings, and on Monday morning the laptops were distributed back to students and staff. The newspaper reported, "Laptop Glitch Fixed." Dr. Scott Smith, his tech team, and our volunteers went way beyond the call of duty and pulled together in a very challenging situation to meet the needs of students, demonstrating the level of "all in" commitment of some often-unsung heroes, our tech team.

STUDENT FEEDBACK   *"You just need your laptop. It makes the book bag lighter. It means our school district really cares about us. They trust us. We each get one. They care about each one of us."*

—Mooresville Middle School student

Forty Years of Enthusiastic Teaching

Carol Caroll, who served as the director of elementary education and federal programs at MGSD for 40 years, until her retirement in 2012, was a constant signpost and model of our "all in" philosophy. In her 36th year of teaching, Carol provided outstanding leadership in the early phases of our digital conversion initiative and beyond. She set the goal of over 90 percent proficiency in math and reading for elementary students, she personally supported a teacher who had a particularly challenging class, and she was the first person to volunteer to sing in the convocation choir.

Carol worked with the energy of a first-year teacher. She laughed together with others at our ups and downs and was thoroughly committed to every student and a model for the "all in" work ethic. We have many outstanding leaders at MGSD, but it was particularly impressive to see our most senior leader and educator become the premier role model for "all in."

On a recent visit to Park View Elementary School, the principal, Mark Cottone, and I both experienced and influenced the "all in" culture as we walked around the school. We thanked each teacher and acknowledged students and their work. We laughed with teachers and students in several classrooms, and I spoke about how lucky we are to have such fine teachers, for all to hear. We chatted with two custodians and complimented them on their work. We went into the kitchen and thanked the food service staff, shaking hands and exchanging small talk. When principals and administrators are out and about, connecting with everyone in their schools, they are fostering and supporting the "all in" culture.

REFLECTIVE QUESTIONS

1. How do you communicate that everyone counts?
2. How do you model desired attitudes?
3. Do your employees go above and beyond?
4. Do your support staff members feel like part of the team?
5. How do you manage counterproductive attitudes?

REFERENCES

Barth, Roland S. (1990). *Improving Schools from Within: Teachers, Parents, and Principals Can Make the Difference.* San Francisco, CA: Jossey-Bass.

Greaves, T., Hayes, J., Wilson, L., Gielniak, M., & Peterson, R. (2010). *Project RED, The Technology Factor: Nine Keys to Student Achievement and Cost-Effectiveness.* Sheldon, CT: MDR.

Heath, Chip, & Heath, Dan. (2010). *Switch: How to Change Things When Change Is Hard.* New York, NY: Broadway Books.

McLearn, Kathryn Taaffe, Colasanto, Diane, & Schoen, Cathy. (1988). *Mentoring Makes a Difference: Findings from The Commonwealth Fund 1998 Survey of Adults Mentoring Young People.* Washington, DC: The Commonwealth Fund.

Ruddick, J., Day, J., & Wallace, G. (1997). "Students' Perspectives on School Improvement," in Hargreaves, A., ed., *Rethinking Educational Change with Heart and Mind.* Alexandria, VA: Association for Supervision and Curriculum Development.

Chapter Ten

Replication and Sustainability

"Success in a digital conversion initiative always results from the confluence of many factors that create a whole greater than the sum of the parts."

Matt Aiken, superintendent of Piedmont City Schools in Piedmont, Alabama, commented in a note to me, "I believe that the model MGSD has created with their digital conversion and mentoring of other districts should be expanded and that this work could be instrumental in transforming public education in the United States."

Since 2008, MGSD has hosted hundreds of visitors from around the country, including teachers, principals, superintendents, journalists, researchers, school board members, and officials from state departments of education and the U.S. Department of Education—most of whom come to learn about our digital conversion initiative and determine whether they can replicate it.

Initially, many schools and districts fear that the cost of digital conversion may be an impassable roadblock. But when they learn that we are a working-class community and not particularly well funded—100th out of 115 school districts in the state—digital conversion starts to look a lot more doable.

Many visitors tell us that they want to move forward, many have embarked on their own digital conversion initiatives, and many are seeing success. In February 2012, *School Administrator* magazine featured several districts that are using the MGSD digital conversion model for planning purposes, including Piedmont, Alabama; Owensboro, Kentucky; Menden, Illinois; Baldwin County, Alabama; and Jerseyville, Illinois. A dozen North Carolina districts have moved forward with digital conversion after visiting MGSD, and several are closely modeling their program after ours.

In addition, organizations such as *Project RED* and publishers such as Pearson are working with school districts nationwide to help replicate MGSD success factors like personalized learning, new instructional practices, and building a technological infrastructure.

Levin and Schrum, in *Leading Technology-Rich Schools: Award-Winning Models of Success*, said,

> "There are many lessons that can be learned from the digital conversion in MGSD that are valuable for other schools and districts, large or small, and these lessons seem especially valuable because they are based on over three years' experience with a one-to-one initiative."

Digital Conversion Critical Success Factors

Educators who visit our schools see for themselves that digital conversion involves far more than technology, although technology is an essential piece of the puzzle. I always tell our visitors they can do it, too. With a firm belief in themselves and their students, districts can accomplish great things and begin to impact the national epidemic of diminished expectations.

Districts may embark on digital conversion at different points and may move differently through the various stages. But I believe that success in a digital conversion initiative always results from the confluence of many factors that create a whole greater than the sum of the parts. Neglect of any one factor seriously diminishes the chances of success.

FIGURE 10.1

Digital Conversion Critical Success Factors

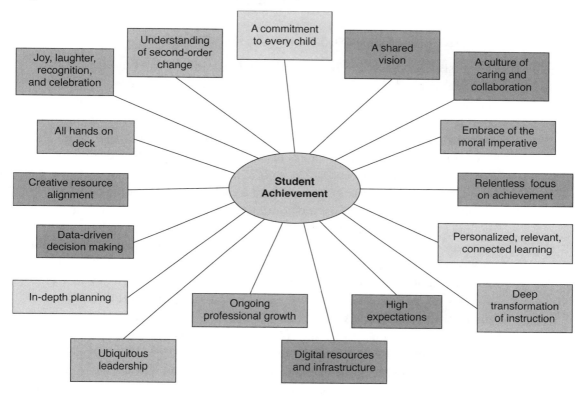

Digital Conversion Checklists

The Steps to Success checklists in this chapter summarize the key factors districts must understand and commit to in order to replicate digital conversion successfully and sustain it over time. The checklists are provided both for initial planning purposes, to help districts get started, and as an ongoing reference tool, to help districts keep the success factors front and center.

Digital conversion is not a short-term fix. It is an ongoing process in which student improvement grows over time, supported by sustained commitment, gradual improvement in practice, and learning together as a team. According to Dr. Steven Webb, superintendent of the Vancouver (Washington) Public Schools, his district is working in a similar vein, gradually developing a new instructional approach: "The lessons learned in Mooresville are helping to shape our district's theory of action as we implement a vision for 21st-century flexible learning environments."

Facilitate Discussion among Stakeholders

The first step in successfully replicating and sustaining digital conversion is to embark on a widespread program of discussion to build understanding and support. If districts are unwilling to invest the time in conversation, dialogue, and debate, the likelihood of success is small. Rushing into a challenging transformational endeavor such as digital conversion does not make sense. Investing time and energy in building community and system-wide buy-in will pay big dividends in the end.

Underlying the discussion must be the recognition that different people develop their understanding and commitment at different rates and that pulling everyone in is challenging and takes time. Digital conversion is highly complex, with huge across-the-board change implications, and it requires input and commitment from all stakeholders—students, teachers, parents, staff, administrators, the school board, and the community. As Frank Florence, senior director for education marketing at Cisco Systems and an expert on change management in schools, commented in a 2012 *School Administrator* article, "It's more than just hardware and software. It's about getting students, parents, staff, the community involved and invested."

Leaders must keep the dialogue open, listen to all points of view, and move toward collaboration as the goal. They must also bear in mind that first impressions are lasting impressions and that initial communications and responses to questions and problems will be very influential over the long haul.

PD TOOLKIT™

Listen to the author discuss the importance of community and parent involvement.

Discussion Steps to Success

- ❏ Hold community meetings on an ongoing basis.
- ❏ Engage with elected and civic leaders and enlist support.
- ❏ Set up school and district meetings on an ongoing basis.
- ❏ Explain the digital conversion concept to all audiences.
- ❏ Outline major steps and major benefits.
- ❏ Continually spread understanding of second-order change.
- ❏ Explain to employees, parents, and students their role in supporting learning.

❏ Post information online.

❏ Issue a news release and build media relationships.

❏ Use parent, teacher, and student advisory committees.

❏ Keep community organizations in the loop.

❏ Take advantage of email and phone messaging opportunities.

❏ Provide ongoing progress updates at school board meetings.

❏ When you hit a bump in the road, be transparent and solve problems together.

Read and Learn Together

Our leadership team has read and discussed many thought-provoking books together, and I highly recommend this practice to other districts as a productive catalyst for change. We can learn much from innovative thinking both inside and outside of education, and it is important to look for inspiration beyond the boundaries of our own schools and districts, to inform the dialogue and spark creative solutions. Books that focus on organizational change, innovation, moral imperative, and instructional improvement offer good places to start.

At MGSD, I have selected books on occasion, and other books have been selected by our leadership team or recommended by colleagues around the country. We have stretched ourselves with authors such as Malcolm Gladwell and John Medina, who have challenged us to think in societal and psychological terms. We distribute books to all district administrators in early summer so that, in our Summer Leadership Meeting, different administrators can lead a Socratic seminar on the new material, incorporating highly participatory activities.

We take this opportunity very seriously and expect everyone to engage as we work on learning together. Throughout the year, we refer back to the books we have read. We have also used book studies and a similar process in our teacher leader seminars, and we generally refer to a book over the course of a year as a point of reference for dialogue and collaborative learning.

Reading and Learning Steps to Success

❏ Start with a book that will stimulate dialogue and that has implications for change.

❏ Use this book and other books on the recommended reading list in this chapter as discussion tools in team meetings.

❏ Provide copies to the leadership team in advance of meeting.

❏ Assign different people to lead the discussion on different occasions.

❏ Allow several weeks to ensure that everyone has ample time to read each book.

❏ List and plan practical steps that arise from your discussion.

❏ Pass on reading suggestions to other staff.

❏ Begin to incorporate the new knowledge into everyday practice.

❏ Share the stories.

Develop Awareness and Motivation

The opportunity to see digital conversion in action can be very helpful in building awareness and motivation. Many of our visiting districts take a strategic approach to their visit, using it as an opportunity to foster courage and commitment among the reluctant and to develop early adopters and leaders. While acknowledging that each team member will come on board at his or her own pace, it is also essential to build excitement and momentum around the need for change.

Allen Lee, superintendent of Baldwin County Schools in Baldwin, Alabama, told us, "We've used the visits to MGSD to inspire and motivate our team. We've left knowing we can do the same kind of work." Judy Kapellen, coordinator of instructional technology in the Sheboygan Area School District in Wisconsin, said, "Our teachers kept asking us what does this new model look like, and now we've seen how the use of data, digital resources, and a team focus on caring can make a huge difference."

Awareness and Motivation Steps to Success

❏ Schedule a visit to MGSD or one of the many districts that have embarked on digital conversion.

❏ Celebrate first steps at faculty meetings.

❏ Acknowledge progress and efforts to learn.

❏ Use digital tools such as email and voice messaging to provide encouragement.

❏ Engage teacher leaders to support others.

❏ Ask parents and community members to support the change effort.

❏ Try to anticipate problems and work on solving them together.

FIGURE 10.2

Recommended Reading

Barth, Roland S. (2001). *Learning by Heart*. San Francisco, CA: Jossey-Bass.

Barth, Roland S. (1990). *Improving Schools from Within: Teachers, Parents, and Principals Can Make the Difference*. San Francisco, CA: Jossey-Bass.

Bolman, Lee G., & Deal, Terrence E. (2011). *Leading with Soul: An Uncommon Journey of Spirit*. San Francisco, CA: Jossey-Bass.

De Pree, Max. (1990). *Leadership Is an Art*. New York, NY: Dell.

Edmonds, Ronald. (1982). "Effective School Research." *Educational Leadership, 40*, 4–11.

Fullan, Michael. (2010). *All Systems Go: The Change Imperative for Whole System Reform*. Thousand Oaks, CA: Corwin.

Fullan, Michael. (2008). *The Six Secrets of Change: What the Best Leaders Do to Help Their Organizations Survive and Thrive*. San Francisco, CA: Jossey-Bass.

Fullan, Michael. (1993). *Change Forces: Probing the Depth of Educational Reform*. Bristol, PA: Falmer Press.

Gladwell, Malcolm. (2008). *Outliers: The Story of Success*. New York, NY: Little Brown.

Greaves, T., Hayes, J., Wilson, L., Gielniak, M., & Peterson, R. (2010). *Project RED, The Technology Factor: Nine Keys to Student Achievement and Cost-Effectiveness*. Sheldon, CT: MDR.

Heath, Chip, & Heath, Dan. (2010). *Switch: How to Change Things When Change Is Hard*. New York, NY: Broadway Books.

LaFee, Scott. (February 2012). "The Affordability Question." *School Administrator*, Volume 69, Number 2,.

Lambert, L. (1998). *Building Leadership Capacity in Schools*. Alexandria, VA: Association for Supervision and Curriculum Development.

Levin, B. B., & Schrum, L. (2012). *Leading Technology-Rich Schools: Award-Winning Models for Success*. New York, NY: Teachers College Press.

Medina, John. (2008). *Brain Rules: 12 Principles for Surviving and Thriving at Work, Home, and School*. Seattle, WA: Pear Press.

Pink, Daniel H. (2009). *Drive: The Surprising Truth about What Motivates Us*. New York, NY: Riverhead Books.

Thomas, D., & Brown, J. S. (2011). *A New Culture of Learning: Cultivating the Imagination for a World of Constant Change*. Lexington, KY: CreateSpace.

Tomlinson, Carol Ann, & Allan, Susan Demirsky. (2000). *Leadership for Differentiating Schools and Classrooms*. Alexandria, VA: Association for Supervision and Curriculum Development.

Wagner, Tony. (2008). *The Global Achievement Gap: Why Even Our Best Schools Don't Teach the New Survival Skills Our Children Need—And What We Can Do about It*. New York, NY: Basic Books.

Wheatley, Margaret. (2006). *Leadership and the New Science. Discovering Order in a Chaotic World*. San Francisco, CA: Berrett-Koehler.

Plan, Plan, and Plan Again

Comprehensive plans provide the bandwidth for organic change and the dynamics for implementation. They serve as living blueprints. Our planning effort positively embraced change, as described by Thomas and Brown in *A New Culture of Learning:*

> "Embracing change means looking forward to what will come next. It means viewing the future as a set of new possibilities rather than something that forces us to adjust."

Our central planning team, which included 12 or 14 people from all areas—instruction, technology, operations, communications, finance, and sometimes service partners—met every week for the first two years of digital conversion, after which we rolled the planning process into a monthly meeting and then into our regular principal meetings. We mirrored much of the planning process with individual school teams to ensure broad-based understanding, shared commitment for the work ahead, and support for the evolving instructional program. The planning process is ongoing, and we still include digital conversion reports and discussion in all meetings—school board, principals, faculty, department and grade level, parent advisory, teacher advisory, Education Foundation, and other meetings.

To ensure that change is always grounded in priorities, we have measured our progress against a list of ongoing reference points ever since the early days:

- Shared vision
- Moral imperative
- Impact on student achievement
- Preparation for today's workplace
- Instructional quality
- Equity and opportunity
- Communication
- Change management

Planning Steps to Success

- ❏ Define the members of your central district planning team and your school planning teams.
- ❏ Define your goals and remember that student achievement must be goal number one.
- ❏ Take a long-term view.
- ❏ Plan your technical infrastructure, including hardware devices, bandwidth, connectivity, deployment, security, and technical support.
- ❏ Invite service partners to present to the team.
- ❏ Select a pilot site.
- ❏ Plan your laptop rollout.
- ❏ Plan for capacity building, with models for coaching and mentoring.
- ❏ Adjust the instructional program based on digital resources.
- ❏ Plan for budget needs.
- ❏ Plan for facilities needs.
- ❏ Develop a communication plan.
- ❏ Embrace and promote the idea of change.
- ❏ Constantly evaluate against reference points.
- ❏ Use feedback loops to adjust and change as needed.

Build a Shared Vision

A shared vision is the foundation that holds together a team, and implementing the vision together ensures a consistent direction. In *Leadership and the New Science,* Margaret Wheatley writes:

> "In a field view of organizations, clarity about values or vision is important, but it is only half the task. Creating the field through the dissemination of those ideas is essential. The dialogue must reach all corners of the organization and involve everyone. Vision statements come off the walls and come alive in classrooms and hallways and provide a shared path for growth."

Vision Building Steps to Success

- ❏ Discuss with all stakeholders why digital conversion is the right thing to do.
- ❏ Identify the needs of at-risk and special needs students and English learners.
- ❏ Develop your moral imperative and use it to drive the discussion.
- ❏ Create a shared vision statement.
- ❏ Connect the vision to goals, benchmarks, resources, and roles.
- ❏ Evaluate all programs and activities against the vision.
- ❏ Work to bring programs and activities into alignment with the vision.
- ❏ Expect constant innovation, exploration, new ideas, and new opportunities.
- ❏ Be prepared for ongoing learning and adjustment.

Ensure a Supportive Culture

Almost without fail, visitors to MGSD leave talking about our culture of caring and our focus on every child every day, which have been key to our

Kindergarten class at South Elementary School

improved student performance—with far deeper impact than laptops or online content alone.

Many districts are taking the caring and "all in" philosophy to heart and adapting it to their own situations. After visiting MGSD, Ed Settles, superintendent of the Jersey Community School District in Jerseyville, Illinois, commented in a *School Administrator* article in 2012, "[Our digital conversion] is truly a community project, not simply a district initiative. I have stressed to our board that we must be 'all in' and dedicate the resources necessary to initiate and maintain the conversion."

Cultural Steps to Success

❏ Evaluate your current culture.

❏ Focus on every child every day.

❏ Promote a culture that cares for every teacher, student, and staff member.

❏ Emphasize the importance of collaboration to get the job done—in teacher evaluations, student activities, and daily work.

❏ Provide staff development on how to care for students.

❏ Develop a strategy for dealing with "negaholics."

❏ Develop practical ways to express gratitude and show recognition, such as awards and celebrations.

❏ Explain and promote the "all in" concept.

❏ Emphasize accountability across the board.

❏ Hold all team members accountable to the standards, the beliefs, the commitment, and the goal of every child every day.

Align Resources

Digital conversion is surprisingly affordable with budgeting strategies that focus on prioritizing and repurposing rather than finding new or more monies. We made digital conversion the priority for instructional spending because we could not afford a parallel program with textbooks. Out of the hundreds of school districts that have visited MGSD, only a few have smaller budgets than we do. This means that digital conversion is within the reach of all.

Resource Alignment Steps to Success

❏ Establish priorities.

❏ Evaluate repurposing options, including staff positions, physical space, and instructional materials.

❏ Repurpose old computer labs as classrooms to avoid the cost of new construction.

❏ Train students to provide help desk support.

❏ Free up textbook funds to purchase online content.

❏ Redefine librarian and lab tech roles.

Focus on Student Achievement

The public will support digital conversion as long as there is a return on the investment, and student achievement is how that return is determined. Strategic plans, school improvement plans, teacher and staff evaluations, policies, practices, and resources must all be tightly connected to annual goals for student improvement. With widespread agreement about focus

Students working on a lab at Mooresville High School

and expectations, a synergistic momentum will support the goals and move efforts forward. When everyone is rowing in the same direction, the boat will move faster.

Aaron Spence, formerly my colleague in Henrico County and now the superintendent of Moore County Schools in North Carolina, is implementing many of our steps to student success. "In my district, we are committed to closing achievement gaps and getting our students future-ready," said Aaron. "My experiences with one-to-one computing tell me that we must focus on these technologies and embed planning and data tools for diagnosis and engagement tools for learning into our work as educators."

Achievement Steps to Success

- ❏ Consistently communicate that improved academic performance is the goal of digital conversion.
- ❏ Evaluate all programs and activities in light of this goal.
- ❏ Define daily expectations for students, teachers, and staff.
- ❏ Engage teachers in mapping out their daily work and how they will work together.
- ❏ Use formative assessments to drive instructional planning.
- ❏ Align plans and policies with student achievement goals.
- ❏ Incorporate individual student data into daily instructional planning.
- ❏ Use a variety of measures to evaluate progress, including graduation rate, state assessments, AP and honors participation, and scholarships.

Foster Leadership

Leaders at all levels are essential to digital conversion success. A top-down approach will not build the necessary buy-in and teamwork. John Tate, of the North Carolina State Board of Education, commented after a visit to MGSD, "You have leaders who do not hesitate to step up. Your grade level and department chairs articulate the work going on and how it connects technology, student achievement, and caring." MGSD has developed a distributed leadership approach in which we recognize, develop, and utilize leaders at all schools and in every aspect of the work of the district.

Leadership Steps to Success

❏ Select teacher and department leaders based on their commitment to the vision, goals, and leadership potential.

❏ Develop leaders at every school.

❏ Develop leaders in every department

❏ Develop leaders in every grade level.

❏ Develop leaders among administrators and staff.

❏ Make sure that central office administrators vigorously embrace a service model.

❏ Encourage parent and community leaders to be "all in" and enlist their input.

Establish the Digital Infrastructure

PD ❿ TOOLKIT™

Listen to the author discuss infrastructure decisions.

Many districts expand their technical capacity after visiting MGSD. Steve Murley, superintendent of the Iowa City Community School District, sent me the following report:

> "I returned to our district with a sense of urgency to augment the digital learning platform necessary to begin the transition to a new framework for teaching and learning. We have embarked on an ambitious plan to install fiber in every school this summer, increase our bandwidth so that our teachers and students have unlimited access to digital resources, and provide the hardware necessary for a 21st-century classroom for every student. Seeing the work in progress throughout Mooresville helped me to better visualize what a difference a 21st-century digital learning environment can mean to students and teachers."

Infrastructure Steps to Success

❏ Select a pilot site and initiate a pilot program.

❏ Select and distribute teacher laptops.

❏ Select student laptops.

❏ Plan a staged laptop rollout.

❏ Develop financial support programs for low-income students.

❏ Build a robust wireless infrastructure with an eye to future needs.

❏ Evaluate cloud computing options.

❏ Develop software evaluation criteria and select online content and tools.

❏ Select and implement a learning management system.

❏ Build a library of multimedia tools.

❏ Develop policies for social networking and required use.

❏ Plan for training, staffing, and support.

Build Capacity

We have embraced the concept that, as digital conversion evolves, we must grow our capacity—meaning our ability to use digital resources and work as individuals and teams to meet goals. Every school leader must be vigilant in ensuring that individuals and teams constantly reflect on how to improve the success of every student. Gary Marx, author and vice president of the Horace Mann League, has commented on our systemic approach to capacity building as follows,

> "Everyone at MGSD, and I mean literally everyone, seems to share in the mission and vision of *Every Child Every Day*, so you see this pervasive effort by teachers, administrators, support staff, and even students to raise their game on a continuous basis."

Capacity Building Steps to Success

❏ Commit to a philosophy of individual and team learning for all adults.

❏ Take the long view and accept different rates of growth.

❏ Develop formal growth plans for teachers and principals.

❏ Encourage students and teachers to learn together.

❏ Expect steady progress and constant effort.

❏ Provide constant encouragement, feedback, and leadership.

❏ Establish meetings to build teams at all levels.

❏ Define professional development goals.

❏ Build a strong program of professional development pathways.

❏ Re-evaluate policies for new hires.

❏ Foster personal reflection to support individual growth.

Implement Data-Driven Personalized Instruction

As we have progressed in our ability to use personalized student information as part of our daily instructional methodology, our teachers have developed a new view of classroom teaching. They now see students and their needs with greater clarity and have the means to make adjustments, to advance or review, based on real-time data.

At the CoSN Conference for Leadership Transformation, hosted by MGSD in October 2012, several guests commented that when MGSD students take online formative assessments, reports are available immediately for students and teachers to use. Real-time data has made the instructional process much more nimble, propelling us toward second-order change. We are now using data in ways that were absolutely impossible in the old world.

Data Steps to Success

❏ Transition to online instructional software that provides detailed data on every student.

❏ Work toward a culture of data transparency.

❏ Systematically align student data with instructional planning.

❏ Assess achievement by students, subgroup, teacher, department, grade level, and school.

❏ Use the data to enable accurate, personalized interventions on a daily basis.

❏ Encourage a team approach among instructional staff.

❏ Use data to inform resource allocation decisions.

❏ Keep parents and students in the data loop.

Rethink the Instructional Process

Engagement, personalization, efficiency, precision, and fun are all part of a new instructional recipe at MGSD that has resulted in a truly enjoyable experience for teachers and students alike. From the youngest to the oldest, our students have a sense that our new ways of learning, researching, building projects, exploring, and discovering are creating conditions they will thrive in. They are encouraged to be creative and innovative, with digital resources providing the underlying support and structure.

Instructional Steps to Success

- ❏ Develop lesson plans that engage students with relevant, personalized, collaborative, and connected learning.
- ❏ Evaluate new teaching strategies appropriate to a digital learning environment.
- ❏ Develop keys to successful group work.
- ❏ Encourage teachers to become "roaming conductors."
- ❏ Empower students with more choices.
- ❏ Extend the time available for teaching and learning.
- ❏ Provide immediate feedback via formal and informal assessments.
- ❏ Promote responsible digital citizenship.
- ❏ Use digital resources to support struggling students.

Replication Tips for Large Districts

- Start small with a group of 10 pilot schools or less.
- Select schools that are physically close to each other and with staff who are open to change.
- Identify principals who can lead change.
- Build common purpose and vision among those schools.
- Provide comprehensive professional development.
- Implement the replication steps to success in the pilot schools.
- Spread the vision throughout the district in preparation for expansion.
- Expand gradually to additional groups of schools.
- Use experienced "signposts" for new staff members joining the initiative.

Collective Problem Solving

At MGSD, everyone has a voice, and consequently staff members are empowered to step up to increased responsibility when circumstances require. Dr. Larry Vick, superintendent of Owensboro City Schools in Owensboro, Kentucky, commented as follows on our culture of collaborative problem solving:

> "What impacted us most when visiting Mooresville was how they brought everyone to the table when making decisions or solving problems. Their emphasis on instruction supported by technology and collaboration, partnership with service providers, and focus toward a clearly defined vision left a major impression on us. Our replication of their approach set us up for a very successful first year of implementation."

One year, we lost electricity during a major thunderstorm on laptop deployment day at Mooresville Middle School. Principal Felecia Bustle and Chief Technology Officer Scott Smith quickly came up with a modified schedule, designating a window of time later in the week for parents who had not made it to school. When power was restored, they sent out an email, thanking everyone for dealing with the situation in a calm and positive way.

Even though the storm shut down all power, the power of people working together was an energy surge. Teachers, administrators, and tech staff spoke to each parent and student waiting in line and assured them they would get their laptops before school started the following week. A quick team decision to provide additional time later in the week diminished the concerns of families that had already waited their turn to go through the deployment process.

Replicating digital conversion can present early and ongoing challenges, and a major ingredient in success is always the ability to solve problems together. At MGSD, we have hit many bumps in the road—online content not aligned with the courses of study or curriculum, integration issues with software sharing, and start-up emotions. A couple of challenges became serious—for example, when our antivirus software started acting like a virus and shut down several hundred machines at a crucial time and when our state online testing process did not work properly in the early days.

At MGSD, we focus on working through issues with teamwork and communication. During challenging situations, leaders with good problem-solving skills often emerge—skills that are fostered in meetings where collective problem solving is a regular activity. Good problem-solving skills can move committed people through any storm—natural, technological, or otherwise. When the North Carolina state pilot for online testing ran into major problems, our teachers and students took it in stride because our collective leadership modeled a calm "we'll get through this" attitude that stood us in good stead when we ran into difficulties.

Problems are going to happen, and being prepared to face them is a big part of the digital conversion process. Organizational troubleshooting, problem solving on the run, and a resilient can-do disposition are all must-have ingredients that leaders must both demonstrate and expect. Schools and districts must be adaptive organizations, working in an environment that is continuously changing and challenging but that offers wonderful opportunities for student success and professional job satisfaction.

Karen Cator, Director, Office of Educational Technology, with the U.S. Department of Education, wrote to me after a visit to MGSD, "Mooresville has combined stellar leadership, a commitment to developing a collaborative school and district culture, as well as a community that has been involved in the transition. Teachers have been supported in evolving their practice. The development and articulation of this replicable model will serve those who are determined to incorporate elements into their own context."

REFLECTIVE QUESTIONS

1. How are you addressing the critical success factors?

2. How do you ensure a constant focus on student achievement?

3. How are you changing your approach to planning?

4. What ongoing reference points can you use to evaluate progress?

5. What is your strategy for addressing problems?

REFERENCES

Gladwell, Malcolm. (2008). *Outliers: The Story of Success*. New York, NY: Little Brown.

Levin, B. B., & Schrum, L. (2012). *Leading Technology-Rich Schools: Award-Winning Models for Success*. New York, NY: Teachers College Press.

Medina, John. (2008). *Brain Rules: 12 Principles for Surviving and Thriving at Work, Home, and School*. Seattle, WA: Pear Press.

Thomas, D., & Brown, J. S. (2011). *A New Culture of Learning: Cultivating the Imagination for a World of Constant Change*. Lexington, KY: CreateSpace.

Wheatley, Margaret. (2006). *Leadership and the New Science: Discovering Order in a Chaotic World*. San Francisco, CA: Berrett-Koehler.

Epilogue

Schools are at the heart of their communities. Good schools build hope, just as poor schools diminish hope. Good schools are possible in every community, and they help to level the playing field and bring us closer to the dream of equality on which our country was founded. Today, I am more confident than ever before that all schools can achieve the goal of *Every Child, Every Day*. The goal must always be to think of how we would want our own children to be treated in school—namely, with care and attention to them as individuals, and with love. The reward is seeing that a caring environment and the right tools make great things happen for every child every day. It is hard work, and it takes several years to build momentum, but every child is counting on us—and you!

Graduations are very special occasions, and in Mooresville, well over 5,000 family members, friends, and community members turn out to celebrate. In 2012, as the students progressed through the ceremony, I recognized a young man approaching the stage. His mom works for our district, and a teacher assistant was walking with him, but she let go of his hand when he reached the base of the platform. I knew that he was drawing particular attention not only from me but also from others who know him. He has multiple physical disabilities and difficulty controlling his emotions and physical actions. I knew he might start yelling, running, or crying at any moment, but we were all smiling and proud of him.

He stopped a few feet short of the high school principal and looked back at his teacher assistant. She urged him on with a smile, and the principal said, "Come on, Trask, you can do it." At that point I noticed a big burly student stand up and slowly start clapping. Soon others joined him, and in a matter of seconds, the entire Mooresville High School graduating class of 2012 was standing and applauding their fellow student. As he received his diploma, his classmates honored him with a standing ovation.

No other student received this kind of peer honor, not even students who had received huge scholarships. As a tear rolled down my cheek, I knew I had just witnessed a remarkable example of students who were "all in." They knew this boy's journey had been full of hardship, they knew that this day was probably the pinnacle achievement of his life to date, and they demonstrated to all 5,000 attendees the real meaning of *Every Child, Every Day*.

Glossary of Terms

At MGSD, these terms are part of a common language that fosters collaboration and leadership at all levels, with staff united by a common vocabulary. Other districts have told us they are developing a common language of their own. For example, administrators in Baldwin County, Alabama, have coined the term "digital renaissance," to personalize the MGSD concepts and make them their own.

All in   The belief that every adult and every student counts in a major way and is counted on in a major way, leading teachers, administrators, staff, and students to go above and beyond the call of duty as individuals and as teams to meet every student's needs.

Calm urgency   The conviction on the part of students and teachers that they should use their valuable time with a sense of urgency but with a calm demeanor.

Cognition ignition   The student engagement, self-monitoring, and increased responsibility for learning that derive from digital resources and collaborative learning.

Collective leadership   Ubiquitous leadership in all stakeholder groups—students, teachers, principals, assistant principals, central office staff, and service staff—that drives the mission forward, based on the belief that we need leaders at all levels in our schools.

Confluence of connectivity   The constant connection of students and teachers to online resources, each other, and the wider world that results in a vibrant new learning energy.

Emotional intelligence   Attention to the needs and emotional well-being of individuals and teams and to the conditions that foster a culture of social and emotional support.

Evolutional capacity   The evolving ability on the part of teachers and administrators to integrate emerging digital resources into daily instruction, address the changing needs of students, develop new instructional strategies, and improve skills.

Forward-focused leadership   Everyday focus on the progress of individual students, teams, and schools, driven by a firm belief in success despite challenges and setbacks

InfoDynamo   The dynamic infusion of data organized by student, teacher, department, and grade level into the instructional process, to drive personalized learning and tailored intervention on a daily basis.

Leaning in   A physical and symbolic demonstration of student engagement, shown by students leaning forward, participating, listening intently, helping each other, collaborating, giving their best, and monitoring their own learning.

Maximum efficacy   Striving every day and at every opportunity for the greatest possible impact on the progress of every child and every teacher.

Physical teaching   Constant movement around the classroom by the teacher to meet the learning needs of individuals and groups, requiring both physical and emotional stamina and energy (comfortable shoes a must).

Precise intervention   Instructional intervention tailored to each student's individual needs, based on real-time data that allows the teacher to help individuals and assign groups that can change as students progress at different rates.

Productive hum   The sound observed in a classroom when students are using digital resources to work on individual and group projects, while the teacher is leading small groups and collaboration is taking place.

Purposeful engagement   The positive engagement that results from students' interaction with the digital world, tied tightly to instructional goals such as grades, content, courses of study, and individual learning needs.

Reflective advancement   The increased competence and capacity that comes from an individual's thoughtful reflection and self-analysis.

Roaming conductor   A new classroom management role for teachers as they move about the room to orchestrate the activity of their class, supporting both individualized learning and project groups, listening, observing, and engaging as needed.

Teaching from the inside out   Teaching primarily from the middle of the classroom, with furniture arranged to allow the teacher to move around freely and assist different groups and individual students as needed.

Appendix A

Sample Meeting Agendas

MGSD meetings focus on team building, collaboration, leadership, and forward momentum toward the goal of improved student achievement, as illustrated in these sample agendas.

Principals' Meeting Agenda

Mooresville Graded School District Meeting Agenda

Group: Principal's Meeting
Date/Time: Wednesday, April 11, 2012
Place: East Mooresville Intermediate School, 9:00-12:00 pm

Agenda Item	Person Reporting	Time	Notes
Facilities Update	Stephen Mauney	10 min.	
McRel Walkthrough Digital Citizenship Information	Todd Wirt	30 min.	
Digital Conversion Update	Dr. Scott Smith	15 min.	
Teacher of the Year Information - HR Referrals for Testing - EC	Dr. Danny Smith	15 min	
EC Staff Development Plans	Sandy Albert	5 min.	
AIG Update	William Parker	10 min.	
Budget Update	Terry Haas	20 min.	
Closing Comments	Dr. Mark Edwards	25 min.	

Important Dates:
April 12 - Digital Conversion Site Visit
April 16-20 - School Informational Meetings
April 24 - Digital Conversion Site Visit
May 8-18 - EOG Testing May 9 - Early Release Day
May 23 - Senior Project Presentations @ MHS
June 5-8 - EOC/VOCAT Testing

Teacher Leader Workshop Agendas

Sample Agenda 1: Grow a Leader—Grow an Organization!

During these three sessions, we will examine processes of instructional leadership and aim to build collective capacity across schools and our school system. Our focus is on improving the work of teacher leaders within their key role(s) that impact the school culture as places of collaboration, teamwork, and professional learning, which lead to increased student learning.

❑ Welcome and introductions.

❑ Distribute book *All Systems Go: The Change Imperative for Whole System Reform* by Michael Fullan.

❑ Opening slide/discussion: Leading questions:
  • What do we expect students to learn?
  • How will we know if they are learning?
  • How do we know we are succeeding?
  • What will we do if they are not learning?
  • Review key elements in our progress.

❑ Dr. Edwards's opening remarks: *All Systems Go!*

❑ *Qualities of Leadership* video.

❑ Think–pair–share activity.

❑ What do you want to gain from these sessions?

❑ Review last year's feedback.

❑ What's on your school's radar screen now (slide of huge tree).

❑ Initiatives, programs, projects, instructional goals.

❑ Each school team will discuss and place initiatives, instructional goals, programs, or projects on the tree (chart).

❑ The school team will determine whether the item is characterized as a seed, blossom, fruit, withering, or compost.

❑ Group explanation/discussion will follow.

❑ In what ways do you believe you have grown as a teacher leader? Ask teachers to give examples.

❑ Show slides displaying district data: Review with teacher leaders three-year trend EOG composite, AYP status, graduation rates, statewide ranking.

❑ Highlight elements within each school's data. Show positive student achievement slides.

❑ Show *Teamwork Makes the Dream Work* video with Al Jarreau's song "We're in This Work Together!"

- ❑ What key components contributed to your school's success last year? Word activity/group discussion.
- ❑ All other factors pale in comparison to the teacher factor!
- ❑ Review student EOG performance data by demographics.
- ❑ Go to NC DPI web site, Accountability Services/ABCs of Public Education/Disaggregation/2010-11, and place data in the chart provided.
- ❑ What do the data tell us? What did we learn? How can we help more students become more successful?
- ❑ Slide chart: How many more students do we need to attain 90 percent success? White, black, Hispanic, multiracial, special education?
- ❑ What is your school's game plan? Tell us how your team plans to achieve 90 percent of students meeting proficiency this school year and explain what you are going to do differently to achieve this goal. Flip chart activity per school.
- ❑ *Every Child, Every Day*: A moral purpose.
- ❑ Song "How Deep Is Your Love?" by the Bee Gees.
- ❑ Leadership homework assignment: The top 10 schools.
- ❑ What can we learn from these schools? Contact the schools and find out what practices/strategies/resources they have in place that are key to their success. Will we do anything differently as a result of this communication?
- ❑ Reading homework assignment: Read Chapters 1–3 by the next session.
- ❑ Check Angel LMS frequently for communications, new content, articles, and assignments.
- ❑ Closing remarks.

Sample Agenda 2: Equity and Excellence

During these three sessions, we will examine processes of instructional leadership and aim to build collective capacity across schools and our school system. Our focus is on improving the work of teacher leaders within their key role(s) that impact the school culture as places of collaboration, teamwork, and professional learning, which lead to increased student learning.

- ❑ Welcome and introductions.
- ❑ Purpose of teacher leaders workshop.
- ❑ Distribute book *Leadership for Equity and Excellence* by James Joseph Scheurich and Linda Skrta.
- ❑ Slide: What do we mean by excellent and equitable schools?
- ❑ School team discussion and definition. Place in Angel LMS.
- ❑ *Leadership for Equity and Excellence* is key to our next level performance slide.

- ❑ Dr. Edwards's opening remarks.
- ❑ Request teacher leaders to read article in Angel LMS and discuss former Governor James Hunt's vision for education in North Carolina and closing the achievement gap. He called on educators to have the will to do it (slide).
- ❑ What are some of the barriers in preventing equitable and excellent schools? Take 20 minutes to discuss in school teams and then report. Use flip charts.
- ❑ Working on the dream (slide).
- ❑ In education, as in other areas of our social life, the dream that Martin Luther King, Jr., was referring to, for equity in our country, has not yet been achieved. It is extremely important that we continue to hold fast to this dream, that we continue to work hard to make it come true in education. This effort is about how to create schools in which the dream of equity comes alive on an everyday basis through the work of ordinary, everyday people. Creating equitable, excellent schools is the right thing to do. Our current inequity undermines our claim to be an exemplary democracy. The civil rights work has come to us as educators. It is not a burden but a gift, something highly valuable that has tremendous implications for society. This effort will increase the dignity, value, and equity of all people. It is up to us to carry the great dream to fruition. It is our moral duty. It is the fulfillment of society.
- ❑ How will your school become a school of equity and excellence (slide)?
- ❑ Give school teams 15 minutes to discuss and list practices and policies they intend to implement to lead to equity and excellence.
- ❑ PUSH: Persevere Until Success Happens (slide).
- ❑ Insert Curtis Mayfield's song "Keep on Pushing."
- ❑ "When you have exhausted all the possibilities, remember this, you haven't," said Thomas Edison.
- ❑ MGSD goals (slide).
- ❑ Highlight district goals.
- ❑ Navigating to 90 percent (slide), highlight key elements. What will it take?
- ❑ "Love Lifted Me" (slide). Carol and Bill sing this traditional song/promote sing-along. Highlight the importance of Capturing Kids' Hearts and building strong relations.
- ❑ The Billy Hawkins story (slide). View DVD and follow up with discussion. What are some of the lessons learned? Never underestimate the human potential. You have to find something a child is good at and build on it. The single most important thing in turning lives around is an ongoing, caring adult. "Love Lifted Me." Are we looking for Billy Hawkins?
- ❑ MGSD performance data four-year trend (slides).

- ❑ School teacher leaders assignment.
- ❑ Review student performance data by demographics.
- ❑ Teachers are to go to NC DPI web site for information.
- ❑ A chart is provided in Angel LMS for teacher leaders' use.
- ❑ Guiding questions while studying the data:
  - What do the data tell us?
  - Is my school a large-gap school or small-gap school?
  - Are we close to becoming both equitable and excellent?
- ❑ Read *Letters from Teddy* (rhinestone bracelet and perfume).
- ❑ Homework assignment: Conduct a school "equity audit." Have each school team bring this information back to the December workshop with a demographic breakdown for each area.
- ❑ What action will you personally and professionally take between now and the December workshop to promote equity and excellence in your school? How will you promote the concept of "all in"? Post responses in Angel LMS dropbox (slide).
- ❑ Reading chapters assigned in preparation for December workshop (slide).
- ❑ Closing comments.

PLC/Department-Level Agendas

PLC Agenda

Department _____   Grade _____

Materials to bring to meeting: Literacy profile cards for your students
PLC Members: Tulbert, Stewart, Gloster, Fingado (tracked out)
Goals/Outcomes:
• Work with student files and grade level data to determine area of greatest need.
• Discuss other sources of data
• Create our next PLC agenda

Meeting Norms:
- Be positive about ideas and the job
- Team work and cooperation
- Compromise and consensus in decision making
- Discuss in the group- say it here!
- Actively listen to all ideas
- Respect backgrounds and experiences
- Stay focused on topics and time limits
- Follow through on topics
- End meeting with next PLT's agenda

Topic for Discussion	Who?	Estimated Time	Minutes
Opening: Review norms; Assign recorder to take and submit minutes, Assign time keeper, etc.	Stewart recording minutes; Tulbert facilitating	1 minute	
Review Literacy cards and determine area of greatest need.	Each teacher	45 minutes	
Discuss other sources of data that we could use as well (once the school year begins)	Each teacher	5 minutes	
Create agenda for our next PLC		10 minutes	

DuFour's Questions that should guide our work?
1. What do we want our students to learn?
2. How will we know they have learned it?
3. How will we respond when a student experiences difficulty?
4. How will we respond when a student already knows it?

Department-Level Agenda

Department _____   Grade _____

Expectations for Agendas and Minutes:

Agendas:
- should be given to all team members at least a day in advance.
- should include goals or expected outcomes.
- should include specific topics for discussion with estimated times listed.
- should include meeting norms agreed upon by team.
- should use the format shown above. File is saved on the shared drive in the **"School" folder labeled PLC's**

Minutes:
- should be typed in the minutes column of the agenda.
- should be emailed to all PLC participants within 2 days.
- should be submitted to Department Administrator within 2 days of the PLC meeting.
- should be read by all PLC participants. When tracked-out staff return, they should read minutes from all missed meetings.

General rule of thumb: The more detailed your minutes; the better. Remember, you will always have team members playing catch up. The more information they have, the more in the loop the will be!

196

Digital Conversion Sample Planning Agendas

21ˢᵗ Century Digital Conversion
March 13, 2008
11:30 a.m. – 1:30 p.m.
Agenda

Special Invited Guest Members:
Blanca Wong-Thomas -- Cisco
Angela -- Cisco
Barbara Nelson – Apple
<u>Guest for March 20th meeting:</u> John Detroye - Cisco

Urgent Items:
<u>Storage and Imaging:</u>
Taking data Ken Stone gave us regarding the laptops - pallet size and stacking capacity to be within warranty and Apple recommendations - we will need 100 sq. ft. per 1000 computers with pallets stacked two high and 200 sq. ft. per 1000 computers with pallets unstacked which is probably what will have to happen if we use the intermediate school media center. This does not account for workspace for imaging. The more workable space we have for imaging will give us more options for moving faster as more sets can be completed simultaneously.

<u>Teacher Assistants – OCS classes</u>

<u>Kim Fields Powell:</u>
Scheduled for April 3ʳᵈ meeting ... bringing John Cormier. What items/topics do we want them to prepare? As far as software is concerned, you have the major ones covered. I also LOVE Explore Learning. You may also want to consider a Learning Management System. We use Angel.

Master Plan Update: Identify urgent items
- Communication/Human Resources
- Deployment
- Infrastructure
- Apple
- AUP/Discipline
- MHS Implementation Team and Launch Date
- Woods Implementation Team and Launch Date
- MIS Implementation Team and Launch Date
- Professional Development
- Curriculum and Pedagogy
- Assessment, Research & Reporting
- Financial Plan/Grants

Updates:
- Discovery Education
- Mi-Connection
- Apple Survey

Next Meeting – March 20, 2008
March 27 meeting canceled due to Spring Break

"The Future is Today!"

21ˢᵗ Century Digital Conversion
May 1, 2008
8:30 a.m. – 11:30 p.m.
Agenda
N.F. Woods

Updates:	**8:30 – 9:00**
• Synching up with the iKid	Ann
• Facilities (Deployment Plan)	Stephen & Cynthia
• Financial	Terry

Burning Questions: **9:00 – 10:00**
- Obtain names for student interns to work this summer (Fall Help desk)
- Angel/Study Wiz Showdown - Need 8 teachers from MIS/MSHS and/or Woods
- Parent Deployment Meetings - May 8 @ MHS
  - Finalize responsibilities

Break   **10:00 – 10:15**

Updates and Discussion: **10:15 – 11:30**

• Professional Development	Danny
• EC	Chuck
• Infrastructure	Robert
• Pilot	Cynthia & Robert
• Assessment	Ginger
• Apple Update	Apple Rep.
• Implementation Team Updates	Todd, Dee & Julie

109 Days to Deployment!
Next Meeting – May 8, 2008

Appendix B

Strategic Plan

MGSD Digital Conversion Master Plan 2008

District Identification

Account: Mooresville Graded School District

Address: 305 N. Main Street, Mooresville, NC 28115

Superintendent/Commissioner: Dr. Mark Edwards

District Strategic Plan Goals and Challenges

1. *Globally Competitive Students:* Ensure all MGSD students are globally competitive by accomplishing the following:
   a. 100% of district schools meet federal AYP benchmarks
   b. 100% of district schools meet expected growth on state assessments
   c. 100% of schools obtain School of Excellence status within the state accountability model.

Strategy	Measure	Responsible	Date
Unpack curriculum across all grade levels to ensure teacher understanding and alignment to instruction to state standard course of study.	Grade, department and district level instructional meetings agenda	School administrators and curriculum directors	2008-2013
Develop and implement pacing guides to support instruction and ensure alignment and coverage of state curriculum.	Pacing guides; subsequent revisions of pacing guides	School administrators, curriculum directors and teachers	2008-2013
Implement a systemic formative assessment system aligned with pacing guides to drive instruction.	Benchmark assessments	Curriculum directors and school administrators	Spring 2008 purchase; Spring and Fall 2008 train; 2008-2013 implement.
Ensure vertical and horizontal curriculum alignment through meetings across grade levels, departments and schools.	Alignment meeting agendas	School administrators, curriculum directors and teachers	2008-2013
Utilize disaggregated data to ensure effective instruction for all students.	Data files (EVAAS), grade level, department level meeting agenda, and mid-year data meetings agenda	Leadership teams, grade and department chairpersons	Annually and ongoing.
Articulate a framework for curriculum and instruction in all major content areas.	Disseminated plan across content areas.	Curriculum directors and school principals	Summer 2008 and 2008-2009 school year

Strategy	Measure	Responsible	Date
Plan for and implement a digital conversion initiative that spans all grade levels.	Deployment plan and artifacts	District administration and curriculum directors	2008-2010
Ensure students experience contemporary methodologies via digital delivery of content, and develop cutting-edge media and digital literacy skills to be globally competitive.	Lesson plans, classroom observations, professional learning communities' work, staff development plans and documentation	Teachers and site-based and district-level administrators	2008-2013
Include goals and strategies for improving academic performance of AYP subgroups within School Improvement Plans (SIPs).	SIPs	School principals, school improvement and curriculum directors	2007-2008 and annually
Create and implement a pyramid of interventions and options for students demonstrating behavioral and/or academic challenges (this may include alternative learning program options and settings).	Program and intervention options lists	School principals with input from curriculum directors	2008-2013
Enhance and align courses and pathways based on job market data.	Registration materials showing course additions/deletions	Directors and school administrators	2008-2013

2. *21st Century Professionals:* Ensure 100% of administrators, teachers and staff possess the skills to lead, teach, assess and support students for success in this 21st century.

Strategy	Measure	Responsible	Date
Provide high quality mentoring support for newly employed teachers.	Mentoring plan, Individual Growth Plans, feedback from ILTs	Principals and HR director	2008–2009 and annually
Develop and implement a comprehensive district professional development plan.	Disseminated plan and agenda for activities	Curriculum directors	2008–2009
Create and implement a plan to recruit and employ teachers and administrators to reflect the diversity of the student population.	Plan and staff demographics database pre-and-post plan comparison	HR director and diversity committee	2007–2008 and annually
Create and implement a plan to recruit and employ teachers within areas of critical need (math, science, and exceptional children).	Recruitment plan and staff demographics annual data review	HR director and district administration	2007–2008 and annually
Recruit and provide support to ensure all staff meet the federal definition as HQ and state licensure requirements.	HMRS report of HQ data	HR director and district administration	2007–2008 and annually
Provide opportunities to develop skills of administrators and teachers, and to ensure retention of staff.	On-site graduate programs; reimbursements for tuition	HR director and district administration	2008–2013
Provide information and training on, and encourage professional development through, site-based professional learning communities.	Professional development meetings agenda and participants rosters	Curriculum directors and school principals	2008–2009 and annually

3. *Healthy and Responsible Students:* Ensure 100% of school sites are safe and caring environments that promote and support developing healthy, responsible students.

Strategy	Measure	Responsible	Date
Develop and update a district safe schools plan.	Dissemination of plan	Director of facilities and operations	2008–2009 and annually
Revise student code of conduct to current issues (e.g., digital conversion, anti-bullying, etc.)	Revised student code of conduct	Director of facilities and operations	2008–2009 and annual revisions
Include aligned goals to district safe schools plan within school improvement plan.	School improvement plans	Principals	2008–2009 and annually
Develop district trainers for energizers implementation K-8.	Training agenda	SHAC chairperson	Spring 2008–Fall 2008
Develop and adopt policies and procedures addressing student health issues and conditions as well as state mandates.	Board adopted policies/procedures	Student services director and school nurses	Summer 2008 and annual updates
Expand opportunities and encourage participation in co-curricular offerings.	Activities list and participant roster	Superintendent, directors, school administrators, school counselors, coaches, teachers	2008–2013
Develop wellness opportunities for staff and students (e.g., partner with local YMCA and gyms to offer staff discounts).	Listing of available discounts and staff enrolled	SHAC and district administrators	2008–2013

4. *Leadership for Innovation:* Provide strong district leadership in all areas that supports our focused vision, guides innovation, fosters collaboration and promotes dynamic continuous improvement.

Strategy	Measure	Responsible	Date
Conduct regular meetings for district administrators that are focused on district initiatives and student performance.	Leadership team agenda	Superintendent and executive team	Monthly 2008–2013
Include leadership enhancement activities within Leadership Team meetings content (e.g., building leadership capacity, utilization of data for decision-making, etc.).	Leadership team agenda	Superintendent and executive team	Monthly 2008–2013
Utilize staff retreats for leadership and team development.	Retreat dates and agenda	Superintendent, executive team, and district administrators	Annually
Utilize community meetings to inform and promote initiatives and vision/mission.	Agenda	Superintendent and executive team	Annually and/or per topic
Include district board members in training on initiatives.	Board minutes and training rosters	Superintendent	Per topic at least annually
Develop partnerships with local businesses to support initiatives.	Listings and recognitions of partnerships activities/projects	Superintendent, executive team, and district administrators	2008–2013

Strategy	Measure	Responsible	Date
Promote the district mission, vision, and values across sites and with all staff and community.	District website, printed materials and other media	Superintendent, HR director, and district administrators	2008–2013
Create and utilize parent and student advisory committees for collaboration and support of vision, mission and initiatives.	Advisory group agenda	Superintendent and executive team	Spring 2008 and ongoing

5. *21st Century Support Systems:* Develop and implement a 21st century comprehensive plan for operations, finances and funding, facilities, transportation and food service that supports teaching and learning.

Strategy	Measure	Responsible	Date
Develop plan for development and use of facilities based on growth projections and capacity analysis.	Disseminated plan	Director of facilities and operations	Spring/Fall 2008 development; Fall 2009–2013 implementation
Develop and implement policies and procedures regarding financial operations and budgeting processes.	Adopted policies and procedures	Finance director	2008-2009
Develop and implement a revised district technology plan commensurate with the digital conversion initiative and including components regarding infrastructure enhancements, financing the initiative, and staff development for a new teacher praxis.	Disseminated tech plan	Technology director, technology staff, and district directors	Spring/Fall 2008 development; Fall 2009–2013 implementation
Provide opportunities for dialogue with and development of classified staff across areas.	Meetings agenda, minutes, action plans	Superintendent and district directors	Ongoing
Provide data on digital conversion components relative to total cost of ownership (TCO) and return on investment (ROI).	Contracts with vendors providing digital conversion tools/resources	Superintendent and finance director	Fall 2008–2013
Review and revise the school calendar to accommodate time for professional development necessary to implement digital conversion initiative.	School calendar demonstrating early release days; staff dev offering lists	Director of facilities and operations	Spring 2008 and annually as needed
Initiate a staff positive recognition (ABCD) program to honor classified staff.	Board meetings agenda including ABCD awards	Superintendent, HR director, director of facilities	Spring/Fall 2008 development; Fall 2009–2013 implementation
Enhance, add to, and improve web-based information at the district level and across sites.	District, school, and Teacher/staff websites/pages	PR director, district administrators, and school-based technology staff	Spring 2008 launch; Fall 2008 (and ongoing) enhancement
Provide online communication and training resources to increase parent involvement to understanding and communications with schools and teachers.	Learning Management System implementation and listing of other resources	Digital conversion implementation team, technology director and staff, school administrators	2008–2013

MGSD Digital Conversion Communication Plan 2008

21st Century Digital Conversion 2008 Master Plan – Communication				
1 *Communication Activity*	*Start Date*	*Finish Date*	*Person Responsible*	*Progress/Update Notes*
2 Determine constituents and methods of communication.			Christy	Partner with Communication Committee
3 Articulate the vision to constituents.		Jun-08	Christy & Jean M.	Letterhead, business cards, website, banners in front of schools (?)
4 Develop district webpages on initiative.	Jun-08	Ongoing	Webmaster	
5 Develop individual school web pages.	Aug-08	Ongoing	Webmaster	
6 Develop public access TV programming.		Jun-08	Christina Nuss	
7 Develop fact sheets and FAQs.		Jun-08	Christy	Utilize Henrico's FAQs
8 Develop district and school newsletters about the initiative.		Aug-08	Christy	Communication Committee
9 District "newsletter" in the Mooresville Tribune (quarterly).		Apr-08	Christy	Communication Committee
10 Prepare letters to parents/guardians regarding deployment plan.		Jul-08		Work with principals
11 Communicate Internet service provider, insurance, warranty, and Internet safety policy to parent/guardians.		Aug-08	Christy/ Cynthia	Need details from Technology Dept.
12 Schedule a PTO meeting at each school on the Digital Conversion initiative.		May-08	Dr. Edwards/ Christy	Discuss at year end Parent Advisory Committee Meeting (May)
13 Develop open houses showcasing 21st-century learning.				
14 Develop and send progress reports to the school board and the community.				
15 Schedule initiative update for each board meeting.		Ongoing	Christy	Monthly board meetings
16 Schedule faculty meetings that include showcasing instructional best practices.		Ongoing	Principals	Use MHS English teachers to "sponsor" meetings

	21st Century Digital Conversion 2008 Master Plan – Communication				
	Communication Activity	**Start Date**	**Finish Date**	**Person Responsible**	**Progress/Update Notes**
17	Communicate professional development opportunities to teachers, staff, and parents/guardians.		Ongoing	Danny	
18	Communicate distribution plans to parents/guardians and the community.		Ongoing	Christy	Newsletter/Website/PAC/ECAC/TAC
19	Communicate help desk procedures and schedules.			Cynthia	
20	Update the District Office receptionists on issues related to this initiative.		Ongoing	Christy	
21	Report Year 1 progress to school board and community.				
22	Code of Conduct changes communicated to parents.		May-08	Stephen	Ready for beginning 08/09 school year material distribution
23	Develop most asked questions to speak with one voice.				
24	Communicate network issues with parents and community.				
25	Public relations spokesperson for questions/answers related to this initiative.		Ongoing	Christy	
26	Designate parent/guardian liaisons as key spokespeople.				Principals??? Or Central Services???
27	Provide parent/guardian workshops.				
28	Provide information on benefits to students and the community, including available research, impact on traditional instruction, detailed funding model, tax impact, implementation plan, security for equipment and students, any costs to parents and responsibilities in addition to current practice, profile of staff and administrative support for the project.				
29	Choose 10 questions and send answers.	Feb-08		Ann	Decision made to give out answers at monthly PD meetings
30	Obtain details from FL district re insurance costs & coverage.	Feb-14	Ongoing	Cynthia	The entire district has reduced their take home computer use to around 2,500. That is how they have a rate of $35.00.

Appendix C

Teacher Evaluation Materials

MGSD Technology Guide and "Look Fors"

	Educator Use of Technology	Leadership	Content of Technology Training	Student Use of Technology	Technology Integration
Developing	• Teachers use email and word processing programs • Technology not used to review student assessment information	• Recognizes benefits of technology in instruction • Limited use of technology	• Teachers become acquainted with technology (i.e., basic computer skills)	• Infrequent use by students as a basic tool for drill and practice, and/or integrated learning labs	• Teacher-centered lectures • Teachers allow students to use technology to work on individual projects
Proficient	• Streamlined administrative tasks (grades, attendance, less on planning, etc). • Technology used infrequently to review student assessment information	• Recognizes benefits of technology in instruction for all students and supports use of technology in instruction • Routinely uses technology in some aspects of daily work	• Teachers learn to use technology in the classroom (i.e., administration, management, and or presentation software; Internet as a research tool)	• Frequent individual use by students to access information resources for communication and presentation projects	• Teacher-directed learning • Teachers encourage students to use technology for cooperative projects in their own classrooms • Teachers use technology projects as an alternative form of assessment
Accomplished	• Technology used for research; creating templates for students; multimedia and graphical presentations and simulations; and correspondence with experts, peers, and parents • Technology frequently used to review student assessment information	• Recognizes and identifies exemplary use of technology in instruction for all students • Models use in daily work including communications, presentations, on-line collaborative projects and management tasks	• Teachers learn to use technology with curriculum/students (i.e., integration skills for creating learner-centered technology projects using Internet, applications, multimedia presentations, data collection; making accommodations with assistive technologies; etc.)	• Students regularly use technology for working with peers and experts, evaluating information, analyzing data and content in order to solve problems, and evaluating individual progress	• Teacher-facilitated learning • Teachers establish communities of inquiry for students to collaborate with community members

(Continued)

MGSD Technology Guide and "Look Fors" (continued)

	Educator Use of Technology	Leadership	Content of Technology Training	Student Use of Technology	Technology Integration
Distinguished	• Teachers explore and evaluate new technologies and their educational impact; technology used for inquiry, analysis, collaboration, creativity, content production, and communication • Technology regularly used to review student assessment information which results in needed changes in instruction	• Promotes exemplary use of technology in instruction for all students; advocates and encourages parental and communal involvement in the training and integration of technology and education • Maintains awareness of emerging technologies; participates in job-related professional learning using technology resources	• Teachers learn about emerging technologies and their uses with curriculum/ students (i.e., creation and communication of new technology-supported, student-centered projects) • Vertically aligned integration of all technology within NCSCOS	• Students regularly use technology for working collaboratively in communities of inquiry to propose, assess, and implement solutions to real world problems, and for evaluating and analyzing their own assessment information to improve learning • Students communicate effectively with a variety of audiences	• Student-centered learning • Teachers act as mentors/facilitators with national/ international business, industry, and university communities of inquiry to develop 21st-century skills • Technology is vital to all curriculum areas and integrated on a daily basis

Personal Development Plan Addendum on Digital Direction

Teacher name: _____

Please take a look at the MGSD Technology "Look-Fors" rubric and circle the statements that apply to you (like a self-evaluation of your own skills). Be honest.

In using this rubric, please begin thinking of some specific and consistent skills you want to learn. You will be meeting with the technology facilitator in the coming week to discuss your self-evaluation and skills you wish to learn that align with your initial assessment. Please have the rubric completed by the time you meet with her.

Beginning the week of October 1 (or earlier if you can schedule appropriately), you will need to meet with the technology facilitator at least once every other week (or twice a month) to co-plan lessons that will help you practice the skills. There is no required time for this; just use your time appropriately for collaboration on how to become a more accomplished teacher with 21st century skills. We will do a status check on a monthly basis to review your progress. Please complete this form as you move forward.

Based on the rubric, what are some of the areas in which you really want to improve?

_____

_____

_____

_____

What skills do you want to consistently practice?

_____

_____

_____

_____

Please keep a running record of meetings with the technology facilitator (dates only):

_____

_____

_____

What other support can we provide to you as we move forward as a school in our use of 21st century tools?

_____

_____

_____

Rubric for Teacher Effectiveness

Rubric for Teacher Effectiveness					
Teacher	Grade/ Subject	Activity Type I - Individual S - Small Group W - Whole Class SP - Student Presentation	Student Collaboration (Rate on a scale of 1-5 with 5 being highly effective dialogue)	Use of Digital Resources R - Research C - Consumption CR - Creation PR - Presentation	Other Observations

Appendix D

Real-Time Data

Math Overview Report

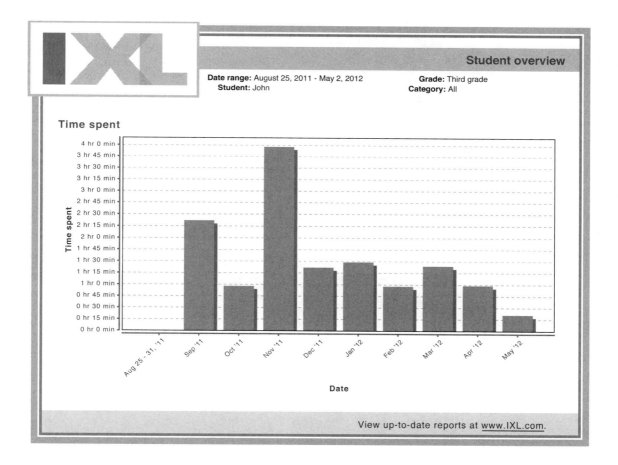

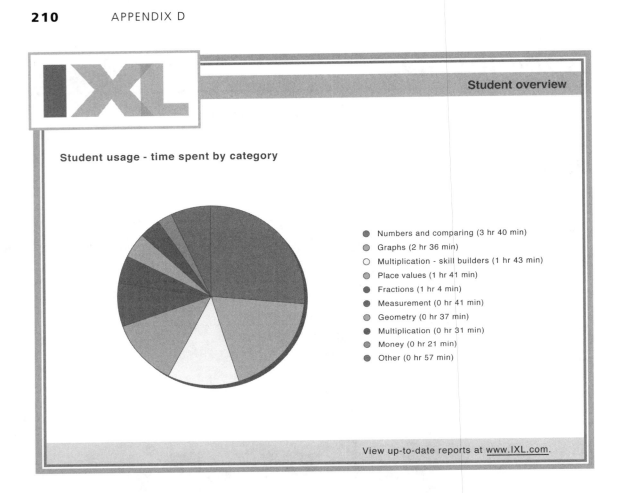

Student overview

Student usage - time spent by category

- Numbers and comparing (3 hr 40 min)
- Graphs (2 hr 36 min)
- Multiplication - skill builders (1 hr 43 min)
- Place values (1 hr 41 min)
- Fractions (1 hr 4 min)
- Measurement (0 hr 41 min)
- Geometry (0 hr 37 min)
- Multiplication (0 hr 31 min)
- Money (0 hr 21 min)
- Other (0 hr 57 min)

View up-to-date reports at www.IXL.com.

Student summary

	School year
Problems attempted	2,940
Skills practiced	60
Time spent	13 hr 51 min
Medals earned	67

News flash

04/30/2012   John has answered 4,500 math problems (across all grades).

Skills practiced

Rank	Skill	Time spent	Problems attempted	SmartScore
1	P.2 Coordinate graphs II	1 hr 19 min	42	81 (good)
2	A.5 Even and odd II	1 hr 8 min	228	83 (good)
3	B.2 Place value names	0 hr 50 min	219	100 (mastered)
4	A.4 Even and odd I	0 hr 43 min	120	100 (mastered)
4	P.12 Venn diagrams	0 hr 43 min	85	89 (good)
6	A.9 Which number is greatest/ least?	0 hr 33 min	70	100 (mastered)
7	A.10 Comparing numbers	0 hr 32 min	234	100 (mastered)
8	P.1 Coordinate graphs I	0 hr 24 min	78	100 (mastered)
9	F.5 Multiply by 4	0 hr 22 min	123	100 (mastered)
10	Q.3 Which customary unit is appropriate?	0 hr 20 min	72	100 (mastered)
11	F.8 Multiply by 7	0 hr 18 min	96	100 (mastered)
11	S.1 Fraction review	0 hr 18 min	55	100 (mastered)
13	A.1 Write numbers in words	0 hr 17 min	77	100 (mastered)
13	S.5 Equivalent fractions: type the missing numeratoror denominator	0 hr 17 min	41	83 (good)
15	A.6 Skip-counting puzzles	0 hr 16 min	40	85 (good)
15	N.1 Count coins and bills - up to $5 bill	0 hr 16 min	38	83 (good)

(continued)

Skills practiced (*continued*)

Rank	Skill	Time spent	Problems attempted	SmartScore
15	Q.2 Reasonable temperature	0 hr 16 min	46	100 (mastered)
15	R.1 Identify planar and solid shapes	0 hr 16 min	61	100 (mastered)
15	S.3 Fractions on number lines	0 hr 16 min	59	100 (mastered)
20	B.3 Value of a digit	0 hr 15 min	70	100 (mastered)
21	B.4 Identify the digit with a particular place value	0 hr 14 min	56	100 (mastered)
21	F.9 Multiply by 8	0 hr 14 min	68	100 (mastered)
21	R.11 Angles: greater than, less than, or equal to aright angle	0 hr 14 min	67	100 (mastered)
24	E.1 Multiplication sentences	0 hr 13 min	30	100 (mastered)
24	S.2 Fraction review - word problems	0 hr 13 min	23	100 (mastered)
26	F.7 Multiply by 6	0 hr 12 min	73	100 (mastered)
27	B.1 Place value models	0 hr 11 min	30	100 (mastered)
27	U.1 Certain, probable, unlikely, and impossible	0 hr 11 min	31	100 (mastered)
29	P.8 Interpret pictographs	0 hr 10 min	16	57 (needs improvement)
30	B.7 Convert from expanded form	0 hr 9 min	30	100 (mastered)
30	E.4 Missing factors - facts to 12	0 hr 9 min	56	100 (mastered)
32	T.1 What decimal number is illustrated?	0 hr 8 min	33	80 (good)
33	E.3 Multiplication word problems - facts to 12	0 hr 7 min	8	55 (needs improvement)
33	L.2 Round money amounts	0 hr 7 min	30	100 (mastered)
35	F.10 Multiply by 9	0 hr 6 min	34	100 (mastered)
35	F.12 Multiply by 11	0 hr 6 min	32	100 (mastered)
35	L.1 Rounding	0 hr 6 min	18	72 (satisfactory)
35	Q.1 Read a thermometer	0 hr 6 min	28	100 (mastered)
35	R.3 Symmetry	0 hr 6 min	31	100 (mastered)
40	A.7 Number sequences	0 hr 5 min	7	43 (needs improvement)
40	C.2 Addition input/output tables - up to three digits	0 hr 5 min	4	36 (needs improvement)
40	D.2 Subtraction input/output tables - up to three digits	0 hr 5 min	8	52 (needs improvement)

(continued)

Skills practiced (*continued*)

Rank	Skill	Time spent	Problems attempted	SmartScore
40	F.4 Multiply by 3	0 hr 5 min	37	100 (mastered)
40	F.6 Multiply by 5	0 hr 5 min	28	100 (mastered)
40	F.13 Multiply by 12	0 hr 5 min	29	100 (mastered)
40	M.1 Guess the number	0 hr 5 min	15	100 (mastered)
47	M.2 Largest/smallest number possible	0 hr 4 min	7	76 (satisfactory)
47	N.2 Which picture shows more?	0 hr 4 min	18	55 (needs improvement)
49	A.2 Ordinal numbers to 100th	0 hr 3 min	7	8 (needs improvement)
49	A.3 Roman numerals I, V, X, L, C, D, M	0 hr 3 min	6	0 (needs improvement)
49	B.5 Convert to/from a number	0 hr 3 min	7	32 (needs improvement)
49	E.2 Multiplication - facts to 12	0 hr 3 min	28	100 (mastered)
49	F.1 Multiply by 0	0 hr 3 min	84	100 (mastered)
49	F.3 Multiply by 2	0 hr 3 min	28	100 (mastered)
49	O.1 Read clocks and write times	0 hr 3 min	4	8 (needs improvement)
56	F.2 Multiply by 1	0 hr 2 min	28	100 (mastered)
56	F.11 Multiply by 10	0 hr 2 min	28	100 (mastered)
56	U.2 Mean, median, mode, and range	0 hr 2 min	5	0 (needs improvement)
56	U.4 Combinations	0 hr 2 min	7	0 (needs improvement)
60	R.5 Reflection, rotation, and translation	0 hr 1 min	7	31 (needs improvement)

Source: Appendix D courtesy of IXL Learning

Appendix E

Helpdesk Procedures for Damaged Student Laptops

The following is designed to be a guide and reference for dealing with issues related to student laptop damage, with the understanding that the goal is for every student to have an operational computer. Typically issues will arise over one of the following: theft, loss, accidental damage, or willful damage/negligence. Administrators' determinations and judgments should be based on the best interests of each student.

Theft

- Administrator meets with student to investigate and discuss.
- Administrator meets with or calls parents to investigate and discuss.
- A police report is required.
- Administrator determines if the student shall be issued another computer.

Accidental Damage

(This is rare, but examples would include auto accident, house fire, etc.)

- Administrator meets with student to investigate and discuss.
- Administrator meets with or calls parents to investigate and discuss.
- After investigation and confirmation of situation, the student will be issued another computer.

Loss

- According to the RUP, the parent/guardian and student have accepted responsibility for the machine and therefore are liable for the cost of the machine.
- Administrator meets with student to investigate and discuss.
- Administrator meets with or calls parents to investigate and discuss.

- To receive another machine:
  - Student can establish status as a day user (check out a machine from the helpdesk each morning and return it at the end of the day) by setting up a payment plan and paying a minimum of 50% of the cost of the machine.
  - Student will be issued a machine to take home when full payment is received.

Negligence/Willful Damage

- According to the RUP, the parent/guardian and student have accepted responsibility for the machine and therefore are liable for the cost of the machine or the cost to repair.
- Administrator meets with student to investigate and discuss.
- Administrator meets with or calls parents to investigate and discuss.
- To receive another machine (MIS, EMIS & MMS):
  - Student can establish status as a day user (check out a machine from the helpdesk each morning and return it at the end of the day) by setting up a payment plan and paying a minimum of 50% of the cost of the machine.
  - Student will be issued a machine to take home when full payment is received.
- To receive another machine (MHS):
  - Day users are not practical with three campuses.
  - Student will be issued a machine to take home by setting up a payment plan and paying a minimum of 50% of the cost of the machine, the cost of the repair, or $50.00, whichever is greater.
  - MHS shall collect all outstanding fees before issuing a diploma.

Multiple offenses should be handled appropriately and in consultation with the CTO if necessary.

Appendix F

Visitors to Mooresville Graded School District

Alamance Burlington School System, Burlington, NC
Alleghany County School District, Sparta, NC
Alton Community School District 11, Godfrey, IL
Anson County Schools, Wadesboro, NC
APTAKISIC-TRIPP C C S D 102, Buffalo Grove, IL
Ashe County Schools, Jefferson, NC
Asheboro City Schools, Asheboro, NC
Asheville City School District, Asheville, NC
Auburn District #10, Auburn, IL
Avery County Schools, Newland, NC
Baldwin County School District, Bay Minette, AL
Bartow County Schools, Cartersville, GA
Beaufort County Schools, Washington, NC
Bibb County, Macon, GA
Bladen County Schools, Elizabethtown, NC
Bushnell-Prairie City Community Unit School District #170, Bushnell, IL
Cabarrus County Schools, Concord, NC
Caldwell County Schools, Granite Falls, NC
Campbell County School District, Rustburg, VA
Carlisle School, Martinsville, VA
Centraila City School District #135, Centralia, IL
Chapel Hill Carrboro City Schools, Chapel Hill, NC
Charlotte Catholic Schools, Charlotte, NC
Charlotte-Mecklenburg Schools, Charlotte, NC
Charlottesville City Schools, Charlottesville, VA
Chatham County Schools, Siler City, NC
Chesterfield County Public Schools, Chesterfield, VA
Cincinnati Christian Schools, Hamilton, OH
Clever School District, Clever, MO
Community Consolidated School Dist 093, Bloomington, IL
Community Unit School District 4, Mendon, IL
Consolidated School District 158, Algonquin, IL
Cumberland County Schools, Fayetteville, NC
Dare County Schools, Manteo, NC
Davidson County Schools, Lexington, NC
Deer Park School District, Deer Park, NY

Detroit Public Schools, Detroit, MI
Diocese of Charlotte, Charlotte, NC
District 50 Schools, Washington, IL
Duplin Schools, Kenansville, NC
Durham Public Schools, Durham, NC
East Alton School District 13, Alton, IL
East Davidson High School, Thomasville, NC
Eastland CUSD #308, Lanark, IL
Edenton-Chowan Co Sch District, Edenton, NC
Elbert County, Elberton, GA
English Montreal School Board, Quebec, Canada
Flossmoor School District 161, Chicago Heights, IL
Forrestville Valley CUSD 221, Forreston, IL
Fort Osage R-1 School District, Independence, MO
Freeburg Comm H S District 77, Freeburg, IL
Gaston County School District, Gastonia, NC
Georgia Department of Education, Atlanta, GA
GRACE Christian School, Raleigh, NC
Granville County School District, Oxford, NC
Guilford County, Greensboro, NC
Harvard Graduate School of Education, Orange, NJ
Henderson County, Hendersonville, NC
Horry County School District, Conway, SC
Howard-Suamico School District, Green Bay, WI
Houston Independent School District, Houston, TX
Iberville Parish School District, Rosedale, LA
Independent School District 318, Grand Rapids, MN
Indianapolis Public Schools, Indianapolis, IN
ISD 317-Deer River Schools, Deer River, MN
Iredell-Statesville School District, Statesville, NC
Jacksonville State University, Jacksonville, AL
Jersey CUSD #100, Jerseyville, IL
Johnston City Community School District 1, Johnston City, IL
Jones County School District, Trenton, NC
Kannapolis City Schools, Kannapolis, NC
Lake Norman Charter School, Huntersville, NC
Leyden High School District 212, Franklin Park, IL

Lake Washington Sch Dist 414, Redmond, WA
Lexington City Schools, Lexington, NC
Lexington School District 1, Lexington, SC
Limestone County School District, Athens, AL
Lincoln, Lincolnton, NC
Little Elm Independent School District, Little Elm, TX
Louisa County Public Schools, Mineral, VA
Magellan Charter, Raleigh, NC
Mannheim School District 83, Northlake, IL
Marengo Community High School District #154,
    Marengo, IL
Marquardt School District 15, Glendale Heights, IL
McAllen Independent School District, McAllen, TX
McDowell County Schools, Marion, NC
McLean County Unit District #5, Normal, IL
Mecklenburg Area Catholic School, Huntersville, NC
Middle GA Regional Educational Service Agency
    (RESA), Macon, GA
Mingo County School District, Williamson, WV
Mitchell High School, Bakersville, NC
Montgomery County Schools, Troy, NC
Moore County Schools, Robbins, NC
Morehead City, Morehead City, NC
Morgan County Schools, Berkeley Springs, WV
Mount Airy City Sch District, MOUNT AIRY, NC
Myrtle Beach High Sch, MYRTLE BEACH, SC
Nash-Rocky Mount School District, Elm City, NC
Natick Public Schools, Natick, MA
New Hanover, Wilmington, NC
Newton Conover, Newton, NC
NC Department of Public Instruction, Raleigh, NC
North Carolina State University, RALEIGH, NC
Northern Region, Greensboro, NC
Northland Community Schools, Remer, MN
Northwest Independent Schools, Justin, TX
One to One Institute, Mason, MI
Orange County Schools, Hillsborough, NC
Owensboro Independent Schools, Owensboro, KY
Oxford City Schools, Oxford, Al
Pell City School District, Pell City, AL
Perquimans County Schools, Hertford, NC
Piedmont Charter Schools, Gastonia, NC
Piedmont City Schools, Piedmont, AL
Pitt County Schools, Greenville, NC
Pittsgrove Township Schools, Pittsgrove, NJ
Poplar Bluff R-I School District, Poplar Bluff, MO
Princeton City Schools, Cincinnati, OH

Richland County School Dist 2, Blythewood, SC
Riverton CUSD#14, Riverton, IL
Robeson County, Shannon, NC
Rochester C U Sch District 3A, Rochester, IL
Rock Hill School District Three, Rock Hill, SC
Rockingham, Reidsville, NC
Rowan-Salisbury School System, Salisbury, NC
Roxana Community Unit School District #1, Roxana, IL
Rutherford County Schools, Forest City, NC
Salem-Keizer Public Schools, Salem, OR
Salem Lutheran School, Tomball, TX
Sampson County School District, Clinton, NC
School of Inquiry & Life Sciences at Asheville, Ashe-
    ville, NC
Scotland County Schools, Laurinburg, NC
Southeast Center for Effective Schools, Flagler
    Beach, FL
Surry County Schools, Dobson, NC
St James School, Montgomery, AL
St. Leo Catholic School, Winston-Salem, NC
Stanly County Schools, Albamarle, NC
Stokes County Schools, Danbury, NC
Talladega County, Talladega, AL
Sylvan Elementary School, Snow Camp, NC
The Riordan Foundation, Los Angeles, CA
Thomasville City Schools, Thomasville, NC
TORCHLIGHT ACADEMY, Raleigh, NC
Transylvania County Schools, Brevard, NC
Trussville City Schools, Trussville, AL
Tupelo Public School District, Tupelo, MS
UGA ETC, Athens, GA
UNC Charlotte, Charlotte, NC
Union County Public Schools, Monroe, NC
University Of Nc At Greensboro, Greensboro, NC
US Dept of Education, Washington, DC
Vancouver Public Schools, Vancouver, WA
Wake County Public School System, Raleigh, NC
Walton County Schools, Monroe, GA
Washington County Schools, Abingdon, VA
Watauga County Schools, Boone, NC
Weaver Education Center, Greensboro, NC
Wentzville R-IV School District, Wentzville, MO
West Carroll CUSD #314, Thomson, IL
Westhampton Beach School District, Westhampton
    Beach, NY
Wingate University, Wingate, NC
Yadkin County School District, Yadkin, NC

Appendix G

League of Innovative Schools

Overview

When it comes to education, America is falling behind. More precisely, we are standing still while other countries outpace us. Over the past several decades, we have tried a host of approaches that conventional wisdom has suggested would work, such as more teachers with a Master's degree and smaller class sizes. The result is the same: test scores, imperfect but reasonable yardsticks, are flat lining.

Too often, what's holding us back is an inability or unwillingness to break the mold of the 19th century schoolhouse and harness 21st century tools—data dashboards, personalized learning, "flipped" classrooms—that can transform the way we educate our kids. In other words, we've failed to harness the power of technology to empower teachers to teach and students to learn.

The good news is that a number of pioneering district and school leaders are committed to doing the difficult work of using technology to deliver results in the classroom. These leaders, the tip of the spear of innovators in American education, have come together to form the League of Innovative Schools. The league connects districts and schools with top universities and entrepreneurs, building a hotbed of innovation where we can demonstrate promising ideas, evaluate them rigorously and rapidly, and replicate what works—accelerating the pace of change in public education. In particular, the League will:

- *Rapidly and rigorously evaluate what works.* Education technology, like all frontiers, is populated by pioneers and hucksters, and it is often hard to tell the difference. There are few reliable, independent places where superintendents, teachers, and parents can turn for trustworthy information about what technologies work. The result is that states and schools are wasting scarce tax dollars on products that are failing our kids. The league will pilot promising technologies and evaluate them rigorously and rapidly across multiple districts, building a reliable body of research about what works and what doesn't.

- *Break down silos and scale innovation.* Right now, districts across the country are developing innovative ways to enhance learning with technology. The problem is that these incidents of innovation are often taking place in isolation without a good way to ensure that the best ideas can be scaled up. The league will be a vehicle for surfacing the most promising ideas and sharing on-the-ground lessons about how to implement them, making it possible to scale innovation in traditional public school districts—big and small, urban and rural—across the country.

- *Transform the market by streamlining procurement, aligning supply and demand, and focusing the decisions of purchasers.* The K-12 market represents a significant—but daunting—opportunity for service providers. The combination of uninformed purchasing decisions, a highly disaggregated market, and a Byzantine procurement process stop innovative tools from making their way into the classroom. Through the league, sellers can learn what buyers need, and buyers can learn what sellers make, paving the way for common technological solutions districts can purchase together.

Why the League Is Unique

The league is an alliance for action rooted in a commitment to deliver results with technology—not just ten years from now, or five years from now, but now. In particular, what makes the league unique are the following defining characteristics:

- *A three-pronged, multi-sector approach.* If we're serious about driving change in public education, we need to unite the people who are in charge of a district with the people who are developing digital solutions, and the people who are studying what works. That's why the league is supported by key leaders from public education, the private sector, and academia. Together, we will pursue cutting-edge research; make the demand side of the market "smarter"; and scale up successful digital innovations.

- *Innovation from the bottom-up.* This isn't about a Washington-driven agenda. It's about transforming education from the bottom-up by identifying the needs of district leaders, harnessing the ideas of entrepreneurs, and leveraging the talents of top-tier researchers. Simply put, we're trying to make it easier for the people who want to innovate—and know how to innovate—to do just that.

- *A focus on school design and implementation.* It's not about the device or software. Even the most sophisticated technologies will fail if they are implemented in the wrong environment or the wrong way. The league will be a place where educators can move from research to practice, learning on-the-ground lessons from peers, researchers, and industry leaders so they can implement promising ideas in a way that delivers results in their districts.

- *A nationally recognized community of excellence.* The league is an initiative of Digital Promise, a new independent bipartisan national center chartered by Congress, supported by Presidents Bush and Obama and Republicans and Democrats in Congress, and governed by an independent board appointed by Secretary of Education Arne Duncan. The league offers a chance to take part in a nonpartisan, nonprofit, nongovernmental initiative with no other interest beyond harnessing technology to deliver results for America's students.

League Activities

There is a wide range of current and planned league initiatives and activities, including:

- Meetings and school visits for participating school and district leaders
- Webinars and online learning opportunities, including an online community to share ideas and aggregate the collective knowledge acquired through the league
- Working groups to develop common standards and technical specifications around education technologies to help provide market signals to developers and expedite procurement
- Rapid, rigorous research through ongoing evaluations, powered by common data-sharing protocols that help ease the burden of research on districts and researchers alike
- Regional entrepreneurial accelerators that match participating school districts with participating research institutions and entrepreneurs, driving innovation from the bottom-up, while sharing lessons nationally
- Prize competitions that leverage partnerships across districts, entrepreneurs, and universities to identify, implement, evaluate, and scale promising technologies and instructional approaches

Participants

The league is currently made up of 26 innovative districts in 18 states that collectively serve almost 2.5 million students. Participants include urban, suburban, and rural districts across the country:

Baldwin County School District, Bay Minette, AL
Blue Valley Unified School District #229, Overland Park, KS
Charlottesville City Public Schools, Charlottesville, VA
Cuba Rushford School District, Cuba, NY
District of Columbia Public Schools, Washington, DC
E.L. Haynes Public Charter School, Washington, DC
Educational Service Center of Central Ohio
Florida Virtual School
Horry County Schools, Myrtle Beach, SC
Houston Independent School District, Houston, TX
Howard-Suamico School District, Green Bay, WI
Indian Prairie School District, Aurora, IL
Iowa City Community School District, Iowa City, Iowa
Lincoln Public Schools, Lincoln, NE
McAllen Independent School District, McAllen, TX
Meridian Joint School District #1, Meridian, ID
Mooresville Graded School District, Mooresville, NC
Napa County Schools, Napa County, CA
New York City Department of Education, New York, NY
Onslow County Public Schools, Onslow, NC
Piedmont City School District, Piedmont, AL
Roanoke County Public Schools, Roanoke, VA
Rock Hill Public Schools, Rock Hill, SC
Utica Community Schools, Sterling Heights, MI
Vancouver Public Schools, Vancouver, WA
York County Schools, Yorktown, VA

Research partners include:

The University of Chicago Urban Education Lab
The Education Innovation Laboratory at Harvard University
The David O. McKay School of Education at Brigham Young University
The Center for Game Science at the University of Washington

Book Talk for Professional Learning Communities and Digital Conversion Planning

Chapter 1: Digital Conversion and Academic Achievement

1. What is digital conversion?
2. What other factors besides technology are essential to digital conversion success?
3. What strategies can educators adopt to address the author's list of critical success factors?
4. How is second-order change different from first-order change?

Chapter 2: The Moral Imperative

1. How does digital conversion equalize students' opportunities for success?
2. Why is it important to have high expectations for every student?
3. What is the relationship between the moral imperative and high expectations?
4. How does student collaboration help to address the moral imperative and raise expectations?

Chapter 3: A Culture of Caring

1. What does the author mean by "a culture of caring"?
2. How does a culture of caring impact student success?
3. What is "persuasive efficacy"?
4. What obstacles might educators face in implementing a culture of caring and how can obstacles be addressed?

Chapter 4: Digital Resources and Infrastructure

1. How can educators determine what resources are necessary for digital conversion?
2. What communications channels can be used to involve different groups in digital conversion?
3. What first steps should schools and districts take as they roll out digital conversion?
4. What factors should be considered as educators develop policies regarding social networking and required use?

Chapter 5: Evolutional Capacity Building

1. How do schools and districts build the momentum necessary for successful digital conversion?
2. What challenges might need to be overcome in order for teachers/administrators/parents/students to embrace digital teaching and learning?
3. How can schools and districts develop formal programs of teacher, parent, and student input?
4. What teams need to be put in place to support digital conversion?

Chapter 6: Instructional Transformation

1. How do relevance, personalization, collaboration, and connectivity impact student engagement?
2. How do instructional methods evolve as schools move toward digital conversion?
3. How does digital conversion change lesson planning?
4. In what ways does digital conversion affect students' academic performance?

Chapter 7: InfoDynamo: A Daily Date with Data

1. Does digital conversion affect accountability?
2. How does the daily collection of data improve student achievement?
3. How can data be used to drive decision making at the classroom, school, and district levels?
4. Why is data transparency essential to digital conversion success?

Chapter 8: Resource Alignment

1. How does second-order change impact financial decisions?
2. What are the valid criteria for evaluating resources to support digital conversion?
3. How can digital conversion save costs, and what costs can decision makers avoid?
4. What are the important considerations in establishing a technical infrastructure to support digital conversion?

Chapter 9: "All In": Collaboration, Synergy, and Momentum

1. What does the author mean by "all in"?
2. Why is "all in" important to student achievement?
3. How can educators foster an "all in" culture?
4. How can teachers, administrators, students, parents, and communities each contribute to an "all in" culture?

Chapter 10: Replication and Sustainability

1. Why is technology only one piece of the puzzle in a digital conversion initiative?
2. What budgeting strategies can affect digital conversion success?
3. Why is distributed leadership a key to success?
4. Who should be involved in solving problems and why?

Pearson's 1:1 Learning Framework

Mooresville Graded School District has become a prominent example of what is achievable when a laptop is provided for every student and teacher. Since implementing their digital conversion in 2007, MGSD has become the second-highest performing school district in North Carolina, and a national success story.

In 2011, Pearson entered into a partnership with MGSD that has since expanded in several areas. Given MGSD's consistent and significant academic gains, Pearson committed to studying MGSD's best practices, with the goal of helping other school districts replicate them. Pearson has learned from MGSD's experiences and combined them with other best practices and research to create a 1:1 Learning Framework that can be tailored to any school system. When effectively implemented, the four core components of Pearson's 1:1 Learning Framework will help accelerate student achievement and better prepare college and career-ready students.

Personalized Learning Environment

An effective Personalized Learning Environment allows students' learning needs to be met anywhere and anytime, while enabling teachers to individualize

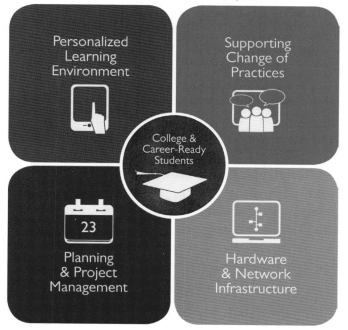

instruction easily. Key components include an Instructional Improvement System (IIS), digital curriculum programs, collaboration environments, and Internet/mobile tools. Interoperability between these components takes on new importance in a 1:1 learning environment. The digital curriculum should be flexible, Common Core–aligned, and support varying levels of teacher technological readiness.

Most districts will benefit from a

onetoone.pearsoned.com

combination of structured (scope & sequenced) and unstructured (teacher created & open educational resource) digital resources. In the digital world, an effective curriculum portfolio will be enriched routinely—be it from curators' enhancements of licensed content, district/teacher-created content, or free high-quality Internet content.

We anticipate a need to coexist with many existing assets and will work to establish an understanding about strengths and gaps in each district. The Personalized Learning Environment should be largely cloud-based to ensure 24/7 access for students and teachers during non-school hours.

Supporting Change of Practices

One of the greatest challenges to achieving success in a 1:1 learning environment is helping educators make adequate and sustained change to their traditional instructional practices. Developing effective instructional practices in a 1:1 learning environment requires regular professional development for teachers so they can become skilled facilitators of learning. In order to do this, teachers must know how to build technology-rich lesson plans, promote student collaboration, effectively use formative assessment data, and utilize good strategies for 1:1 classroom management.

Leadership should systematically support these changes by learning how to model good instruction in a 1:1 learning environment, modify teacher evaluation protocols to formally include facilitation and technology skill sets, lead the annual professional development planning process, and provide a rich set of support resources for teachers. Inter-rater reliability training ensures consistency in evaluating the effective use of technology in practice.

Many of the resources and data used to support educator development will come from the Personalized Learning Environment. The most obvious teacher resources are the Common Core–aligned digital curriculum resources that promote personalized learning and individualized instruction.

Most districts have teachers that span the continua of technical readiness and instructional orientation. When implementing a 1:1 learning strategy it is generally a good idea to promote the concept of teacher-authored lessons. While the promotion of teacher-created digital content can be beneficial, it needs to be implemented thoughtfully, otherwise it can be frustrating to teachers and add unintended costs.

To build and sustain teacher effectiveness, online support tools and collaborative environments for planning and professional development are important. Teachers can improve best practices and technology literacy by sharing experiences, observing tutorials, and improving professional curiosity. Data analytics, adaptive learning technology, and systems reporting will play increasingly more important roles in supporting change of practice.

Pearson has added the following new professional development workshops to its 1:1 Learning Framework, based on Dr. Mark Edwards's experiences and success in MGSD:

Digital Conversion: Every Child, Every Day   This workshop is a foundational overview based on this book and on the dramatic improvement in student achievement in Dr. Edwards's district. Achieving success in a digital conversion involves much more than introducing technology. It means changing the expectations of teachers for their teaching, and of students for their learning. It means identifying needed resources, setting up a technological infrastructure, and asking teachers to invest in self-improvement and in preparing new ways to teach. It also means raising the bar for accountability and a need to collect data methodically to ensure the digital conversation improves student achievement, and to make changes when needed.

Leading a Successful Digital Conversion   This workshop is for leadership teams in districts contemplating or undergoing a digital conversion. It focuses on how to establish the vision for digital conversion and how to lead the change that will be required to get there, based on best practices created by Mark Edwards in his district's highly successful digital conversion. It also explores the role that administrators can play in supporting and coaching teachers through their change of instructional practice.

Teaching 1:1 for Student Success   This workshop is for teachers in districts contemplating or undergoing a digital conversion. It focuses on how to impact classroom-level change in student achievement and excellence, based on the highly effective model created by Dr. Edwards. Teachers will explore the vision for digital conversion and how to participate actively in the change required to support "every child, every day." It also explores how the role of the teacher changes from the "Sage on the Stage" to the "Roaming Conductor" in support of an engaging and interactive classroom environment.

Planning and Project Management

Without a detailed plan, most complex cross-functional initiatives will fail. It is important to invest in a project manager with expertise in 1:1 deployments, a 1:1 proven project plan and associated project schedule, and a formal and active communications plan that promotes awareness, stakeholder buy-in, and dialogue.

Pearson has invested in a prototypical 1:1 learning project plan that helps define the necessary steps, actions, owners, and timeframes of a digital conversion. Having a dedicated and experienced 1:1 learning partner with a broad base of proven capabilities will help ensure the success of a digital conversion. When districts decide to move forward with a 1:1 learning initiative, but are not accustomed or structured to take on this work, they run the risk of massive waste and unrealized or stalled student achievement gains. Having a 1:1 learning partner whose focus on accelerated student achievement is aligned to yours, temporarily expands the district's capacity and syndicates project risk and ownership.

Hardware and Network Infrastructure

Pearson's strategy with regard to devices and infrastructure is to be agnostic, but to provide advice and support in several areas that can impact a district's success. Ensuring your network has adequate capacity and is configured to support the demands of 1:1 learning activity should be an important early step in every district's 1:1 learning project plan. If this is your technology staff's first attempt at 1:1 learning, they will benefit from an experienced and skilled 1:1 learning network infrastructure partner.

Many districts are reallocating district budgets so they can lease computers and/or tablets for each of their students and teachers. The cost of providing a device for every student typically represents 1/3 to 1/2 of the total annual per-pupil cost of a district's 1:1 learning initiative. Devices depreciate quickly and obsolescence is unavoidable, so it is important to delay device acquisition until your Personalized Learning Environment, Supporting Change of Practice strategy, and 1:1 Learning Project Plan are all in place. Defining the 1:1 learning strategy is the first step to ensuring a district does not inadvertently select a device type that is incompatible with their learning strategy.

Please contact the Pearson 1:1 Learning Group at **onetoone.pearsoned.com** if you would like more information on the Pearson 1:1 Learning Framework or specific Pearson Professional Development programs noted within these pages.